To Warren
With Love
Dorothy

THE CHRISTIAN SCIENCE WAY OF LIFE

with

A CHRISTIAN SCIENTIST'S LIFE

The CHRISTIAN SCIENCE

With A CHRISTIAN

WAY OF LIFE
by DeWitt John

SCIENTIST'S LIFE
by Erwin D. Canham

Prentice-Hall, Inc., Englewood Cliffs, N.J.

CONTENTS

About This Book

Our times call for a deeper understanding and mutual appreciation among those of differing races and religions. People thirst for a sense of humanity's oneness. They long for greater compassion, charitableness, and a spirit of generosity. They hunger, too, for a sure faith and a practical idealism. Rebirth of those healing elements nearest the heart of Christianity and of other great religions, and their demonstration in practical life, is the need of today. The age cries out for reassurance that spiritual values can survive the onslaughts of scientific materialism, and that spiritually-oriented moral and ethical standards are workable in a space-age civilization.

One naturally hopes that this book may help to answer these needs.

One wonders if any individual could fully portray the Christian Science way of life. He can tell what his religion means to *him,* and what he thinks it means to others. But such a book as this could not attempt to offer a full statement of the teachings of Christian Science, nor could it give any final picture of how Christian Scientists live and think and worship.

If ten different Christian Scientists had been asked to write on this topic, ten very different books would have resulted. The fundamentals of the religion would be the same throughout, though perhaps differing in expression; but the application of these fundamentals to human experience is as diversified as human experience itself. Consequently, I hope my fellow Christian Scientists will not assume that I try to speak definitively for them. And I hope the reader will realize that this book is only an introduction to a vast subject.

Without the invaluable comments of a number of able and talented friends, this book would not be. Some of them are people devoting their lives to the work of Christian Science. Others, in the natural sciences or other professions, have brought to the appraising of the manuscript a wealth of background in specialized fields. The comments of all these people were trenchant and discerning, and I thank them deeply, though I do not ascribe to them any responsibility for what I have written.

I wish also to thank those kind friends and acquaintances who have allowed me to use their personal experiences as illustrations. I appreciate their patience in answering countless questions of one who sought to report every detail faithfully.

My thanks also to the Trustees under the Will of Mary Baker Eddy for their kindness in permitting quotation of copyrighted material from Mrs. Eddy's writings, and to the owners of other copyrights, including the Trustees of The Christian Science Publishing Society, who have given similar permission. The reader will find the fact stressed, throughout these pages, that the authoritative statement of the teachings of Christian Science is to be found in Mrs. Eddy's writings.

DeWitt John

Lincoln, Massachusetts
October 1961

Chapter One

What Kind of People
Are Christian Scientists?

Perhaps the first thing to be said is that Christian Science comes to people exactly where they already are in the endless variety of human life. Sometimes it comes like a blaze of light, sometimes as a gentle influence, sometimes like a hand reaching out to one in the depths. Often it comes with transforming impact, but it finds people right where they are. And though it sometimes works remarkable changes in them, it does not claim to make them perfect overnight.

Christian Science comes to all sorts of people. It comes to the rich and poor, the talented and the simple, the old and the young, the pure and the impure, the sick and the well, the beautiful in character and those whose dispositions are scarred with ugliness. It comes to people of many races and many backgrounds and at varying stages of progress.

It is hard to generalize about what kind of people Christian

Scientists are. Their diversity is outwardly evident in their occupational backgrounds. Here is a random list of a few I know: a lawyer, a dentist, a professor of physics at a large university, a woman chemist in an atomic laboratory, a historian, a biologist; a carpenter, an automobile mechanic, a farmer, a rancher, a weigher of ship cargoes; an artist, an actor, a leading movie director; a professional football player, a dress designer, a music teacher, a cattle broker; a German baron, a lady-in-waiting in the Japanese imperial court, a British earl; a janitor, a clerk, a laborer; a banker, the president of a topflight advertising agency, a former major-general in the United States Army, a well-known corporation president, a United States senator, a university president, a former medical student.

To these might be added any number of engineers, schoolteachers, writers, housewives, businessmen, retired people, students, clerical workers, artisans, and salaried people. Here and there you will find a Christian Scientist in politics, and from time to time a figure of eminence in his chosen field.

But who these people are, or what they are, is not nearly so important as what Christian Science has done for them, and what it has done to them. Surely this is one gauge of any religion, and it helps to disclose the distinguishing characteristics of Christian Scientists.

Many a person has found the direction of his life altered from the day he first accepted Christian Science. Sometimes the change in direction is immediate; often it is much slower. But Scientists regard the working of this religion as somewhat like the leavening effect of yeast in a mass of dough. They find that it brings deep changes in the lives of its people.

Many who turn to Christian Science yearn to be different from what they are. They are weary of the perversities of human nature. They know they have a lot to outgrow. After all, there are a good many rough spots in human character wherever you find it. As the Discoverer and Founder of Christian Science, Mary Baker Eddy, once wrote: "Human lives are yet uncarved, —in the rough marble, uncumbered with crude, rude frag-

ments, and awaiting the hammering, chiselling, and transfiguration from His hand" (Misc. 360:2).

Many individuals have come to Christian Science for
physical healing. Many have found it. Sometimes quickly,
sometimes slowly. Yet physical healing is neither the primary
purpose of Christian Science nor its main effect upon the lives
of those who embrace it.

The same could be said of Christ Jesus' words and works,
which Christian Science emulates. Healing the sick characterized his mission. But his influence extended much farther.
He enriched human life by bringing to men a deeper and more
immediate sense of Deity, a profoundly transforming revelation
of God as Love.

Many have come to Christian Science for help in some crisis,
but have not known what it was they really needed. Often such
an individual has found, in this new-old interpretation of practical Christianity, the answer to his deepest questions: Who am
I? Why am I here? What is life's purpose? What is Truth? What
is God?

Sometimes the inquirer has been surprised to discover that
when he gained a new light on these questions, his body was
healed and a tangled life made over.

Most of those who accept Christian Science feel that whatever the impact this religion may have had on their lives, they
have only begun to experience its redemptive power. One often
feels that there is a challenging distance between the fullness
of the teachings and the degree to which he has learned thus far
to live them.

Yet one could not drink in daily the deep teachings of the
Saviour, striving to assimilate them and live them, without ex-
periencing in some measure a rebirth. Ideas have tremendous
power, especially when they glow and flash with the light of
the divine. Anyone who studies Christian Science discovers
that he is dealing with immensely powerful spiritual forces. He
finds the healing elements in the Scriptures sharply etched in
dynamic Science. He learns to analyze thought with new in-

sight, and gains a stronger desire to bring his living into harmony with God.

Many have found that Christian Science tends to bring out the best in one—to enlarge the abilities, expand the capacities, enrich the nature, deepen one's love and humanity—to nurture whatever is good. But at the same time, this purging influence serves to uncover and expose whatever is at variance with the standard given in the Sermon on the Mount. Thus it calls upon the student to grapple with evil and cast it out.

One finds an example of this stirring action upon human character in the letters of St. Paul to the early Christian congregations. Paul awakened the people to the high goal of Christian perfection. He nurtured every germ of goodness. Gently and patiently he watered the green shoots of righteousness. But at the same time—with the insight and courage of a true Christian warrior—he exposed the sins and perversities of the people to the naked light of Christian revelation.

And this is as it should be. The coming of day brings out the beauties of the countryside—the sparkle of the dew, the flower-studded hillside. But it also exposes the tasks awaiting the gardener—the unkempt hedge and the weedy flower patch.

And so today, Christian Science touches human character with the irradiance of the divine and uplifts it. But it also throws into bold relief the frailties needing correction. This is something the church member finds it helpful to recognize; it makes him more patient with his fellow members, and shows him the need for Christian love.

As we have seen, there is great diversity among Christian Scientists. But a common denominator among them is the fact that somehow a spark within them has been touched into light. Within every individual there is a spark; he may be aware of it only as a vague yearning for something better than the concerns of mortal existence, a spiritual hunger. Perhaps it is a sense that God is not the source of human suffering, with all its injustice and bitterness. Perhaps it is an intuitive feeling that God is Love. Perhaps it is a yearning for a way of living better than aimless drifting, perhaps a thirst for something higher than material goals. It may be a gnawing desire to know absolute Truth. Some modern thinkers would interpret it as a deep anxiety or insecurity, prompted by the questions Where do we come from? Where do we go? What are we to do with life? The preoccupations of human living never quite silence the yearning. One still knows intuitively that somehow and somewhere he will gain an inspired awareness of God—and realize the potentialities of his own being.

The writer of Proverbs tells us that "the spirit of man is the candle of the Lord" (Prov. 20:27); and Moffatt translates this passage: "Man's conscience is the lamp of the Eternal, flashing into his inmost soul." Something happens to one's life when the spark is kindled into light by the understanding of God and man. Something happens when he discovers that the spark within him is actually "the lamp of the eternal." This discovery transforms thought. It brings a sense of man's intimate relationship with God; and one gains an inkling of what the Psalmist glimpsed when he sang: "As for me, I will behold thy face in righteousness: I shall be satisfied, when I awake, with thy likeness" (Psa. 17:15).

It was something of this sort that happened to Jacob when he wrestled with the angel at Peniel. It happened to Moses at the burning bush. It happened to Saul of Tarsus on the road to Damascus. It happens to every individual, in some measure, when an awareness of God dawns upon him.

It is this quickening of the spark that attracts people to Christian Science and holds them to its teachings. With this illumination of consciousness often comes a physical healing, or a sense of freedom, an expansion of one's capacities, a sense of fulfillment, a transformation of one's whole world—based upon a new sense of man's unity with God as His likeness.

The Christian Scientist recognizes that the outward benefits are but surface evidence of a deeper transfiguration going on in his nature. For him, they are a natural outcome of true religion because they bear witness to the coming into his life, here and now, of the redeeming Christ.

2.

We have spoken of how a spark within is quickened into light. Undeniably such an experience can make over a life. Let me give you an actual example. It happened to a friend of mine, who told me about it himself.

As a young man, he was a run-of-the-mill salesman for a retail floor-covering business in New York. He firmly believed in the necessity of drinking with his customers to get business, and the drinking developed into a habit. He began spending much of his income on liquor. More and more frequently he would get drunk and disappear for periods of two or three days, to the distress of his young wife and his employer. No longer was he considered dependable. Liquor was rapidly robbing him of his standing and promise in business, and his home of stability and happiness.

One night, as a peace offering to his wife, he agreed to visit a Christian Science church with her. After the testimony meeting, someone introduced him to the First Reader, who was pointed out to him as one who had been cured of alcoholism through Christian Science.

His curiosity mildly aroused, he decided to ask the Reader about this healing. The Reader confirmed it.

"Well, you probably never did any really serious drinking," commented the skeptical inquirer.

The Reader looked him squarely in the eye. "Did you ever sweep out a barroom for just one more drink?"

This impressed my friend. He wanted to talk further. They made an appointment for the next Sunday afternoon. When the time came, he went to the home of the Reader, who was also a Christian Science practitioner.

While they were talking, a strange interruption took place. A young woman came to the house, with a desperately ill three-year-old child she was carrying on a pillow.

She was a distant relative of the practitioner's. Her child was ill with tuberculosis and rickets. It had been in a charity hospital in midtown New York. But finally the hospital authorities had called the parents and asked them to come and take the little girl away, saying they could do no more and that she would live only a few days. She weighed only seventeen pounds.

At this point the mother thought of her relative who, she remembered, was interested in a religion which healed people. She decided to bring the little girl to his house. She appealed to him to take the child into his home, and to do whatever he could for her. The practitioner agreed and the sick child on the pillow was laid on the living room sofa.

Several Sundays later, my friend again attended the Christian Science church. While there he was utterly astounded to see the same little child *walk* into the Sunday school! He was told she had been healed through Christian Science. Years later, incidentally, he learned that she had grown to be a strong, healthy woman with two or three children of her own.

Having seen this amazing transformation with his own eyes, he began seriously studying Christian Science to find out how such a miracle could take place. He was beginning to conclude that this religion which healed through prayer might hold the answer to his own demoralizing problems.

He went to see the practitioner often. Before very long the practitioner discerned that he was carrying another terrible burden besides the drinking. He was nursing a violent hatred.

The man he hated was the credit manager of a customer firm. The hatred was mutual. The man used tactics that appeared to be deliberately designed to injure the salesman and cause him embarrassment in his company.

The practitioner pointed out that hatred is a barrier to progress and a foe of health and well-being. He urged the young salesman to study an article entitled "Love Your Enemies" in *Miscellaneous Writings* by Mrs. Eddy.

My friend read and studied this article hundreds of times. One statement struck him with profound impact: "Can you see an enemy, except you first formulate this enemy and then look upon the object of your own conception?" (Misc. p. 8)

This was a challenge! It put the matter squarely up to him.

He was hating his own mental conception of the other man. It didn't matter what the other man was doing, or whether the other man was hating him. What did matter was the state of his own mental household—whether his own thoughts were filled with hatred, or with the love that comes from God. He set to work to change his thinking.

Through a deeper study of the Master's teachings, and the explanations of God as Love to be found in Christian Science, he was successful. He gained some understanding of man as God had created him—upright, just, pure, free, whole. He was able to imbibe in some measure the spirit of Christian love which Jesus taught. As a result of earnest study and prayer, his heart was cleansed forever of the hatred.

The drinking tapered off but still he wasn't able to get rid of the habit. Then one night some months after he had started studying Christian Science, he stopped at a bar as usual on his way home from work. He ordered a drink. It came. He sipped it. It tasted "just as bitter as quinine." He pushed it away, and walked out. That was the end of the drinking.

All this was only a beginning. With the burden of hatred and alcoholism removed fom his heart by the touch of the Christ, he became a better salesman. His home became happy and he progressed in business. After some time he was made a vice president of his company.

Years followed during which he served ably as an executive in several large industrial corporations. He became recognized as a member of the upper echelons of the American business community. During wartime he served in the army in a position of large responsibilities. After the war he served his country in an important overseas assignment.

Finally, as the capstone of a distinguished career, he was appointed assistant secretary of the army for logistics, a post he held for five years. It was an assignment of vast complexities and worldwide responsibilities, involving the spending of billions of dollars.

He discharged his responsibilities with unusual distinction, earning the respect of the administration in Washington from the President on down. When he retired after five years in office, his departure was the occasion of a governmental ceremony which reporters said was seldom equaled in Washington. Among other things, there was a seventeen-gun salute and he was awarded the civilian Distinguished Service Medal. Today this man is a management consultant to some of the largest industrial enterprises in the United States.

All this followed that first encounter with Christian Science. "Any success that has come to me," says this man, "the privilege of serving my Government, the opportunities I have had—all of this I feel has stemmed directly from my study of Christian Science."

3.

There are certain distinguishing characteristics of Christian Scientists which lie just below the surface. Let us cite a few.

Practically every Christian Scientist is a Christian Scientist because he has made a deliberate personal choice to be one.

Being a Christian Scientist is not like being an Irishman or a Texan: an Irishman is an Irishman by birth; a Texan is a Texan by geography.

Not so with the Christian Scientist. He is not a Christian Scientist by birth, by geography, or even by association with others. Nor is he one by an outward ceremony of christening or baptism. If he joins the church, it will be because he wants to; but even church affiliation, by itself, could not make him a Christian Scientist.

Even if he was born into a Christian Science family and has attended the Sunday school from infancy, there comes a time sooner or later when he has to think through its teachings for himself, and make the deeply personal decision whether or not he will embrace them.

There are perhaps two reasons for this. One is that the teachings of Christian Science are so radical they challenge the deepest convictions of the human mind. They run utterly contrary to the external appearances of things in this world. One can accept them as true only by thinking deeply—pondering them, searching his own thoughts, reasoning perceptively and proving what he learns in practice.

It is true that some people do accept the teachings without much effort at the start. But these people are quite rare, and sooner or later comes the demand for perceptive reasoning. The teachings are so revolutionary that it would be difficult to accept them and be faithful to them, unless one thought deeply and made the choice for himself.

The other reason is that to be a genuine Christian Scientist requires continual study, prayer, and striving. This is not a faith one can successfully embrace in name only. It is not a religion in which, like a sponge, one can soak things up without much effort. It calls for daily effort and self-immolation. Its benefits are vast but they must be earned. The only way one can really absorb the teachings sufficiently to benefit very much from them is to make a persistent and courageous effort to live them.

Of course there are some who attend church services but have never really committed themselves to the teachings. Others, outside the church, lightly assert that they are Christian Scientists, because this suits their fancy. But this is like claiming to be a musician when one never plays music.

On the other hand, it is known, from sales of Christian Science literature, that many individuals, some of them churchgoers of other faiths, privately and even secretly study the teachings of Christian Science and try to live them.

The point is that being a Christian Scientist means adopting a way of prayer and a way of life—not merely a label. The result is that the real Christian Scientist is a worker. He studies daily. He prays—in his home and in free moments during his work. He schools himself in the art of turning to God, divine Mind, in every circumstance for guidance and inspiration.

For example, the active Christian Scientist studies daily the Christian Science Lesson-Sermon for that week, comprised of selected passages on a given subject from the Bible and from the Christian Science textbook, *Science and Health with Key to the Scriptures,* by Mrs. Eddy. To read the lesson takes about half an hour. To study it thoroughly takes more time. Many devout Christian Scientists spend an hour or more daily in study of the lesson and in prayer.

It is not uncommon for a Scientist to rise at a very early hour each morning for the sole purpose of such study before the day's activities begin. I recall one time I happened to mention this to some personal friends, a university professor and his wife. The wife's reaction was one of unrestrained merriment. She could not understand why anybody would get up early in the morning to study his religion!

But as a Christian Scientist sees it, no subject could be more important or more interesting than the nature of God, and man's relationship to Him. What we call the material universe is so vast that men often spend a lifetime studying one tiny facet of it. If one feels his religion reveals the real universe of Spirit—the Science of his own being and the answers to all his problems—then it is natural for him to think of study as a normal part of religious practice.

So far as getting up early in the morning is concerned, the Scientist feels there's a good deal of logic here, too. A good housekeeper straightens up the house in the morning. The Scientist finds it even more important to keep his thinking straight. To him, it doesn't make sense to leave one's mental home untended, rushing madly into the day's activities with a confused or untidy mentality. He finds that earnest prayer can take away the fears, frustrations, annoyances, discouragements, hurts, resentments of human living, so that they don't accumulate in his mental household like cobwebs and old shoes.

So he turns in prayer to God. He cultivates a sense of God's presence, strives to gain a better understanding of Him, drinks in the joy and inspiration so richly provided in his religious source-books, and endeavors to remove from his thoughts whatever is base or unworthy.

Hand in hand with this goes the conviction so marked among Christian Scientists—so fundamental to their religion, in fact —that human nature actually can be improved, and that the improvement must start with prayer for oneself. If one has a bad temper, for example, he will not conclude resignedly that he has always been that way, that it runs in the family anyhow, that it really is the result of circumstances, and that he is always going to be that way. On the contrary, the Christian Scientist's outlook will be characterized, in the degree of his spiritual growth, by a refusal to accept evil as inevitable, and a positive conviction that he can do something about his frailties because divine good has unlimited power.

He bases his conviction upon the understanding that after all, man's real nature in the image of God must be good, pure, upright, spiritual, perfect—and that anything contrary to this is an illusion.

In a remarkably high percentage of instances, the conviction that prayer is effective is based upon personal experience as well as religious teaching.

Suppose you were to select ten church members at random and persuade each one to tell you the story of his life and his religious experience. It is safe to say that nine of them, but more likely that every one of them, would include in his narrative some physical healing he himself has experienced through prayer, or would tell you of other kinds of problems which he has overcome through specific, systematic prayer as taught in Christian Science.

In fact it goes even further than that. A substantial percentage of the people who become Christian Scientists have, at some point in their lives, been considered beyond hope because of physical maladies. That is the reason, and often the only reason, why they decided to "try Christian Science." Quite large numbers of such people have been restored, entirely by spiritual means, to lasting health. The result is that in any typical group of Christian Scientists, you are likely to encounter a number who have found themselves at the portal of death and then been rescued by the prayer of absolute reliance on God—or who have had a close relative who has gone through such an experience.

The healings are not only of neurasthenic conditions, or maladies now termed psychosomatic by doctors, but are also of cancer, tuberculosis of the bone, arthritis, or other organic conditions, sometimes far advanced. Often the diagnosis was fully established by exhaustive medical tests before Christian Science was resorted to. And many times, too, the patient has had occasion, after his healing, to seek a medical examination for insurance purposes, employment purposes, or other reasons. Such examinations, together with successive years of good health, have attested to the completeness of the healing. These facts go a long way to explain the steadfastness and consistency with which Christian Scientists rely upon divine help.

4.

Again let me cite an actual example. This one is quite close to me, but it is typical of what has happened in many Christian Science families.

From early childhood, the person of whom I speak had been perplexed by the enigma of life, its meaning and purpose. As a little girl she sometimes would leave her play to run to her mother and ask, "Mother, who am I and why am I here?"

Her mother didn't know what to say, except, "You are my little girl and you are here because I love you." But the question persisted as the child grew older.

During her years at the university she became active in church work and in the work of interfaith groups. But there were doctrines she could not accept—in particular the view that God knows disease and disaster and visits these evils upon His helpless creation.

On one occasion, while attending an interfaith conference, the young student heard a prominent religious teacher tell a seminar group that God sends calamities to make us love Him, and also to purify and strengthen us. Hearing this she set the class in an uproar by remarking that the less she had to do with that kind of God, the better off she would be. She went home from the conference with doubts more bitter than before. These multiplied until finally she left the church and became a militant atheist.

A few years later, as a county high school teacher in a remote settlement in Colorado, she lived with a family whose chief topic of dinner conversation seemed to be criticism of a strange religion called Christian Science. The young teacher had never heard of it. Curious as to what could arouse such ridicule, she went one Saturday afternoon to see the only Christian Science practitioner in the area.

The practitioner recommended the study of Christian Science. The young teacher responded that the subject of religion was strictly taboo with her; that she had studied them all, except Christian Science, and they had all turned to dust. "And so will Christian Science," she added.

"But do you feel it is fair to pass judgment on a religion you admit you know nothing about?" asked the practitioner. Reluctantly the young teacher accepted a loan of the Christian Science textbook, *Science and Health,* and promised to read it.

The young woman was struck by the beauty of the little leatherbound volume, but she argued her way strenuously through its pages. Then she returned it with relief.

But she could not quite forget it. Thinking it a beautiful volume to look at, she finally bought a copy. Admiring its appearance, she would notice a sentence here and there. Slowly it dawned upon her that the statements she was reading were irrefutable. Her interest increased. Occasionally she read other Christian Science literature. But her resistance was strong and her attitude changed but slowly.

A year or so later, she and another teacher boarded a train in El Paso, bound for Chicago, to visit relatives during the summer. Before long the other teacher fell violently ill. So extreme was the condition that they left the train at Hutchinson, Kansas, and went to the Bisonte Hotel, which was near the railroad station.

Not knowing anybody in town, the young teacher recalled that she had in her suitcase a copy of *The Christian Science Journal,* with its directory of practitioners. She asked her sick friend if she would care to have her call a Christian Science practitioner, and the friend agreed.

The practitioner came to the hotel room and prayed until after midnight. The sick girl fell asleep. Next morning she was perfectly well. The two travelers resumed their journey.

The young woman who had witnessed the healing was deeply impressed. A few years later, after she had married and settled down in a lonely desert village of Arizona, she happened one day to tell her husband the details of this episode.

A little while after that, their first child, a boy, was born. Six weeks later the mother fell ill with what the doctor described as malignant blood poisoning. For seven weeks she lay in a semicoma. All that kept her alive was her determination that she must live to take care of the child. The doctor, a deeply sincere and kindly man, did everything he knew how to do. Five times he operated. But after the fifth operation the patient lapsed into a deep coma and then all hope was abandoned.

At this point the distraught husband remembered the strange story his wife had told him of the healing of the schoolteacher in that hotel room in Hutchinson, Kansas. He could even recall the name of the practitioner. He got on his bicycle and rushed to the telegraph office, where he urgently wired to that same practitioner for his help through prayer.

This was on a Tuesday. On Thursday his sick wife rallied and unaccountably regained consciousness. When the doctor came she was sitting up in bed. On Saturday morning the patient insisted on getting up. When the doctor came that day she was dressed and out in the yard, wheeling her baby in its carriage.

The doctor was astonished. He asked her if he could make an examination. He found that the wounds in the woman's left side and breast, which had been the seat of the trouble, had healed. He saw that only slight scars remained. He said in sincere humility, "Mrs.———, I don't know what has healed you. But one thing I do know, and that is, that I didn't. It is a miracle!"

Physical healing had never been this woman's primary interest in Christian Science. Until this illness she had always been considered a rugged type. True, she had suffered violent headaches from childhood, and often they had lasted two or three weeks. But as she relates now, "Such difficulties were regarded as more or less normal in those days, so nothing had ever been done about it."

But after this healing the woman embraced Christian Science and began to study it more carefully. Gradually the headaches disappeared. So did other illnesses in the family, including a persistent condition of eczema.

From that period onward illness gradually faded from the family history, and there was steadily unfolding well-being and happiness, though not without severe crises at times.

But it was not the healings, or the outward well-being, that meant the most to the woman. By her own statements today, it was the answer she found in her study of Christian Science to those questions that had troubled her from childhood. She gained a new concept of God—a God she could trust, a God she could love, because now she understood Him to be infinite Love, unfailing good, and always near. She gained a new insight into the nature and purpose of man—an understanding that man lives because God lives; that man's purpose is to bear witness to God's nature; that life is a glorious adventure in which the spiritual resources available to man are boundless and his possibilities for good are without end.

She had come a long way from the bitter frustration and despair of atheism. She had experienced the change of outlook epitomized by the Psalmist when he said, "I shall not die, but live, and declare the works of the Lord" (Psa. 118:17).

To many people, healings like this one seem incredible. Are they really true? Are they exaggerated? Are they miracles? Even if they are true, how can one safely rely upon the religion that produced them? What is their explanation?

These are questions we shall consider. So far as this particular experience is concerned, I know that it actually happened just as related—and that the woman is hale and hearty today, active, healthy, more useful to others than ever before.

I well remember the headaches this individual used to have during my early childhood. But they are indeed a remembrance of things past. I don't think she has had a headache in thirty-five years.

5.

Now let us be a bit more specific about some of the outward characteristics of Christian Scientists.

Most of the Scientists I know are calm, balanced, thoughtful, quiet, prayerful people. Their outlook is characterized, in some degree at least, by devoutness, faith, spiritual conviction, and joy, and all this tends to show in their lives and attitudes.

It is true that many unhappy people have turned to Christian Science for help, just as have many well-adjusted persons in blooming good health. Not all who come for help have been healed quickly; but the fact is that a great many have regained excellent health and increased harmony in their daily living. Many have gained encouragement to look outside of themselves, to exchange selfish interests for unselfish purposes.

There are not so very many poor people who are Christian Scientists, but there are quite a few who used to be poor before they felt the influence of this religion in their lives. Such people have found that this religion has removed from their lives the causes of their poverty: ill health, alcoholism, lack of opportunity, inferiority, insecurity, resignation, personality problems. Many have been able to prove that such things as lack can be overcome by earnest prayer just as can hate and physical suffering—even as Christ Jesus taught and demonstrated.

So far as education is concerned, it is true that Christian Science appeals to those who are willing to read and study and think and improve themselves, whatever their schooling may have been. It calls for patient effort and disciplined thinking. But individuals of very limited formal education have embraced it. Many of its students have found over the years that its influence tends to expand their horizons and bring deeper culture to their thinking. There are comparatively few poorly educated Christian Scientists, and a rather high percentage are college-educated.

There are some families which have included Christian Scientists among their members for as many as four or five generations. And many individuals have been practicing Scientists, relying wholly upon their religion in matters of health and in other needs, for more than half a century. On the other hand, some of the churches are composed largely of young families, and many of the Sunday schools are bulging.

Many young Christian Scientists have embarked upon careers in business, the arts, and the professions; but some, putting aside other interests and promising secular careers, are choosing to devote their lives to healing the sick and the sinner through prayer, as Christian Science practitioners.

Because of the fact that Christian Science teaches exclusive and complete reliance on God for healing, it is sometimes assumed that Christian Scientists are "against doctors." This, however, is misleading and oversimplified.

It is true that relying concurrently on Christian Science and medicine does not work out well; the two systems are so vastly different in diagnostic approach, in their concept of the nature of disease, and in their healing procedure, that they cannot work in cooperation; this would be unfair to both systems and dangerous to the patient. The fundamental assumptions of Christian Science are opposite to those of medical theory: for example, that all disease is essentially a mental condition, and that man, in his true nature, is essentially a spiritual being and not a material organism.

It is a fact, also, that Christian Scientists have a positive desire to help all mankind into the world of spiritual therapy; for on the basis of their own experience they feel that much good for mankind lies in this direction.

But Christian Scientists do not question medical methods for those who wish them. They would not attempt to force their convictions on anyone else—nor would they "close all the hospitals if they had the chance," as is occasionally asserted by critics. They deeply respect the right of every individual to make his own choice in health matters. They do not question the right of anyone to depend on medical methods.

Furthermore, Christian Scientists respect and appreciate the sincere and conscientious efforts of the medical profession to alleviate human suffering and stamp out disease. Their appreciation of this humanitarian goal is especially deep because they themselves share it and are working in a different way to achieve it.

What they are "against," however, is dictation by the state or by organized private interests to accept medical methods. Over the years they have resisted efforts to compel them to adopt medical measures, on the ground that they should have the right to live their religion and rely upon it for healing. It is this resistance which may have led some to think they are "against doctors."

There are some other ways in which a Christian Scientist's basic attitude toward health tends to shape his behavior. For one thing, his religion teaches that not just some kinds but all kinds of disease can be healed through spiritual means; that all physical discord is amenable to divine power when this power is understood and utilized properly. Consequently the Christian Scientist, if confronted with serious illness, is not likely to accept it as incurable.

Some people in such circumstances tend toward an acceptance of the situation, a mental attitude of accepting without question the medical prognosis no matter how discouraging it is. As a result there are many of the seriously ill who are resigned and even gloomy about their prospects. Some fight but many don't.

On the other hand the Christian Scientist is inclined to view the situation, no matter how dire, with a noticeable hope, faith, and expectation of healing. On the basis of his religious insights he will refuse to accept the physical evidence as final. He will make a strenuous effort to avail himself of those mental and spiritual resources which resist disease and ward it off. He is likely to show a marked degree of both optimism and fight. Instead of building up disease by thinking about it and talking about it, looking at its manifestations, and impressing it vividly on the mind, he will strive to turn his thoughts to the contemplation of God's goodness, perfection, and supreme power, and to understand Him better.

Rarely can a Christian Scientist be drawn into any extended discussion of sickness. There are many people who have a tendency to discuss their operations, their allergies, their expectations of illness. The genuine Christian Scientist strives to avoid sick thinking and talking, however, because in his view sick thoughts make sick bodies.

This view, of course, is not exclusively limited to Christian Scientists. Most doctors recognize that discouragement has a depressing effect upon recovery, and that a patient who feels his life has meaning is more apt to get well. It is commonly acknowledged today that many kinds of sickness have their origin in sick thinking—in fear, bitterness, grief, frustration, maladjustment, tension, anxiety, guilt, and so on.

As noted physician Dr. Paul Ernest Adolph writes in *The Evidence of God in an Expanding Universe*:

My own experience happens to coincide with an awakening in recent years within the medical profession as to the importance of psychological elements in the science of medicine. For instance, today it is recognized on reliable authority that 80 per cent of all the illnesses encountered in general practice in our large American cities have a predominantly psychic causation, and that half of these 80 per cent involve no demonstrable organic causative factors whatsoever. In this connection it should be mentioned that it is the concept generally accepted by the medical profession that these diseases with the strong psychic, or so-called nervous, component, are not imaginary in any way.

The Christian Scientist, as mentioned earlier, traces *all* disease to mental factors, and especially to fear. Consequently he regards a detailed conversation about sickness with about as little relish as other people would regard a contagion. In taking this position it is not that he is trying to live in a fool's paradise. He is simply convinced that one's life tends to be filled with the kinds of things he thinks about.

If one were to feed constantly a morbid interest in stealing, very likely he would either feel the temptation to steal or would find himself living in fear of being victimized by thieves. One's thoughts tend to father his actions, and they shape the kind of world he makes for himself. This seems all too apparent in an age when a steady diet of television crime dramas is often cited as a contributing factor to juvenile delinquency.

There are some other conversational earmarks of the Christian Scientist. Every field of activity has its own special language. That applies to baseball fans, lawyers, and many other groups. Some of the terms Christian Scientists commonly use among themselves—"mortal mind," for instance, meaning what Paul called the carnal mind, or carnal-mindedness—are derived from Mrs. Eddy's writings. Another example is the word "demonstration," meaning a proof of divine power in terms of healing or some other victory over discord. Other terms, such as "protective work," which refers to prayerful mental work of a preventive character, have grown up in usage but have no particular authority.

It may be noted, too, that profanity is conspicuous by its absence among Christian Scientists. While there may be individual exceptions, the generally accepted standard among them is literal obedience to the third commandment of Moses.

Another generalization we can safely make is that Christian Scientists do not smoke or drink. There are individual exceptions, especially among those who are nominally Scientists but do not work at it very hard. But Christian Science churches do not ordinarily grant membership to those who use tobacco or alcohol, and in overwhelming majority the members do live strictly by this standard.

A Christian Scientist does not view this as a deprivation. Nor does he take an attitude of "holier than thou" toward those who do smoke or drink. His reasons are grounded in the logic of his religion as well as its spirit.

His religion teaches him that the way of salvation is a way

of triumph over dependence on matter. As he views it, the winning of salvation includes the establishing of his dominion over his own body through spiritual power; not that the body shall rule him. He learns that the divine energies available for the saving of humanity can and should be utilized to win this freedom. The practice of his religion includes reliance on these energies to overcome whatever would enslave him. His goal is to exchange the servitude of materialism for what Paul called "the glorious liberty of the sons of God."

People sometimes wonder why smoking, so generally considered to be morally acceptable, should bar a person from membership in a Christian Science church, when there are so many things so much worse—selfishness, domination, or hate, for instance. The answer is that smoking, or drinking, are acquired appetites—voluntarily acquired. Now one starts with the easiest steps in Christian progress. Broadly speaking, one might logically be expected to avoid the voluntary acquiring of an undesirable appetite, and then go on from there to win his freedom from the more deeply rooted sins of human nature.

So far as alcoholic beverages are concerned, the Christian Scientist feels that whatever happiness and elation they seem to bring is essentially deceptive. They work against clear thinking.

Occasionally a Christian Scientist is asked why it is necessary for religion to "take all the joy out of life." From his viewpoint, however, his religion does not take the joy out of life; it brings joy into his life. True, he does not turn to a cigarette for relaxation and social poise or to a cocktail for release and good fellowship. But the reason is that he feels he has found a much better way to bring these values into his experience.

From his point of view, poise, freedom, spontaneity, inspiration, the spirit underlying true fellowship—all these are native to man's genuine selfhood. They are inherent in his real individuality as the likeness of God. They derive from the infinite source of all good—God, divine Love, the infinite Giver—and are bestowed upon man unfailingly and impartially, permanently and without measure. The Scientist finds all this to be demonstrable here and now in practical ways, insofar as man's relationship to God is scientifically understood. As a result he prefers to draw upon the wellsprings of spiritual good for the qualities that make one a well-rounded and well-adjusted person.

With generally accepted social standards being what they are today, the ranks of Christian Scientists include large numbers who have been released from the smoking and drinking habits through Christian Science. They have permanently lost any desire whatever for either tobacco or liquor. I have yet to find a single one who regrets it.

One will also find among his Christian Scientist friends a noticeable absence of gambling. While undoubtedly some individuals are exceptions, the generally accepted standard among Christian Scientists would prohibit gambling.

There is much more to this than a "Thou shalt not. . . ." A Christian Scientist thinks of his religion as setting forth immutable laws, the eternal laws of God. He conceives of these unvarying laws as demonstrable by anyone who understands them and is willing to follow the rules in relying upon them.

Adopting as his standpoint unchanging Science, or divine law, in which accidents are unknown, the Christian Scientist feels it would be insincere and self-defeating to follow so-called laws of chance. The deliberate acceptance of uncertainties runs counter to reliance upon the divine Principle, which knows no uncertainty. The result would be a divided loyalty, a divided heart, a mental household at war with itself. The fact that gambling is sometimes habit-forming would only intensify the conflict. If one makes the so-called laws of chance his bosom companion in his social life, his sports, or for financial gain, he cannot very logically expect, in other areas of his life, to overcome the uncertainties of mortal existence by resort to spiritual law. A double standard is unworkable. Thus the Christian Scientist feels that when he avoids gambling, he is contributing to stability in every avenue of his life.

We have noted the importance of joy in the religious outlook of the Christian Scientists. It is safe to say, as a general statement, that Christian Scientists are an unusually joyful people. There are exceptions, of course. But as a general rule, the working Christian Scientist draws from his religion the honest conviction that good is supreme, man is immortal, and evil is doomed. He cultivates daily a sense of his own direct relationship to God, and conceives of his own real self as being always in harmony with God.

All this brings a growing sense of quiet joy and deep peace. This joy is bound to be expressed in an outer warmth and good humor. Fundamentally he is serious, thoughtful, reverent. But to most Scientists, laughter and fun are not strangers.

In view of the multitudes of taut, fearful, unhappy, bitter faces one sees on the streets of some of our cities, it is small wonder that a sense of closeness to God, with the joy this brings, means so much to Christian Scientists.

Some observers have wrongly concluded that this buoyancy is merely a shallow optimism or a selfish lack of concern for the afflictions of mankind. It is anything but that. It is something quite different and much deeper. Some of the most joyful people I have ever known have been exceedingly busy Christian Science practitioners who, in their compassionate efforts to help others, come face to face every month with more trouble, more suffering, more misery, and more human perversity than most people encounter in a decade.

Their buoyancy is based upon their experience of seeing patient after patient released from prisons of suffering or sin by means of prayer. It comes from a deep conviction that good is supreme, that life is triumphant. The wellspring of their joy is the awakened sense that the absolute reality of being is wholly good; that a good God is all-powerful and that this can be demonstrated in the healing and saving of mankind. They draw inspiration from their spiritual conviction that final victory never lies on the side of disillusionment, frustration, loneliness, defeat, death, but inevitably on the side of salvation and joy, goodness and freedom, dominion and harmony. To the Christian Scientist, the central fact of Christianity is victory over the flesh. His joy comes from the deep realities of Christian revelation—truths which he nurtures in his own heart with the reverence of daily communion and the quiet gratitude of humble prayer.

Chapter Two

What Kind of Religion?

The Christian Scientist is a Christian Scientist because he finds in this religion a satisfying answer to his deepest questions. Most of us share those inner yearnings, common to humanity, to understand basic truth: the nature of God and the explanation of who we are and why we exist. We yearn to *know*—to know what is really true, and to feel it so surely and so profoundly that Truth becomes real and living to us, transforming our lives.

Many have been attracted to Christian Science because they have found in it a religion which rejects the proposition that God is the great unknown, or the unknowable. From the viewpoint of its adherents, Christian Science reveals God, and it makes the understanding of God practical in human experience.

But the Christian Scientist would be the first to agree that the full understanding of God is not to be gained in a few easy lessons, or even in a limited span of years. Manifestly the truth of God is as infinite as God Himself; the unfolding of it makes eternal life itself a grand adventure. But one can grow a little each day in this understanding; and when the fundamentals are right, this growth uplifts human experience and illumines the road to salvation.

Thus it should be stressed that no summary like the present one could fully cover the subject. While the fundamentals of this religion remain the same for all students and are universal, each individual approaches the subject from where he is, assimilates what he is ready to grasp, and demonstrates the fundamentals progressively, step by step, in his own experience. Consequently any chapter of this sort, even though couched in general terms, must express the vantage point of its author.

For an understanding of God the Christian Scientist turns to two textbooks he considers authoritative. The first is the Bible. He uses the King James Version, known in Britain as the Authorized Version. He studies it daily, and hears it read at all the church services. Many Scientists also use various modern translations and Bible commentaries for reference purposes.

In the Christian Scientist's search for God, the scriptural message is of central importance. To him the Bible occupies a unique place; it records the unfolding revelation of the nature of God. It contains within its pages the way of salvation.

Used in conjunction with the Bible is the Christian Science textbook, *Science and Health with Key to the Scriptures*, by Mary Baker Eddy. In no way does this textbook replace the Bible. The phrase *Key to the Scriptures* indicates the relationship. This book sheds new light on the Bible—a light which reveals the Science contained in the Scriptures from Genesis to Revelation. It presents rules and precepts which enable the student to practice the Master's teachings in healing the sick and in other demonstrations of spiritual power.

In Christian Science the words and works of Christ Jesus are foundational. The Scientist's view of the Saviour's mission differs in certain important respects from traditionally accepted doctrines in the older churches, but one finds the Master's teachings pervading the whole of Christian Science.

It has sometimes been asserted that Christian Science "denies every doctrine of apostolic Christianity." But this is far from true. A distinction needs to be made between the outward forms and the inward meaning of Christian worship. Many can testify that as they have explored this Science more thoroughly, they have found their appreciation of Christ Jesus growing profoundly, and their grasp of essential Christian concepts to be clarified and spiritualized.

As a result of the explanations given by his religion, the Christian Scientist accepts Christ Jesus as the Saviour of the world. He believes that Jesus was born of a virgin, lived in the flesh, healed the sick and reformed sinners, suffered, sacrificed, and triumphed in order to show forth the nature of the eternal God, divine Love, and reveal to mortals the way out of sin.

The Scientist accepts with joy the fact that Christ Jesus indeed dwelt among us, overcame death, rose from the grave with his selfsame body, and then ascended beyond human perception—leaving the spirit of Truth to bear witness in our hearts that he "hath abolished death, and hath brought life and immortality to light through the gospel" (II Tim. 1:10).

The Christian Scientist comes to regard the Master with the greatest gratitude and affection, because of what Jesus has done for humanity and because this religion brings out so clearly the meaning of the Saviour's earthly career. This estimate of his work is indicated in *No and Yes* where Mrs. Eddy writes: "Jesus' sacrifice stands pre-eminently amidst physical suffering and human woe. The glory of human life is in overcoming sickness, sin, and death. Jesus suffered for all mortals to bring in this glory; and his purpose was to show them that the way out of the flesh, out of the delusion of all human error, must be through the baptism of suffering, leading up to health, harmony, and heaven" (No. 33:22).

As the Christian Scientist sees it, Jesus was indeed a man who walked among men; but he was one whose consciousness was so perfectly in unity with God that he revealed the Christ, the ideal Truth, which redeems humanity. The Scientist does not espouse either the Docetic view, which holds that Jesus' body was a phantom, or spirit, or the humanistic explanation of him as only a man like other men. He understands the Saviour as having a dual nature—the man seen by other men, and the unseen Christ, or spirit of Truth and Love, which was "made flesh" in Jesus' mighty works.

Mrs. Eddy speaks of Jesus as the human man and of Christ as the divine idea, and she writes in *Science and Health:* "Christ expresses God's spiritual, eternal nature. The name is synonymous with Messiah, and alludes to the spirituality which is taught, illustrated, and demonstrated in the life of which Christ Jesus was the embodiment" (S&H 333:9). And further: "This Christ, or divinity of the man Jesus, was his divine nature, the godliness which animated him" (S&H 26:12).

Such terms as the "divinity of the man Jesus" and "the godliness which animated him" could only refer to that which is eternal and inseparable from God. They refer to the spirit of Truth, which Jesus exemplified—the Christ, or Way. As the Christian Scientist views it, it was the Christ—the very nature and presence of God made manifest to humanity through Jesus —that enabled Jesus to say, "He that hath seen me hath seen the Father" (John 14:9).

One finds all this throwing a light on the question of the incarnation. The Scientist does not accept the view that God took the form of a material man and walked the earth, because he understands God to be the eternal and all-encompassing creator. But he does accept the incarnation, if by this is meant that the incorporeal Christ, or divine idea of God, was revealed, taught, shown forth, demonstrated in healing and in other mighty works—and thus embodied in the flesh—by the man Jesus.

Through his study the Scientist comes to realize that the truth the Saviour taught and demonstrated is eternal; it is always present everywhere, needing only to be understood. On this basis he is satisfied that the incorporeal Christ is always here—not as a bodily presence, but as the practical truth, which is of God. Mrs. Eddy refers to the everpresence of the Christ, Truth, when she writes:

> Throughout all generations both before and after the Christian era, the Christ, as the spiritual idea, the reflection of God, has come with some measure of power and grace to all prepared to receive Christ, Truth. Abraham, Jacob, Moses, and the prophets caught glorious glimpses of the Messiah, or Christ, which baptized these seers in the divine nature, the essence of Love (S&H 333:19).

Through the healing and transforming experiences which come to him and to others through prayer, the Christian Scientist finds that we may know this everpresent divine influence in our hearts and lives by drinking in the spirit of Jesus' teachings, assimilating and digesting the truth he taught. While Scientists do not celebrate this with literal use of the bread and the wine, they do observe it through deep and humble prayer. For them the sacrament of communion takes place daily in one's own heart and thoughts and actions, insofar as one imbibes the spirit of Christ and thus acknowledges man's true unity with God.

Many have found that this divine influence, received and welcomed into one's thinking, brings a purging and uplifting of thought. This purifying process, going on continually and expelling evil and error from consciousness, is what baptism means to the Christian Scientist. He feels that one can truly experience baptism only insofar as this genuine purging, or Christian regeneration, takes place in his innermost thoughts, through his own prayerful efforts and the transforming power of the Christ.

Thus the Christian Scientist recognizes that he must do his individual part in working out his salvation, but he also recognizes with great gratitude that these efforts are crowned with success through the grace of God as expressed in Christ.

Paul expressed this thought when he wrote to the Philippians: "Work out your own salvation with fear and trembling. For it is God which worketh in you both to will and to do of his good pleasure" (Phil. 2:12,13).

Christian Scientists do not subscribe to the view that Jesus endured the crucifixion in order to appease an angry God and thus expiate our sins; they do not view his sacrifice as a vicarious atonement for the sins of those who had gone before and those who would come after him. Rather their understanding is that by his suffering, his resurrection and ascension, he revealed the nature of God as ineffable Love, and showed mortals the *way* of redemption from sin—through tears, toil, and the joy of divine Truth understood and demonstrated as supreme over all. For the Scientist, the meaning of the atonement is to be found not in a bargain with an estranged God, but in Christ's revelation of the all-power of divine Love and of man's spiritual birthright of unity with this Love.

The Scientist finds that this view of the atonement does not diminish his appreciation of Christ Jesus but magnifies it. Nor does it cancel one's debt to the Master, since he said, "If ye love me, keep my commandments." Far from lessening the meaning of the cross, it heightens it by calling on each follower to take up the cross in daily life and *live* the teachings of Christ. Mrs. Eddy speaks of the cross as the central emblem of human history.

The standard emblem on authorized Christian Science literature is the Cross and the Crown. Every true Christian Scientist cherishes this emblem in his heart. He accepts not only the crucifixion but also the resurrection and the ascension as literal facts. And so his appreciation of the Saviour embraces not only the sacrifice but also the unparalleled victory over the flesh; not only the agony of Gethsemane but also the empty tomb; not only the gloom of Calvary but also the joyful news: Christ is risen!

One's appreciation of Jesus' work for humanity grows stronger as he realizes that by the resurrection Jesus revealed the power of Truth as absolute, final, supreme—and thus he showed to mankind God's way of salvation. The Saviour proved that man's life is deathless. He demonstrated, step by step, that divine Love can overrule hatred, pain, physical law, matter, and death. He proved that the Christ is not at the mercy of material conditions, but is above the reach of malice. He showed that the Christ is able, through Truth, Life, and Love, to triumph over sickness, sin, and death.

As one ponders this line of thought he begins to realize that Jesus tore the mask from evil and proved it to be deceptive and fraudulent. The Master showed that evil is not final, not supreme; that it has neither sanction nor foundation in the law of God. He proved that in the final analysis all evil must bow before the power of Truth, Life, and Love. Once and for all he proved that, in his own words, the devil, or evil, "is a liar and the father of lies" (RSV John 8:44).

This indicates what the Christian Scientist means when he holds evil to be "unreal." He means that it is a pattern of lies; that it has no basis in the all-inclusive God, who is Life, Truth, Love; that it is temporal and delusive, a false consciousness of existence; that in the omnipresence of God, who is Good, this self-deluded dream cannot really exist; that its nothingness can be proved here and now—to human sense, it can be annihilated —by resort to the law of God, the law of Spirit, which Jesus demonstrated.

To give this sublime example was the reason, as the Scientist sees it, for our Master's patient and selfless human sacrifice. As Mrs. Eddy explains in *Science and Health:* "Jesus could have withdrawn himself from his enemies. He had power to lay down a human sense of life for his spiritual identity in the like-ness of the divine; but he allowed men to attempt the destruc-tion of the mortal body in order that he might furnish the proof of immortal life" (S&H 51:6).

Even though agony, sin, and death belong solely to the nightmare of materiality, still this great fact had to be proved to humanity in order that the way of salvation might be re-vealed. How could it be revealed except by annihilating these evils through divine power?

Patiently the Master did this. He proved the power of Chris-tian love and understanding to come squarely to grips with the demonic power of evil and to destroy it—proving its unreality. To the Scientist, the glory of the Saviour's mission lies in the realism of omnipotent Life, Truth, and Love, which he proved so unmistakably for mortals.

No element of escapism is involved here, from the viewpoint of the Scientist, because he commanded his followers to do as he did and he gave them the means of doing so. The teachings of Christ, when understood, bring victory "over all the power of the enemy."

As Jesus himself declared: "These signs shall follow them that believe; In my name shall they cast out devils; they shall speak with new tongues; They shall take up serpents; and if they drink any deadly thing, it shall not hurt them; they shall lay hands on the sick, and they shall recover" (Mark 16:17,18). From the Scientist's viewpoint, the great import of the Master's teaching is best confirmed in the "signs following."

The Protestant theologian Karl Barth voices a central concern of Christianity. Writing in *The Word of God and the Word of Man* about why people go to church, he recognizes all the superficial and conventional influences which may take them there, but deep underneath it all he sees the innate human craving for positive assurance of the God revealed through Christ Jesus. What the people are really asking, he says, is: *Is it true?* He explains:

Is it true, this talk of a loving and good God, who is more than one of the friendly idols whose rise is so easy to account for, and whose dominion is so brief? What the people want to find out and thoroughly understand is, *Is it true?* . . . Let us not be surprised that this want of theirs seldom or never meets us openly with such urgency as I have indicated. People naturally do not shout it out, and least of all into the ears of us ministers. But let us not be deceived by their silence. . . . There is no wisdom in stopping at the next-to-the-last and the next-to-the-next-to-the-last want of the people; and they will not thank us for doing so. They expect us to understand them better than they understand themselves. We are misled not when we assume that they are brought to us by the last and profoundest questions, but rather when we think that when they come to us they may really be put off with next-to-the-last and less-profound answers.

Is it really true? Is it true that Christ's Gospel is more than a hallowed legend? Is it true that the Christian revelation of God, properly understood, can reach down to the very roots of one's being and meet his deepest cravings?

To these questions Christian Science answers with a mighty shout of joy: *Yes, it is true!* It is true that Christ Jesus literally rose from the dead. It is true that he overcame the final arguments of evil, matter, mortality. It is true that he revealed the supreme goodness of God and the immortality of man. It is true that the deathless Christ, Truth, is always present, always available to heal and save.

Out of nearly one hundred years of spiritual healing—out of the life experience of multitudes whose bodies have been restored, whose wounds have been bound up, whose sins have been purged, their tears dried, their lives filled with hope and faith—out of all this, Christian Science confirms: *It is true!* It is true that the transcendent power of Truth, which Jesus demonstrated, is effective today—for us of the twentieth century. It is true that this saving power of divine Love can be known and understood and felt and demonstrated—by us today.

Every Christian Scientist has felt, in some measure, the glorious thrill of these tidings. Many of them have felt the power of the Word in actual Christian works. They can say with the writer of John's first epistle: "That which was from the beginning, which we have heard, which we have seen with our eyes, which we have looked upon, and our hands have handled, of the Word of life. . . . That which we have seen and heard declare we unto you, that ye also may have fellowship with us: and truly our fellowship is with the Father, and with his Son Jesus Christ" (I John 1:1,3).

2.

We have said that Christian Scientists are a praying people. The opening chapter in *Science and Health* is entitled

"Prayer." It is of exceptional simplicity and tenderness; its clarity and depth throw much light on this subject.

When the Christian Scientist thinks of prayer, which is often, he thinks of wholehearted reliance on one infinite God, who is universal good—illimitable, unalloyed, perfect; boundless Love tenderly sustaining His children; supreme Mind, dwelling in infinite harmony. As the Scriptures say, "God is light, and in him is no darkness at all" (I John 1:5). Working from this premise he reaches the inevitable conclusion that evil—being utterly unlike Him—has no place, power, nor reality in God's universal presence.

It is never the Christian Scientist's aim in prayer to somehow change God, or to obtain His special intercession in some human situation. Rather, it is to bring human consciousness into communion with Truth, which annihilates discord.

This approach to prayer is indicated in *Science and Health* in these words: "Prayer cannot change the Science of being, but it tends to bring us into harmony with it" (S&H 2:15); and again: "It is our ignorance of God, the divine Principle, which produces apparent discord, and the right understanding of Him restores harmony" (S&H 390:7).

Since the purpose of the Christian Scientist's prayer is to bring human thinking into harmony with the divine Principle, Love, his method of praying is not limited to petition. It also includes acknowledgment—acknowledgment of the nature and power, the glory and goodness and presence of God. It includes the affirming of who and what God is, and of the true nature of man in His likeness. This in turn calls for mental rejection, or denial, of whatever opposes God or is unlike Him.

But the Christian Scientist feels that the only way he can truly acknowledge God is to understand God. And so he strives for the understanding of God which underlies all prayer in this religion. He seeks a clearer and deeper grasp of the Science of Love. He does not think of prayer as an emotional trust in the unknown. He does not think of God as inscrutable, hidden in mystery, forever concealed from humanity. On the contrary, he accepts at face value the Master's statement: "This is life eternal, that they might know thee the only true God, and Jesus Christ, whom thou hast sent" (John 17:3).

Insofar as he gains an understanding of the nature of God, and employs the reasoning which flows from it, the Christian Scientist feels he has available to him the spiritual power which moves mountains.

But this is not to imply that faith is of little importance to the Christian Scientist. Quite the contrary. In fact, he recognizes that a feeble or halfhearted faith is not enough. When the disciples asked Jesus why they could not heal the lunatic boy, he answered, "Because of your unbelief." As the Scientist sees it, the faith that moves mountains is wholehearted and absolute because it is based on understanding. It entertains no doubts as to the willingness and power of God to maintain universal harmony.

Since the purpose of prayer is to bring human consciousness into unity with the divine, the Scientist makes every effort to live the precepts his Master taught, and thus express the divine character. In Christian Science prayer is answered only insofar as we put our spiritual desires into practice.

Hand in hand with this element goes the importance of motives. A Christian Scientist does not pray for *things*. Nor does he mentally outline a specified solution to his problem. He strives to give up fear, pride, selfishness. His goal is to realize man's true and everlasting oneness with God. Love for God and man must be paramount. Prayer is worthy of answer only if it meets the Christly standard: "Seek ye first the kingdom of God, and his righteousness; and all these things shall be added unto you" (Matt. 6:33).

From all this it will be clear that to the Christian Scientist, prayer is an activity of mind and heart. This is typified by the silent prayer used in the churches, in which the whole congregation unites for a few moments before saying the Lord's Prayer together. So far as the individual Scientist is concerned, usually he will be alone when he prays; but he also will continue to pray in the silence of his own thinking as he goes about his work. When alone he usually will not kneel, but he will attach great importance to humility and an honest willingness to listen for God's direction. He may or may not close his eyes, clasp his hands, study passages in his textbooks, or speak out loud. But whatever he does, his aim will be a deep and wholehearted communion with God, a listening for the impulsion of Love, a knowing of divine Truth, which Jesus said would make us free.

The purpose and results of prayer are briefly summarized in this sentence from the chapter on "Prayer" in *Science and Health:* "Simply asking that we may love God will never make us love Him; but the longing to be better and holier, expressed in daily watchfulness and in striving to assimilate more of the divine character, will mould and fashion us anew, until we awake in His likeness" (S&H 4:17).

3.

We have said that a Christian Scientist's faith is based on an understanding of God. The more he advances in this understanding and in the proofs it brings of God's love, the more distinctly does he come to recognize God as the very center and circumference and essence of all being. This outlook is in sharp contrast to some of the prevalent thought trends of these times.

We live in an era which has largely lost touch with God. Millions have abandoned the faith of their fathers, feeling that symbols and dogmas once literally accepted no longer have relevance to the needs of the times. Many of the unchurched live by a sort of secular humanism, and scarcely ask the deepest questions—though these questions still linger below the crust of conscious thought and worldly concern.

Even within the churches there are multitudes who have no definite concept of God. Large numbers of children grow up to be spiritual illiterates. Broadly speaking, the present-day outlook of Western man seems characterized by a medley of doubts

as to the very existence of God, and an unquestioning conviction that if He exists, He cannot be expected to impinge upon
present-day human affairs as a tangible influence.

Yet rationalism and skepticism are not enough. This fact becomes increasingly apparent in the deepening shadows of world
crisis. Neither technology nor material strength can substitute
for a living faith in God. Christianity has largely shaped the
ethical, juridical, and social concepts upon which our civilization is built. Even though certain traditional dogmas and rites
are outmoded, it is a question whether our civilization could
retain its cohesiveness or its sense of purpose without the worship of God.

The Christian Scientist believes profoundly in the existence
of God. He holds the deep conviction that the power of God
is immediately demonstrable in human experience. He feels
that what is needed in order to bring this power to light in human situations is a clear and correct understanding of God, and
he finds this understanding attainable through Science, which
explains God.

As he explores Science he finds there is nothing vague about
the concept of God it presents. But this concept differs fundamentally from many widely accepted concepts of Him. As understood by the Scientist, God is absolutely unlike anything
mortal, material, or human—and cannot be described in such
terms.

Some religions, observing the nature of mortal man, have
attributed to Deity human qualities and even a physical form.
Others, accepting as literal certain Biblical statements which
Christian Science considers symbolic or figurative, have
thought of God as a Being who loves and hates. They have
thought of Him as someone who dispenses to individual mortals, on the basis of His knowledge of their specific deeds and
misdeeds, certain punishments or rewards, damnation or salvation. Other systems, contemplating the wonders of nature, have
conceived of God as an unknown essence of the natural world
and the material universe.

But from the viewpoint of the Christian Scientist, such concepts seem rather earthbound. It is characteristic of the human mind to think in terms of limits, to clothe all things with finite conceptions, and even to measure God in terms of time, space, human qualities, physical limitations, and material forces.

As a result of the approach given by this religion, the Christian Scientist does not start with limited concepts, mortal man, or even with the material universe in order to find an explanation of God. On the contrary, he recognizes that we can understand Him only as we detach thought from this material world and begin to explore the heights and depths of the infinite. He realizes, more and more clearly, that God can be understood only with thoughts derived from His own infinite nature, not with thoughts derived from the carnal mind.

In other words, he finds that Christian Science does not start with the material world and then try to discover what kind of God would have made it. Right here it parts company with rationalist theories, human philosophies, and, indeed, most religions. Christian Science starts solely with God, as the infinite, all-pervading, supreme, eternal, omnipotent, original Cause of all that truly is—and it shows the student how to deduce from His nature the real and essential character of man and the universe.

So the Christian Scientist feels the understanding of God is not to be found in human theories about Him. God is known only through revelation. And the Scientist finds this revelation to be recorded in the inspired teachings of the Scriptures and *Science and Health.*

The Christian Scientist does not regard God as a remote and unfriendly Being to be approached in fear or dread. True, the Bible admonishes us to "fear the Lord," but here the word "fear" means a call for a deep reverence that hears and keeps the divine laws—an interpretation not only accepted by the Christian Scientist but given by leading Bible scholars.

To the Christian Scientist, God is to be loved and adored, known and understood, worshipped and obeyed, expressed and reflected, trusted and relied upon, confided in and companioned with; enshrined in our hearts as the one Ruler who makes and governs all that really is.

Here is a brief definition of God given in *Science and Health:* "God is incorporeal, divine, supreme, infinite Mind, Spirit, Soul, Principle, Life, Truth, Love" (S&H 465:9).

Mrs. Eddy goes on to say that the terms of this definition are synonymous, that they refer to one absolute God, and that they express His nature, essence, and wholeness.

Here the student finds a cardinal point where the theology of Christian Science contrasts with that of some other Christian faiths: Christian Science presents God as the triune Principle—Life, Truth, Love—but does not accept the trinitarian Christian view of the Godhead as three Persons in one; it presents Him as one God, who is indivisible.

The student of Science soon discovers that the seven synonyms for God, capitalized in the definition given above, indicate vastly more than can be discerned at a glance. They are primary and basic in the study of Christian Science, and their meaning is infinite. As one goes deeper into this Science, he finds these synonyms continually opening new vistas for thought. In any given situation along the way of his progress, he is likely to turn to the study of them and to derive such insights into the nature of God as he is ready to grasp.

It is noteworthy that all of these synonyms are drawn directly from the Bible: they are either used explicitly therein or clearly implied.

For example, Jesus used the word "Spirit" for God when he said, "God is a Spirit," or, as given in the Revised Standard Version, "God is spirit" (John 4:24). The Scientist gains from this word a keener sense of God's boundless character, His omnipotence, omniscience, and pure omnipresence. The Psalmist spoke of the everywhereness of the Almighty when he wrote, "Whither shall I go from thy spirit? or whither shall I flee from thy presence?" One thinks of omnipresent Spirit as having no limits in time or space or matter, encompassing all that exists, and not having physical form or dwelling in a localized place.

To the Christian Scientist, "Spirit" is that which nothing can destroy. He finds that as used in Christian Science literature it often connotes the inexhaustible energies of the Almighty, the endless resources of God giving life, strength, and continuity to all that He creates. It is often linked with the word "substance," but this does not refer to matter. The student soon finds that matter is the opposite of Spirit and that Spirit is expressed only in spiritual man and a spiritual universe.

As to the word "Principle," some religious thinkers have questioned Mrs. Eddy's use of this term for God, asserting that it reduces Him to something resembling a cold, lifeless, unfeeling, inert principle of mathematics. But the student discovers that this word has a higher and quite different meaning. As used by Christian Scientists it refers to perfect and unchanging Love, expressing itself in its dynamic science of man and the universe—in other words, to the creative cause, source, and origin of all good and all being.

Nor does it imply something static. On the contrary, the Christian Scientist is more apt to think of "Principle" expressing itself in harmonious and orderly action manifesting exact spiritual law—symbolized, in a way, by the natural law that keeps the planets swinging majestically through their orbits.

The term is not explicitly used in the Bible, but the Scientist feels it is clearly implied in various statements of His nature. For instance, we read in Malachi, "I am the Lord, I change not" (Mal. 3:6). The Apostle James speaks of Him as "The Father of lights, with whom is no variableness, neither shadow of turning" (Jas. 1:17). The Psalms speak of God frequently as the source of law, as do other parts of the Bible.

Many have seen in Mrs. Eddy's use of the word "Principle" one of her outstanding contributions to religious thought. To them it has come as a new and inspired revelation of the divine nature. Surely it offers insights of special interest to an age steeped in scientific methods. The Scientist gains from it new views of God as unerring, without any mistakes; perfect in government, permitting no exceptions or disobedience; self-maintaining in His absolute power, and therefore always to be relied upon; good in essence, cause, and effect. One recalls that the very nature of evil—deceitful, divisive, fraudulent, contradictory—is to be without Principle.

Through a study of Mrs. Eddy's writings many have found that the term "Principle" helps them to look above and beyond the whims, vagaries, and injustices of human nature in seeking to grasp the character of the Most High. The word introduces a sense of Love so ineffably good and pure, tender and divine, unchanging and beneficent, that this Love eternally knows neither limit, flaw, discord, nor evil result.

The shining concept of God as Love is one shared by Christian Scientists and many other Christians. So strongly does this religion emphasize this synonym that it has often been called a religion of Love. For the Scientist, Love is not simply an attribute of God, but the very essence of the divine Being; Love is the fountain of infinite goodness. Not a molecule of evil could exist anywhere in the perfection of Love, for Love could not permit any opposite of itself to exist anywhere in its infinite presence.

When one explores deeply the nature of God as Love, he finds he is losing the sense of evil and gaining a sense of man's eternal unity with all-embracing good. Thus he gains some perception of what it means to say that God is All-in-all.

The Christian Scientist feels that the word "Love," used so clearly in the New Testament as a synonym for God, tells of God's nature as Father and Mother, forever sustaining, upholding, guiding, preserving His children, giving all good to His creation. It tells of the will of our heavenly Father never to afflict His offspring, but to bless them with life eternal.

As the Scientist sees it, the Master gave the supreme illustration of Love—Love, the universal solvent, the unquenchable Light, the liberator, the Giver of life, the source of comfort, healing, redemption. As the Master himself said, "God sent not his Son into the world to condemn the world; but that the world through him might be saved" (John 3:17).

The Master also gave the supreme demonstration of God as

Life. To the Christian Scientist, this word for God opens a new realm for understanding and demonstration, a realm of immortality, joy, freedom, and endless possibilities.

The physical sciences conceive of life as the product of molecular actions, biochemical reactions and processes, which culminate in organic matter. Viewed as the product of matter, life becomes subject to death and returns to dust.

But the Christian Scientist finds that these theories do not go to the root of the question, because they deal only with material phenomena. What lies deeper? What is the eternal First Cause? What is the infinite reality of which material existence at best could be only a hint? From the viewpoint of the Christian Scientist, to say that Life is God is to say that Life is ageless, diseaseless, forever conscious, irrepressible in its self-expression, manifested as continuous right activity. As stated in *Science and Health*, "Life is the everlasting I AM, the Being who was and is and shall be, whom nothing can erase" (S&H 290:1).

The Scientist learns to think of Life as Spirit, not matter; Mind, not material molecule; as infinite, not organic; the creative One governing His creation through His laws of universal all-inclusive harmony, not the interaction of physical forces. This gives him a growing sense of Life as forever unfolding and expressing itself, without any destructive element within it. To him it becomes increasingly clear that since Life includes the infinite forces of Being in a universal and harmonious symphony of action, Life must be perfect Love.

If the inquirer into this religion comes from a background of the older Christian denominations, he is very likely to ask whether the use of such words as "Life," "Love," "Principle," "Spirit," leaves any room for a concept of God as Person, a sense of Him so precious to many Christians.

It is true that Scientists do not think of God as a person in the ordinary sense of the word, as it is used in referring to a physical form or a finite personality. But they do think of Him as individual conscious Mind, the all-knowing, all-wise, supreme Intelligence. They think of Him as the Ego, or infinite I AM, the creator to whom we can always turn for comfort, inspiration, guidance. All this is indicated when a Christian Scientist speaks of God as Mind.

As Mrs. Eddy writes in *Science and Health:* "If the term personality, as applied to God, means infinite personality, then God *is* infinite *Person*—in the sense of infinite personality, but not in the lower sense. An infinite Mind in a finite form is an absolute impossibility" (S&H 116:27).

Modern science considers mind or intelligence to be a phenomenon of matter, working through electrical impulses of the brain, and largely confined to the higher primates. Each individual is considered to have a mind of his own, which empowers him in greater or lesser degree with the faculty of comprehending himself and his environment. But what of the original divine Being who knows all Truth, the all-embracing Intelligence which launched the universe, the Mind which is primal and fundamental? To the Christian Scientist, this one omnipotent Mind—which creates its own likeness in ideas, and of which the real man and the spiritual universe are the perfect expression—is God.

On exploring this Science one encounters a fundamental distinction between the perfect divine Mind, or Spirit, and the phenomenon called conscious matter. The material mentality, faulty and mortal, is viewed as a distorted concept of Mind, involving limits and believing in evil. It is the opposite of Spirit. It is the opposite of Truth—namely, a lie. Paul called it the carnal mind, and the learner in Christian Science finds it explained as an illusion, or nothingness.

To human sense it appears that the elements of the carnal mind, or mortal mind, meet in conflict with the truths of divine Mind, and that the battleground is human experience. But the Scientist finds a metaphorical explanation of this in the Master's parable of the tares and wheat. The temporal and worthless nature of carnal-mindedness is indicated by the tares, which are to be gathered and burned, while God's ideas, like the wheat, are to be gathered and preserved.

Through his religion the Scientist gains some present perception of the truth that the carnal mind is a self-deluded dream and that all reality is to be found in the divine Mind and its conscious expression, including man.

The Christian Scientist uses another term for God which tells of His nature as the author of lovely and exquisite expressions of perfect intelligence—including spiritual beauty, radiance, melody, joy, perfection, identity. This term is "Soul." As the Scientist sees it, no word for God could be more interesting.

While "Soul" means divine consciousness, it does not imply a sort of vague Nirvana in which all is absorbed. Quite the opposite: one finds, through a careful study of its usage in Christian Science, that the word conveys a sense of God as the source of infinite individuality and identity, forever expressing His nature in distinct and multifarious spiritual forms. Each of God's ideas expresses the divine nature in its own individual way. Each manifests light, law, intelligence, strength, loveliness, consciousness—the various elements of the divine nature —and so expresses its own God-given identity.

To the Christian Scientist, "Soul" is a word that opens the doors of his thought to the absolute perfection and purity of God's creation: the luminous clarity of the infinite understanding; the harmony, beauty, lucid outline, and satisfactory relationship of all of God's ideas.

As many Scientists have found, this is a divine synonym of tremendous practical import, especially for anyone concerned with the creative arts. Properly understood, it awakens one to see that through prayer he can look deeply into the kingdom of heaven, and drink deep draughts of inspiration, originality, perception, vitality, and beauty. It leads one to look beyond the sensuous, or material, expressions of beauty to the divine essence, of which these are only a promise. The word conveys the realization that genuine beauty and identity—whether of star, leaf, rainbow, or man himself—is something beyond matter. It is spiritual and can only be, in essence, the reflected light of the divine Being.

The views of the divine nature which unfold in Science are not mere theories; they become vivid and demonstrable to the student when he reminds himself, as he frequently does, that God is Truth, and that everything true has its origin in Him.

When a Christian Scientist says that God is Truth, he means something much deeper and indeed much different from what the world calls truth. Ordinarily people think of truth as either good or bad, permanent or changeable, relative or universal, depending upon the circumstances and the frame of reference.

But to the Christian Scientist, Truth means God Himself, including all that God knows of His spiritual creation. It refers to that which is absolute, fundamental, immutable, original, eternal. He reasons that because of the perfection of Truth, there could be no error in Truth, consequently no mistakes in God's creation. Since God is all-inclusive Truth, it is impossible to have any truth that is at variance with Him; either it is in harmony with His all-encompassing nature as infinite good, or it is not true at all and is only a deception.

Thinking of God as Truth helps one to see the logic of calling this religion Science. Laws derived from divine Truth—that is, truths expressing the divine order—can be known, understood, and demonstrated.

It is this demonstration to which the Scientist devotes his prayers and his energies. Knowing that all the goodness and glories of God's wondrous creation are universally true, and knowing that everything true is essentially demonstrable, he views this demonstration as a practical possibility to be realized progressively through spiritual growth. He views this not only as the most satisfying of all life-goals, but also as the very essence of salvation.

4.

The world is convulsed with the question What is man? Every day's headlines echo the turmoil; it is one of the great issues of our times. The Communist movement denies man's spiritual identity and declares him to be a biological organism shaped by physical, economic and social forces which can be manipulated by the state. The long-slumbering peoples of back-ward areas rebel at their chains and reject the theory that certain races are inferior; they grope for a sense of human dignity, and demand their right as human beings to work out their own destiny. The civilization which has been illumined by the insights of Christianity struggles for the dignity of individual man and his spiritual integrity under God, but seems unable thus far to communicate this vision in sufficiently meaningful terms to the non-Christian world.

But not all of the denials of man's spiritual nature are to be found in the tediously systematized materialism of Communist theory. In the past century, Western thought has become deeply imbued with concepts portraying man as a physical organism governed by natural forces, his personality a composite of inherited instincts and environmental influences. The ideas of Darwin and Freud, interpreted and modified by their successors, permeate the language, morals, economics, politics and jurisprudence of our times. In fact, the whole edifice of modern scientific thought regarding the nature of man shares this materialistic foundation—depending, as it does, upon physical observation and experiment for its data.

Yet the non-Communist world has never fully accepted the implications of scientific materialism. There still exists the intuitive conviction that man includes more than the techniques of laboratory investigation can measure or even identify. It is a question, for instance, whether any of the sciences could explain conclusively the nobility of a Lincoln or the genius of an Einstein. The consensus has been, and still is, that man is much more than organized matter; indeed, many would agree in greater or lesser degree with the writer of Job, who said, "There is a spirit in man: and the inspiration of the Almighty giveth them understanding" (Job 32:8).

But how much more than clay? So long as science or religion starts from the premise that matter is basic reality and that man is a physical organism living in a material world, can it ever explain the ultimate questions regarding man? What is his source and his destiny? Who is he and why? Even from the premise of materialism, man is still a mystery; and the warring elements of human thought still wrestle with the riddle, What is man?

In approaching this question the Christian Scientist starts from a totally different premise. He starts with God, the divine Principle, or Mind, as the sole creator. Beginning with God's nature, Science shows one how to follow a straight line of pure logic in deducing the actual nature of man as His offspring. Like a blaze of light, this spiritual logic reveals a new view of man, as the image and likeness of God. As one follows it he begins to realize that every constituent element of man's true being is derived from pure Soul and not from gene or chromosome. He gains a new view of man—as the conscious, individualized reflection of supreme intelligence and not a physical organism.

Such conclusions are wholly contrary to the evidence before the physical senses. But the physical senses are notoriously limited and misleading, as can be shown even in the physical realm; they are not adequate to answer the fundamental questions regarding God and man. The Christian Scientist feels that the answers proceed from beyond matter, and must come to human apprehension through revelation, reason, and demonstration.

The underlying Christian Science approach is indicated in these words from Science and Health: "The universe, like man, is to be interpreted by Science from its divine Principle, God, and then it can be understood; but when explained on the basis of physical sense and represented as subject to growth, maturity, and decay, the universe, like man, is, and must continue to be, an enigma" (S&H 124:14).

Reasoning from the basis of divine Principle one learns that man is idea, the object of Mind held in divine consciousness. He is wholly mental and spiritual and not the inhabitant of a mortal body, though it so appears to mortal view. He is encompassed in divine Love as Love's own object and offspring. As Paul wrote: "In him [Mind, or Love] we live, and move, and have our being. . . . For we are also his offspring" (Acts 17:28).

The statement that man is the image and likeness of God has

its origin, of course, in the first chapter of Genesis and elsewhere in the Bible. Accepting this, the Christian Scientist concludes that every element of man's being springs from eternal Mind. As God's own expressed image, man must show forth all the qualities and character of the divine; his every thought must be derived from God. All his faculties are divinely perfected; they are spiritual, not material, and forever indestructible.

As seen from the viewpoint of Christian Science, Christ Jesus described the scientific relationship of Mind and its idea, Father and Son, when he said: "The Son can do nothing of himself, but what he seeth the Father do: for what things soever he doeth, these also doeth the Son likewise. For the Father loveth the Son, and sheweth him all things that himself doeth" (John 5:19,20). While the passage is often interpreted to refer solely to the Saviour, the Christian Scientist finds in it a statement of the nature of the true man. For as the Apostle John said, referring to man's spiritual selfhood, "Beloved, now are we the sons of God" (I John 3:2).

Thus one learns, as he explores Christian Science, not to accept the outward human sense of things but to recognize man as spiritual and coexistent with God, inseparable from Spirit, harmonious as IIis divine Principle. Answering the question "What is man?" in *Science and Health*, Mrs. Eddy replies in part:

Man is not matter; he is not made up of brain, blood, bones, and other material elements. The Scriptures inform us that man is made in the image and likeness of God. Matter is not that likeness. The likeness of Spirit cannot be so unlike Spirit. Man is spiritual and perfect; and because he is spiritual and perfect, he must be so understood in Christian Science. Man is idea, the image, of Love; he is not physique. He is the compound idea of God, including all right ideas; the generic term for all that reflects God's image and likeness; the conscious identity of being as found in Science, in which man is the reflection of God, or Mind, and therefore is eternal; that which has no separate mind from God; that which has not a single quality underived from Deity; that which possesses no life, intelligence, nor creative power of his own, but reflects spiritually all that belongs to his Maker (S&H 475:6).

This description of man's present perfection may be questioned by those who accept as historical fact or literal religious tenet the fall of man as portrayed in the second and subsequent chapters of Genesis. But from the Christian Science point of view this scriptural narrative is an allegory, a portrayal by symbols of deep metaphysical teachings.

The first chapter of Genesis, recording the creation of the firmament, the earth, living things, and man, is accepted by the Scientist as a metaphorical description of the perfection, beauty, diversity, and completeness of God's wholly spiritual and good creation. Likewise, the subsequent account—recording the rising of the mist from the ground, the creation of Adam and Eve, and their sin and condemnation and punishment—is viewed by the Christian Scientist not as literal history but as a deeply perceptive analysis of the fundamental elements and assumptions of error: a fallible God, a sinning mortal man, and dominant but self-destructive evil.

While the Christian Scientist draws deep and exact metaphysical lessons from this second account, the view of it as an unusually penetrating allegory is accepted by many modern thinkers of other persuasions. For example, Paul Tillich speaks of "the symbol of the Fall of Man, which points to the tragic estrangement of man and his world from their true being." He calls the scriptural account "one of the most profound psychological descriptions of the general human predicament." But the Christian Scientist finds his religion going further. Since evil is "a liar and the father of lies," a deceiver from the beginning, this picture of tragic estrangement is presented as the description of an illusion. The purpose of the scriptural account is to expose the nature of this illusion by uncovering its basic assumptions and its consequences.

Thus the Christian Scientist holds to the understanding that man as God's likeness is forever pure, upright, sinless, having immutable identity, which cannot be subverted. He finds this understanding progressively revealing to him man's infinite possibilities but lack of either the capacity or the desire to sin. No such capacity could be engendered by God. Such a capacity —limiting, negative, condemnatory, self-destructive, valueless— certainly would add nothing to the scope and power of God's man, but if real and true would reduce him from the image of the Most High to the status of a worm. As the Scientist sees it, this would be utterly unlike the perfect and infinite intelligence, which is Love.

It should be stressed that this does not for a moment mean that the Scientist thinks of mortal man as sinless. Such a statement applies only to the real spiritual man of God's creation— of which sinning mortal man is only a counterfeit, or distorted picture.

Nor does the Scientist conclude that since sin is unreal, one may go right on sinning without punishment. Mrs. Eddy specifically repudiates such a doctrine: "To get rid of sin through Science, is to divest sin of any supposed mind or reality, and never to admit that sin can have intelligence or power, pain or pleasure" (S&H 339:28-31). In one of the tenets of Christian Science she also states that the belief in sin is punished as long as the belief continues.

At this point one might ask: But is not the view of man as really sinless, spiritual, and perfect a very idealized concept? What relevance does it have in a world wrestling with poverty, strife, oppression, hate, nationalism, and racialism?

To the Christian Scientist, the answer is that this understanding reveals the true basis of human progress: not matter or biological evolution, but man's real status as the idea or likeness of creative Mind. The understanding of man's God-given dominion is demonstrable in terms of greater freedom. His spiritual inviolability is demonstrable in terms of greater dignity, integrity, mutual respect, and uprightness. His divinely endowed individuality can be proved progressively in terms of greater respect for and value of the individual. His imperishable substance can be shown forth in more health and greater longevity. His pure goodness as the son of God is demonstrable in terms of deeper humanity and brotherly love.

Does all this make religion "man-centered"? Far from it. The fruits of this understanding of man are wonderful—in terms of expanded capacities, greater peace, higher joys, more abundant living, sounder health, freer unselfishness, deeper Christianity. But not one iota of these blessings could be won by putting man first. They can only be realized by putting God first. The only way to heaven is literal obedience to the Master's first command: "Thou shalt love the Lord thy God with all thy heart, and with all thy soul, and with all thy mind, and with all thy strength" (Mark 13:30).

Man's only reason for being is to glorify and express God.

5.

The more a Christian Scientist learns of the nature of God, the more he begins to understand that an infinitely good God could create only good. And since God is all-inclusive and the only creator, evil is nowhere, nothing, a nonentity. From the Scientist's point of view, evil is the opposite of God *in every sense*: essentially negative, not real, not true, contradictory, illogical, nonintelligent, insubstantial, chaotic, deceptive, mythological; having no creator and not actually present.

Evil is often compared by Christian Scientists to the mirage on the desert or the break in the pencil standing in a glass of water. It is that which seems to be and is not. It appears real only to the limited, misguided, distorted consciousness of things which mortals regard as their own.

It is hard for the human mind, so steeped in its own limited conceptions, to grasp the unreality of evil. The student of Science finds that he grasps it only by degrees. It can be grasped only by accepting those thoughts derived from God, which so illumine one's understanding of His nature that he sees evil's claims being annihilated in his experience.

The necessity for turning from human views to God-bestowed ideas, if one would understand the unreality of evil, is illustrated by a story I once heard from the Harvard astronomer Dr. Harlow Shapley. He told of a seminar in which he was attempting to explain to a group of graduate students the concept of modern astronomers that the universe has limits. The class seemed reluctant to accept this idea, and one after another, the students raised their hands and questioned it, asking in various ways what lay outside the "limits." Finally a girl in the back row spoke up and said, "But Dr. Shapley, suppose I were to go to the very edge of the universe, the limit you speak of, and *poke my finger right through!*"

"Well, I wish you would!" shot back the astronomer. "You see, you are trying to understand a four-dimensional problem with your three-dimensional mind!"

Similarly it is impossible to grasp the unreality of evil with the "three-dimensional human mind"—or with a four-dimensional one, for that matter. In other words, this profound truth cannot be grasped by thinking in terms of the limited conceptions native to the fleshly mind. It can be understood only by deriving one's conscious thoughts from the divine Mind—that is, by accepting the reasoning and conclusions based wholly upon one infinite God, the All-in-all, who is supreme good.

Physicists tell us that their concept of space as curved can only be understood mathematically; one finds in Christian Science that the unreality of evil can only be understood spiritually.

Some religions have maintained that God sends afflictions to His children, or permits them to be imposed upon them, because they serve a divine purpose, such as discipline. To the Christian Scientist such explanations seem to subtract much from the all-power, glory, and perfection of God, and from His orderly and intelligent government of His creation. They seem more like the efforts of the human mind to rationalize the evils it accepts as real and then cannot explain, than the light of divine revelation.

The disease that condemns an innocent child to suffer, the accident that strikes down a loving and upright parent, the destruction that engulfs a whole town or a whole nation without regard to justice—how can these be attributed to a God who is infinite, perfect Love? How can they be called "acts of God," as our legal jargon, with a touch of medievalism, still holds?

To the Christian Scientist these discords have no place in God's creation; and the law of Truth and Love, when sufficiently understood, will bring exemption and safety from them. The more one learns of the infinite God, the stronger and deeper becomes his sense of the reality of good alone, and the weaker his sense of sin and evil.

The insistence of Christian Science that God is All-in-all has led some of its critics to describe it as pantheistic. But this is quite contrary to the facts; one finds that this religion is totally different from pantheism, in any accepted usage of that word.

Certain phrases or sentences in *Science and Health* may be made to sound pantheistic by separating them from their proper context, but this involves a twisting of the essential thought.

The student finds that a fundamental point in Christian Science is this: all-inclusive Mind, Life, Spirit, does not create matter. So Spirit is not expressed by matter, through matter, in matter, or as matter; for matter is the opposite of Spirit and is described in Christian Science as an illusion. While one finds many useful symbols in the physical universe which serve to illustrate something of the nature of God—for example, the beauty and orderly movements of the stars—these are never, to the Christian Scientist, more than illustrative and imperfect symbols; the physical universe is not the medium by which God expresses Himself.

Holding the physical universe to be a misconception of being, the Christian Scientist rejects the pantheistic doctrine that God is to be found in its combined forces, laws, and other phenomena.

Historical forms of pantheism share in common the doctrine of a general might, or being, which swallows up individual beings. But as one explores Christian Science he finds that a fundamental distinction is made between God and the spiritual universe. Mrs. Eddy speaks of the universe as secondary and tributary to Spirit, from which it borrows its reflected light, substance, life, and intelligence; of Soul as giving existence to the universe; of the divine Principle expressing Science and art throughout His creation; and of the universe, Mind's infinite idea, *reflecting* God as He is.

From all of these statements and many others, the student finds a clear distinction emerging between God and His universe, though they are inseparable. God is cause; universe is the effect, or expression, of that cause. The relationship is that of Mind and idea, Life and expression, Love and object, Spirit and its reflection.

Nor is man's identity and individuality absorbed in Deity. Mrs. Eddy specifically states in *Science and Health* that man is not God, and God is not man. She further writes: "This scientific sense of being, forsaking matter for Spirit, by no means suggests man's absorption into Deity and the loss of his identity, but confers upon man enlarged individuality, a wider sphere of thought and action, a more expansive love, a higher and more permanent peace" (S&H 265:10).

The learner finds that these points, among others, wholly separate Christian Science from pantheistic systems, including those of Hinduism. They open the door to the endless wonders of the kingdom of heaven. Their expansiveness and inspiration are by no means limited to the realm of theory. When properly understood, their effect is to enlarge human individuality, heighten human vision, deepen one's nature, and illumine human experience with joy.

Chapter Three

What Kind of Church?

If you were to enter any of the more than 3,200 Christian Science churches in the world, you would find an auditorium of basically simple character. It is true that these churches cover the spectrum of architecture, from plain to imposing, Tudor to New England colonial, California Spanish to contemporary. So great is their diversity that there just isn't any such thing as a typical Christian Science church building. But all of these churches contain essentially the same simple facilities and functions.

In the auditorium there will be a rostrum with a high desk broad enough for the two Readers to stand side by side during the service (sometimes there are two individual desks). There will be space for the soloist, who usually stands near the Readers during the solo and hymns. There is no choir.

Inscribed on the walls, usually at each side of the platform, will be a short quotation—one from the Bible and one from *Science and Health*. Often used are Jesus' words "Ye shall know the truth, and the truth shall make you free" (John 8:32); and frequently these words of Mrs. Eddy: "Divine Love always has met and always will meet every human need" (S&H 494:10-11). There will be no pictures, icons, or images.

Typically the decor and atmosphere of the auditorium will be light and free, in contrast to the dimness sometimes associated with churches. There will be pews or seats for the congregation, sometimes upholstered and sometimes not. There is no prayer book and no provision for kneeling, but there will be racks containing the *Christian Science Hymnal,* and for the Sunday services there will be copies of the *Christian Science Quarterly,* containing the Lesson-Sermon.

Usually there is a separate room, or auditorium, for the Sunday School, which may meet during the morning service. It will be attended by pupils up to the age of twenty. The classes usually convene around work tables furnished with copies of the Bible, *Science and Health, Quarterly,* and *Hymnal.* The size of these classes could be anywhere from two or three pupils up to fifteen or so. Sometimes the classes are mixed but sometimes the boys and girls are separate.

There is no provision in the Sunday School for games, art projects, or other diversions. Christian Scientists feel that even toddlers can be taught rudimentary truths regarding the nature of God. Little children have an innate sense of love, of good, of conscience, and they can learn to look to God, divine Love, as the source of all right and true expressions of these attributes. They can begin to become familiar with the Bible characters and what they stand for, and with the simplest meanings of the Ten Commandments and Beatitudes.

Often there will be a nursery, where the infants of those attending church can be cared for in cribs and playpens.

Sometimes the Reading Room will be in the church edifice; often, however, it will be located in the business section of the town, or on a well-traveled street easily accessible to the public.

If the church is large there will be rooms in the edifice for the executive board and for committee meetings, and also a lobby adjoining the auditorium, where those attending the services can mingle afterward. But there will never be kitchens, gymnasiums, or any provision for social events. It is characteristic of these churches that they are devoted solely to religious activities.

Reflected here is the underlying Christian Science concept of the function of the church. The Christian Scientist thinks of his church as devoted solely to activities concerned directly with the worship of God. These include the services, lectures, and also the membership meetings to discuss church business. The Scientist does not think of his church as a center of purely social activities. No suppers, rummage sales, or social hours take place there, nor do weddings, or funerals. (The denomination does not have ordained ministers, who are legally authorized to perform marriages. Wedding ceremonies for Christian Scientists are usually performed by an ordained minister of another faith.)

This does not mean that the Christian Scientist thinks of his church as removed from the needs of society. On the contrary, he views it as making an essential contribution to the stability of the community. As Mrs. Eddy wrote when the cornerstone was laid for The Mother Church, in Boston: "The Church, more than any other institution, at present is the cement of society, and it should be the bulwark of civil and religious liberty" (Misc. 144:32-2). The Scientist thinks of this contribution as stemming not from social activities—which other organizations can and do provide—but from those peculiarly religious and spiritual activities which the church alone can carry forward.

The Sunday service centers around the reading of the Lesson-Sermon by the two Readers, and also includes a short scriptural selection, hymns, and prayer. There are no personally prepared prayers; silent prayer is used, together with the Lord's Prayer and its spiritual interpretation given by Mrs. Eddy in *Science and Health*. Even the benediction is always taken from the Bible.

There is no personal preacher and no personal sermon. As

brought out in the "Explanatory Note," read by the First Reader just before the reading of the Lesson: "The Bible and the Christian Science textbook are our only preachers. We shall now read scriptural texts, and their correlative passages from our denominational textbook; these comprise our sermon. . . ."

As the Scientist sees it, each individual can gain direct personal access to God through understanding the divine truths revealed in these books; he does not gain it through ritual or person.

The Lesson-Sermon consists of a Golden Text and brief Responsive Reading from the Bible, and of six "sections" dealing with aspects of the central subject. Each section consists of several selected passages read from the Bible by the Second Reader, and several correlative or explanatory passages read immediately thereafter from *Science and Health* by the First Reader, who also is in charge of the service.

This gives the Bible an unusually prominent place in the service. The scriptural texts constitute approximately half of the sermon, and they are presented in such a way that the Bible is never far from the attention of the congregation.

These Lesson-Sermons are prepared in Boston. On a given Sunday the same one will be used throughout the world. Here is a list of the twenty-six subjects that are used in rotation: God; Sacrament; Life; Truth; Love; Spirit; Soul; Mind; Christ Jesus; Man; Substance; Matter; Reality; Unreality; Are Sin, Disease, and Death Real?; Doctrine of Atonement; Probation After Death; Everlasting Punishment; Adam and Fallen Man; Mortals and Immortals; Soul and Body; Ancient and Modern Necromancy, Alias Mesmerism and Hypnotism, Denounced; God the Only Cause and Creator; God the Preserver of Man; Is the Universe, Including Man, Evolved by Atomic Force?; and Christian Science. These subjects were established by Mrs. Eddy and are used twice each year, though the content is new each time.

Use of the Lesson-Sermons at church services means that on a given Sunday a modest little band of half a dozen people in the Australian bush will hear a sermon just as substantial and authentic as that heard by a congregation of several hundred on Park Avenue.

One accustomed to the diversity of preaching in other churches might wonder whether adherence to the Lesson-Sermons imposes limitations upon the Sunday services. The Christian Scientist would not feel that it does. The subjects are so broad that there is plenty of variety in context.

In fact the content for any given week is so varied and substantial as to meet a wide range of individual tastes and needs. The system enables one to hear a sermon read in his church on Sunday which he has studied thoughtfully as a lesson every day of the week; as a result he is prepared to gain meaning and inspiration from the service.

It is true that the lessons do not provide an opportunity for expression of personal opinions or interpretations; but on the other hand, they open to the individual's understanding the unsurpassed riches of the Bible. They constitute a thorough course in the fundamentals of Christian Science. They provide a systematic means of spiritual education. Thus they nourish the student's spiritual growth. They also provide subject matter for the teaching of the older classes in the Sunday school.

If one goes a little further into the character of the Christian Science church, he finds that in striking ways it is designed to promote the spiritual development of the individual member. This, after all, is its essential purpose, together with spreading the teachings to others.

Nowhere is the concern for the progress of the individual more obvious than in the character of the Wednesday testimony meetings. The visitor will find that such meetings include selections from the Bible and *Science and Health,* chosen and read by the First Reader, and hymns and prayer; also that the latter half of each meeting is devoted to testimonies of healing and the narrating of other personal experiences which illustrate the practical application of Christian Science.

The Reader customarily arranges his selections so that they deal with a particular subject of his choice. Thus the Wednesday meetings will cover a tremendous range of practical topics. Typical subjects would be Christian wisdom in bringing up children, overcoming selfishness, the fundamentals of effective prayer, or how cultivating an understanding of God can expand one's horizons and abilities.

During the period reserved for testimonies, members of the congregation will rise spontaneously in their places to tell of the proofs they have experienced of God's power and goodness, and found through prayer as taught in Christian Science.

It would be difficult to overestimate the importance of these midweek meetings in shaping the religious outlook of the Christian Scientist. Here, built inextricably into the structure of the church, is a perpetual symbol of the fact that Truth is demonstrable—in healing, the overcoming of sin, and the gaining of freedom over every kind of human discord. Very often someone struggling with a problem will gain a great deal of encouragement from hearing others tell how they have faced similar challenges and worked them out through prayer.

The Wednesday meetings are a living admonition to the Scientist never to think of his religion as a set of abstract theories. They are a reminder of the trenchant words of Mrs. Eddy, "The error of the ages is preaching without practice" (S&H 241:17).

An important theme of a typical Wednesday meeting is gratitude. The Christian Scientist thinks of gratitude as the seeing and acknowledging of good from the great Giver, immediately at hand and always available. He thinks of gratitude as an element indispensable in healing. The ungrateful heart is also the closed heart, barren and empty. It is incapable of blessing others and being blessed.

The Wednesday meetings are a perennial reminder to the student of the importance of gratitude and joy. And as such, they tend to be a catalytic agent for all the other Christian graces, such as humility, kindness, unselfishness, purity, spirituality, honesty, sincerity.

The element of regeneration is so important in Christian Science healing that rarely can one sit through the testimonies in a Wednesday meeting without hearing something of the necessity and the fruitage of replacing the seamy traits of the carnal mind with the graces of Spirit. Hearing others speak, in modesty and thankfulness, of the improved ways of thinking which prayer has brought to them in some Gethsemane or some resurrection of their own, one is impelled to search his own thoughts a little deeper and to strive a little harder for Christian perfection.

So the Wednesday meetings place a demand upon the individual member. Their content is such that their continuance depends upon the success of the members in healing. And they could not continue without the active participation of the members in telling of their experiences.

This last fact is characteristic. Active participation in church work is generally considered to be an important element of progress for the Christian Scientist. He is likely to be called upon to serve in various capacities: on committees for certain activities—Reading Room, literature distribution, lectures, maintenance, prison and institutional work; and as an usher, Sunday-School teacher, executive-board member, or Reader.

A local Christian Science church is conducted exclusively by laymen. The Readers are elected from the membership, usually for a term of three years. So are those who serve on the executive board, which usually consists of from five to ten persons, depending on the size of the church. Lay members alone staff the other activities.

The practitioners listed in *The Christian Science Journal*—persons devoting their time to the work of Christian Science healing and having no other occupation—are the nearest thing to what in other faiths might be termed professional religious workers. But they hold no office and no administrative responsibility in the church by virtue of being practitioners; their role in the church is simply that of individual members.

A local Christian Science church is organized on a distinctly democratic basis. Every member is eligible to serve his church in any office, subject solely to his qualifications and the decisions of the membership. Every member has an equal voice in these decisions. Every officer, every committee, and the executive board itself, is answerable to the sovereign authority of the membership. Every important decision either is made by the membership directly, or is subject to review at membership meetings.

Sometimes this means that the membership as a whole must decide complex financial or technical questions. For example, in a church building program day-to-day decisions on details might be delegated to the building committee or the executive board, but all major questions would be referred to the membership. In fact, the system of church government is remarkably similar to that of a New England village, with its town meeting at which every citizen has a vote and the right to speak.

All this means that the individual member has a maximum opportunity to participate in church government. It also means that in order for church business to go forward, the members must rise to a rather exacting standard. How much easier it would seem sometimes to let a strong leader make the decisions! The way of democracy demands individual responsibility, integrity, and mutual respect and trust. Its success depends upon the continuing loyalty of the minority, and upon perpetual respect for minority rights by the majority. Often it calls for uncommon patience, love, and courage on the part of the individual member. In a direct democracy one does not have the luxury of leaving difficult questions to his elected representative. But how much this demand can mean for the development of the individual!

At this point we come upon a fundamental value of church membership for the Christian Scientist. His church is a laboratory for working out problems of human relationships. Church membership sometimes brings tests, trials, challenges, opportunities to work with others and for others. This may not always be a pathway of flowers—partly, perhaps, because the members love their church so deeply and take it so seriously.

But in this very challenge lies the supreme value of the church in fostering the growth of the individual. Surely the meaning of Christian progress is found in the redeeming, tem-

pering, purging transformation of character described by Paul
when he urged the Colossians to put off the old man with his
deeds and to put on the new man—and which the Master referred to when he said simply, "Ye must be born again"
(John 3:7).

So as the Scientist sees it, the church is a crucible for the
Christianization of human character. The transacting of church
business, the choosing of officers, the serving on boards and committees with others of diverse backgrounds and views—all such
activities, carried on in the context of an exacting Christian
ethic, place demands upon the individual to rise to spiritual
maturity. The call of the Saviour to "love one another, as I
have loved you" (John 15:12) constitutes a ceaseless lesson for
the individual member. In essence the church symbolizes the
standard of love.

On the one hand, the individual member is the beneficiary
of this love. The church provides encouragement, inspiration,
protection; a feeling of belonging, of association with others
sharing the same ideals; a haven where one's most precious
aspirations will, in some measure at least, be understood and
tenderly valued by others.

On the other hand, the member will be called upon to give
in full measure of the same coin, in terms of appreciation, for-
bearance, understanding. Human nature being what it is, he
may even find himself needing to remove the stones of resentment, jealousy, apathy, from his own thoughts or from his relationships with others—to dissolve them with what Mrs. Eddy
calls the universal solvent of Love.

But the glory of the church lies in the fact that here is an institution whose purpose is to help its members learn how to dissolve these jagged stones of selfishness, through the irresistible
God-derived qualities of thought shown forth in the Christ.

These are deep lessons. They go to the roots of human
nature. But as the Scientist sees it, they are the quintessence of
Christianity. They make the church an active Christianizing influence in the lives of its members. Without this—without the
specific call upon the individual to look within himself and to

cultivate love, kindness, gentleness, patience, forgiveness, trust, honesty, moral courage, humility, integrity, purity, unselfishness, spiritual strength—where would the Christianizing power of the church be found? It is through this redemptive work of purging and uplifting human character that Christian healing takes place.

Thus for the Christian Scientist, the church exerts a positive spiritualizing influence in the lives of its members. It carries on the work of the incorporeal, everpresent Christ. What Jesus did individually, in redeeming and uplifting human lives through the power of the Christ, the church does collectively for all who will accept its help.

In its deepest sense the church is spiritual; or, as Mrs. Eddy defines it, "The structure of Truth and Love; whatever rests upon and proceeds from divine Principle" (S&H 583:12-19). But its mission is of great practical import. To quote the second part of the definition: "The Church is that institution, which affords proof of its utility and is found elevating the race, rousing the dormant understanding from material beliefs to the apprehension of spiritual ideas and the demonstration of divine Science, thereby casting out devils, or error, and healing the sick."

And it is interesting to note that healings, taking place in the lives of members, give impetus to the church. In the eighty-odd years since the Church of Christ, Scientist was founded by Mrs. Eddy, it has spread to all the continents and to most of the countries of the free world. What has largely blazed the trail and given the movement its momentum is the healing work— even though, as indicated earlier, physical healing is only a token of the power of Truth. If one studies the early histories of individual Christian Science churches in a given country he finds that in a majority of cases, remarkable healings led to the holding of services and this in turn brought the establishment of a church. In some instances the healings came about when a copy of *Science and Health* somehow found its way into unfamiliar hands; in other cases it was when a student or perhaps a practitioner came to a new area to live.

In more recent years many of the new churches have grown up in suburban areas near cities where Christian Science is already well established. But in modern times, too, it is the healing work which has often provided the foundation.

To cite an example, there is a small town in Oklahoma which had no church group until a few years ago. The events that led to its establishment began one day when a woman I know found a discarded magazine in her yard. Evidently someone had tossed it away. Painfully she bent over to pick it up, for she was becoming a cripple. She wore a special steel corset, and braces in her shoes. She also suffered from anemia and heart trouble.

The magazine proved to be a copy of the *Christian Science Sentinel,* a publication she had never heard of. The woman's condition had been called incurable, and it had been expected that in time she would be confined to a wheelchair. But she began the study of Christian Science—which to her brought a new interpretation of the nature of God. In a few months' time she was completely healed.

Being a long-time resident of the town, she was well known and the word of her healing spread. From time to time others, braving the strong religious tradition and bias of the town, came to her with their problems. Over a period of several years the number of those studying Christian Science grew until today there is a Christian Science Society—the forerunner of a full-fledged church—in the town. The woman herself finally gave up a highly successful career as a music teacher to devote her time to the practice of Christian Science healing.

Second only to the healing work in furthering the spread of the Christian Science movement has been the exceptional devotion of members. This loyalty has been expressed in various ways. Of greatest importance, from the viewpoint of Christian Scientists themselves, it is expressed in faithful systematic prayer for the church—a form of support that is common among working Christian Scientists. Then, too, it is expressed in willingness to shoulder the tasks of operating a church. Many a business or professional man of demanding responsibilities has put aside other interests sufficiently to serve a three-year term as Reader in his church. A great majority of Reading Room librarians serve gratis or for only token remuneration.

A Scientist usually expresses the sense of loyalty he feels in the form of financial contributions. While formal tithing is not required, most Scientists give regularly and generously to their church. Contributions are apt to be particularly large during a building program.

Some years ago a couple I know belonged to a church group in Texas which was raising funds for a building project. When the members were invited to pledge contributions, somebody put a diamond ring in a pledge envelope with a notation quoting the words of Peter at the temple called Beautiful: "Such as I have, give I thee" (Acts 3:6). A church member who was a jeweler sold the ring for the church.

Word of the incident got around among the members and soon a number of them contributed jewelry to be sold. The couple I mentioned gave two gifts. The wife gave her engagement ring, with her husband's permission, and to this day she does not wear one. The husband, then a young practitioner with very little cash to his name, put in a pledge slip for five hundred dollars.

As a sequel to the story, the very next morning a patient came to his office, a man who had just consummated an important business transaction. Full of thanks for the prayerful help he had received over quite a long period of time, he asked the practitioner for his bill, which was ninety-five dollars. Then he wrote out a check for $595, insisting he wanted the practitioner to accept this as a token of his gratitude.

It is the gratitude of thousands of individual members which has given momentum to the Christian Science movement. This gratitude is neither an emotional religiosity, nor an obligatory attitude. It is typically a natural outpouring of thanks for blessings received. If a man has come out of invalidism, or been released from alcoholism, or found the answer to a tangled business or home problem, or gained a new sense of meaning of life, he can't very well help feeling grateful.

The growth of the Christian Science movement has stemmed

from practical proofs of Christian power. Up to the present time this growth has been continuous and far-ranging. It has dotted the globe with churches, all woven together into a single organization: The Mother Church, the First Church of Christ, Scientist, in Boston, Massachusetts, and its branches around the world.

The agency which holds the movement together in unity is the governing instrument for the entire denomination: *The Manual of The Mother Church*, by Mrs. Eddy.

2.

The *Manual* is to The Mother Church and its branches what a constitution is to a state. It crystallizes basic goals, provides a governmental framework, locates responsibility, establishes lines of authority, and defines basic functions.

For the individual member, it prescribes certain duties and opportunities and gives guiding rules.

For the local church it sets up certain standards, prescribes the basic character of its government and operations, and defines its relationship as a branch of The Mother Church.

For The Mother Church, it establishes a system of continuing executive direction and provides a broad range of activities to meet the needs of the movement.

The *Manual* is the symbol of Mrs. Eddy's achievement as the Founder of Christian Science, and the means through which her leadership of the church organization is perpetuated.

Under *Manual* provisions an individual anywhere in the world may become a member of The Mother Church and/or of a local branch church. The *Manual's* rules and precepts for the individual member are typified by the "Rule for Motives and Acts," which, incidentally, is read in all Christian Science churches on the first Sunday of every month:

Neither animosity nor mere personal attachment should impel the motives or acts of the members of The Mother Church. In Science, divine Love alone governs man; and a Christian Scientist reflects the sweet amenities of Love, in rebuking sin, in true brotherliness, charitableness, and forgiveness. The members of this Church should daily watch and pray to be delivered from all evil, from prophesying, judging, condemning, counseling, influencing or being influenced erroneously (*Man.* 40:5).

Manual provisions relating to branch churches are illustrated by the requirement that in order to form a branch church there must be not less than sixteen loyal Christian Scientists, of whom at least four must be members of The Mother Church and at least one must be a Christian Science practitioner. Smaller groups may band together as a Christian Science Society, and the *Manual* also provides for establishment of Christian Science organizations at colleges and universities.

While each branch church is democratic and autonomous within the realm of its own affairs, those broader matters which concern the welfare of Christian Science as a religious denomination are centralized in The Mother Church, whose activities are worldwide and whose administrative responsibility rests with the five-member Christian Science Board of Directors. This board, which fills any vacancy arising within its own membership, supervises a tremendous range of day-to-day activities.

Certain of the activities of The Mother Church can be grouped under the general heading of preserving the authentic teachings of Christian Science and making them available. This is a function of considerable importance—partly because of the scientific exactness of the teachings, partly because they have so frequently been misunderstood and misrepresented, and partly because of the many offshoots and imitations of Christian Science which from time to time have gained temporary notoriety.

Publication of Mrs. Eddy's writings, authentic source of the teachings, is a function of the Trustees under the Will of Mary Baker Eddy, and these trustees are the five members of the Board of Directors. Publication of the Christian Science periodicals, which deal with the application of the teachings in healing and other practical ways, is a function of the Christian Science Publishing Society, an agency of The Mother Church, and located in Boston. Ultimate editorial responsibility for them is exercised by the Board of Directors, which appoints the editors.

The religious periodicals include *The Christian Science Journal*, official organ of the Mother Church, published monthly; the *Christian Science Sentinel*, published weekly; *The Herald of Christian Science*, published monthly and quarterly in a number of languages other than English; also the *Christian Science Quarterly*, containing the Lesson-Sermons.

The religious publications also include a great many pamphlets and some books, including the *Christian Science Hymnal*. The Publishing Society is also one of the world's largest distributors of Bibles.

Under the general heading of preserving the authentic teachings also comes the maintenance of the system of teaching of formal classes in Christian Science. Every third year a class, limited to thirty experienced Christian Science practitioners selected from all over the world, convenes in Boston under the auspices of the Christian Science Board of Education for special instruction in the fundamentals of Christian Science. The members of this class graduate with the designation of C.S.B. and thus become teachers of Christian Science. Returning to his own field, each teacher holds one primary class annually, limited to not more than thirty pupils and lasting two weeks. There are several hundred of these teachers, located in many countries.

Primary class instruction is usually a major milestone in the progress of a Christian Scientist. It is in some degree unique. Few lay members of other faiths ever have had the experience of devoting two full weeks exclusively to the orderly, comprehensive study of the nature of God and man under the guidance of a trained and experienced religious teacher. The course of study, based upon the chapter entitled "Recapitulation" in *Science and Health*, is thorough and concentrated. Class sessions usually last several hours daily and a great deal of homework is assigned. The instruction is so deep and absorbing that it often changes one's outlook and leaves an impression that lasts a lifetime. Class instruction is customarily a requirement, though by no means the only requirement, for listing in the *Journal* as a Christian Science practitioner.

Once a student chooses a teacher and goes through class, the relationship is a permanent one. Each year the teacher calls all the members of his association of students together for what is called the annual Association Meeting. This meeting, which often lasts all day long, is really a refresher course. It is devoted to further instruction in the practice of Christian Science healing. Students' associations continue to hold annual meetings even after their teacher has passed on, inviting an experienced Christian Scientist to address them. There are many hundreds of such associations throughout the world.

While the content of the class teaching is derived entirely from the Bible and from *Science and Health* and the other published writings of Mrs. Eddy, it has special impact because of its systematic and thorough character, and because it is based upon years of actual experience on the part of the teacher in the practice of Christian Science healing. Class teaching is certainly one of the most important means of maintaining the vitality and integrity of the teachings of Christian Science.

Another of the major functions of the Mother Church is to make the teachings of Christian Science as widely available to the public as possible. The religious periodicals help to fulfill this missionary function; so do the Reading Rooms, and the literature-distribution committees of branch churches, which, among other things, place literature in racks in public places. But there are other means too. While The Mother Church does not maintain missionaries, it does maintain a board of about twenty-eight lecturers who travel all over the world wherever Christian Science groups are located.

Each year the members of the Board of Lectureship deliver an aggregate of about 4,500 public lectures on the subject of Christian Science. Their lectures, sponsored by local churches and societies, are open free to all. They also speak before Christian Science organizations at colleges and universities. Some of the lecturers speak also in languages other than English. The groups they address cover a tremendous range—from a cultivated audience in a lecture hall at Oxford or Cambridge to a group of barefoot natives clustered around an outdoor platform on an island off southeast Asia.

Somewhat allied to the Board of Lectureship in function, but far more diversified in scope, is another department of The Mother Church, the Committee on Publication. Established by Mrs. Eddy long before anybody had ever heard of "public relations," this agency is assigned the task of dealing with various media of public communication—newspapers, magazines, books, radio, television; and also with students, researchers, teachers, theologians, ministers, authors, publishers.

The Committee on Publication functions as an office of public information, with the underlying purpose of correcting misconceptions and misrepresentations of Christian Science. Its activities range from correspondence with sociologists or theologians involving questions of scholarship to the planning and production of a continuing series of radio and television programs. These programs have been heard regularly for many years over 700 or 800 radio stations and 150 to 200 television stations.

Like all the activities of The Mother Church, the Committee on Publication has its headquarters in Boston but is a worldwide organization. It has a manager in Boston and several thousand representatives in many countries. Each state, province, or country has its own committee on publication—no longer a group as originally, but a single individual appointed annually by the Readers of one of the three largest churches in the area. This committee, answerable to the manager in Boston as well as to the churches in his own field, functions as a representative of the Mother Church, handling public relations matters. He has an assistant committee—also a single individual—in every community where a branch church, or society, is located and sometimes in other localities as well.

The Committee on Publication carries out another vital function for the Christian Science movement—that of dealing with public officials and legislators on matters affecting the welfare of the church and the freedom to practice Christian Science healing. Over the years these committees have done a great deal to safeguard and strengthen for all citizens the basic human right of freedom of worship and conscience, which is recognized as fundamental by most free nations. They have worked to deepen and clarify the meaning of this freedom so as to ensure that it includes not only the right of assembly and formal worship but also the right of the individual to practice healing by prayer and to depend, if he so chooses, upon prayer and spiritual means alone for healing. Probably no other group is doing more actual day-to-day spadework with public agencies on behalf of freedom of religion for all.

The concern of the Christian Science movement with public affairs is by no means limited to the work of the Committee on Publication. It is most clearly illustrated, perhaps, by the publication by the Christian Science Publishing Society of *The Christian Science Monitor,* a daily newspaper established in 1908 by Mrs. Eddy.

Because of its responsible coverage of national and world news the *Monitor* is widely known in the United States and abroad, particularly among statesmen and governmental officials, teachers and professional workers, newspapermen and others dealing with public affairs. It is edited in Boston, printed in London, Los Angeles, and Boston, and circulated in several dozen countries. Many read the *Monitor* who know or care little about the religious organization which produces it; some who admire its standards fail to realize how literally these stem, in day-to-day decisions, from Christian Science in action. Most of the professional staff and all of the key editors are Christian Scientists.

The Founder herself approved the description of it as "a newspaper for the home," and in later years it adopted the subheading "An International Daily Newspaper." Taken together the two phrases aptly describe the scope of its purpose and outlook; both phrases take on redoubled meaning in the light of the motto its founder gave it in the first issue: "To injure no man, but to bless all mankind" (My. 353:17).

In proportion to its total content, the *Monitor* is characterized by a comparatively high percentage of cultural fare. Contrary to some stories about it, it does report crime news—in terms of the social significance when such news has significance. It has even won a national award as a result of its coverage of a murder trial. But it carries no crime for crime's sake, no blatant headlines. It does not trade in sensation. It is a newspaper any parent can always trust to the children in his home. And it is known, too, for its perceptive and politically sophisticated grasp of world issues.

Establishment of the *Monitor* consummated a desire voiced by Mrs. Eddy as early as 1883, when her church was still in its infancy. It is generally assumed that her purpose was to provide the public and particularly her own followers with an example of clean journalism and a source of reliable and constructive news. Whatever precise motives she may have had in mind, it is an empirical fact that the *Monitor* has had a tremendous influence upon the religious outlook of Christian Scientists.

It is worth imagining what the viewpoint of the Christian Science movement as a whole might be if the *Monitor* did not exist. Christian Science is a religion that teaches the individual to keep evil far from his thoughts, and that keeps him busy working out his salvation. It teaches him to lift his gaze from the sordid, the mundane, the merely material, and to center his interest in spiritual realities.

But the *Monitor* stands as a constant reminder to the Scientist to keep his feet on the ground in the practical application of his religious teachings to the present-day needs of men. It reminds him to think beyond his own personal problems—to think intelligently about the problems of his country and mankind. It helps to educate him to assume his proper responsibilities as a citizen.

Nobody could read the *Monitor* day after day and still take an ostrich-like attitude about public affairs. In fact, a daily stint of reading it is a considerably more sobering experience than reading an average newspaper which seeks to entertain—because in the *Monitor* issues are so thoroughly and analytically discussed. Nobody could read the *Monitor* regularly without gaining a realistic insight into the present plight of the human race and a renewed sense of unselfish concern for mankind's welfare and also an increased appreciation of the utility of moral and spiritual resources.

Thus the influence of the *Monitor* has been constantly to remind Christian Scientists that Christianity is not merely a set of theories, but a positive spiritual force which can and should be applied to solve mankind's problems. Its effect has been constantly to remind them that their responsibility as Christians is not merely to themselves or their families, but to their community and to all mankind. It is not an accident that the average Christian Scientist thinks of his religion in terms of universal salvation as well as individual salvation. Actually, he gradually learns to think of the two as one, and he feels an obligation to embrace in his own life purpose the goal expressed in the *Monitor*'s motto, quoted earlier: "To injure no man, but to bless all mankind."

The practical concern of The Mother Church for the social needs of mankind is expressed in a number of ways. It maintains a large department of armed-service activities, which supplies chaplains to the armed forces and special ministers to several hundred military installations. The Mother Church also maintains a home for elderly Christian Scientists at Pleasant View, Concord, New Hampshire, and two sanatoriums where Christian Science nursing care is available. (Many other sanatoriums and nursing homes, and a number of institutions caring for the aged, are maintained as nonprofit institutions by committees and private groups of Christian Scientists.) The Mother Church makes financial contributions toward disaster relief in time of major emergencies in the United States and abroad, and has contributed many millions of dollars toward war relief. Christian Science branch churches, singly and cooperatively, often provide workers who visit prisons and other public institutions to hold services and to provide religious counsel.

But basically, the approach of the denomination to social

needs rests on the conviction that what is most deeply needed is greater individual demonstration of Christian power. To this specific goal the church devotes itself primarily, for this is the task for which it exists and by which it can make its contribution most effectively.

There are many other activities carried on by The Mother Church, but for the most part they fall within the broad general areas sketched above. For example, as part of its relationship with its branches, The Mother Church maintains a staff of workers who travel the field constantly, conferring with branch churches regarding local problems. The purpose is to encourage and nurture the branches. A similar staff works with young people in the Christian Science organizations at colleges and universities; and every other year, a conference for young people from these organizations all over the world is held in Boston.

But in the last analysis, all the diversified activities of the church organization—the holding of services, the publishing of periodicals and newspaper, the negotiating with public officials and legislators, the teaching, lecturing, and administrative policies—all are aimed at the goal of nourishing the individual spiritually and promoting his progress, filling his spiritual needs; and at bringing the gospel of Christian Science to those many who still cry in the darkness of suffering for new light and faith.

Chapter Four

What About the Bible?

For many people the Bible is a mystery. Beyond doubt it has influenced Western civilization more profoundly than any other book; centuries of the most searching examination and criticism have failed to destroy it. Yet many persons feel its imagery is obscure, its events incredible, its history jumbled, its idiom and illustrations remote from the world we know. Some have dismissed it as of doubtful value for a world of rationalist free-thinking and an industrialized social context. Yet it lies at the heart of religion for hundreds of millions of people.

The Old Testament is the religious literature of a little band of people caught in the endless conflicts of cruel and predatory Mideastern empires of long ago; the events of the New Testament took place among humble folk in an obscure frontier area of the mighty Roman Empire. Yet the Scriptures burst upon the Western world, after the time of Christ Jesus, with such power and illumination that they have radically influenced the whole course of Western history.

Beyond any doubt the Bible is unique among mankind's books—even among its religious books. Its scope and stature are attested to by its role in history. Yet because so much of it is unexplainable in ordinary human terms, all sorts of interpretations have been offered. These have ranged from the view that every word put down by the scriptural writers was literally dictated by the Holy Spirit, to the view, shocking to religious people, that the Bible is a fountainhead of superstition. Many people today, frustrated by their unanswered questions about religion and unable to fathom the Scriptures, have put the Bible on the shelf, where it silently gathers dust, figuratively and literally a closed book.

But like many devout thinkers of other faiths, the Christian Scientist finds in the Bible a vast and priceless treasurehouse of spiritual teaching. It is much more than magnificent literature; it is the record of the clearest spiritual insights in mankind's history; and it is filled with meaning for the modern world. Not only does it point to deep and absolute Truth; it shows unmistakably that this Truth is demonstrable in human experience. It reveals the nature of spiritual laws; and when its spiritual meaning is understood, there emerges from its pages a pattern of spiritual logic—fundamental, universal, eternal, and provable as Science.

To consider only the literal meaning or the material circumstances recorded in the Bible would be to overlook its real message. The historical background is important; but quite clearly the Scriptures are centrally concerned with the things of the Spirit. They are concerned with the nature of God and man's relationship to Him, of good and evil, and of mankind's redemption from mortality. The Bible contains a record of spiritual discovery and it cannot be understood from a material standpoint. *Science and Health* states that the one important interpretation of Scripture is the spiritual interpretation.

"Take away the spiritual signification of Scripture," writes Mrs. Eddy, "and that compilation can do no more for mortals than can moonbeams to melt a river of ice" (S&H 241:14-17).

So the spiritual meaning is of paramount importance to the

Christian Scientist. Here it will be useful to give an indication of what this refers to. Let us take a panoramic view.

From the standpoint of Christian Science, the first commandment of Moses, "Thou shalt have no other gods before me" (Ex. 20:3), is foundational to an understanding of the Scriptures. It constitutes a point of departure for the spiritual teaching throughout. It is a shining thread visible from the very first words of Genesis—"In the beginning God created the heaven and the earth"—to the majestic imagery of the Apocalypse.

In a thousand different ways the Bible unfolds the meaning of the commandment and explains its application to human experience. Historical incidents and illustrations are presented in such a way as to show its significance for human action. Various literary forms are used to elucidate its heights and depths of meaning: precept, proverb, psalm, parable, praise, allegory, admonition.

The Great Commandment constitutes the basis for the whole Decalogue. Its evolving lesson is richly unfolded in the teaching of the prophets, and it reaches its climax in the words and works of Christ Jesus.

The Scriptures portray the consequences of obeying the commandment and the consequences of disobeying it. And in the process they reveal the nature of God and man's true relationship to Him.

The immediate application of the commandment, at the time Moses gave it to the Children of Israel, was to forbid the worship of idols, to turn them from the many pagan deities of that era—to establish the concept of monotheism. The God of Moses had made himself known to Abraham as the Almighty, possessor of heaven and earth; it was the God who had revealed Himself to Jacob at Peniel and thus changed Jacob's nature.

But it is well to emphasize what a radical departure this concept of one God represented from anything known to the rest of mankind at the time Moses gave the commandment to his people (about 1290 B.C.).

All of the great nations of that day had highly developed forms of polytheistic worship. Nearly a century before the Exo-

dus, Egypt had witnessed the attempt of Amenophis IV to replace the Egyptian pantheon with the worship of one god, the
sun; but the attempt was abortive. Witchcraft and magic
abounded in the religion of the Egyptians. The Canaanites, inhabitants of the Promised Land, toward which the migratory
little band of Hebrews was moving, also had a system of idolatry as elaborately developed as that of later Greece or Rome—
though it involved much lower moral standards. The whole
world of that era was filled with idol worship and assorted tribal
deities.

But Moses' own experience in the Arabian desert had prepared him to give a new commandment to his people. There
while in exile, keeping the flocks of Jethro, he had made the
spiritual discovery which fitted him to be the great leader of
Israel. In the wilderness God revealed Himself to Moses as "I
AM"—causative Being conscious of itself; not a god associated
with sun or star, but the creative power behind the whole universe; not one of many potentates, but the one and only God,
of transcendent power and authority. Moses identified Him by
the Hebrew name of YHWH, or Yahweh: "He (who) causes
to be."

This discovery was a Great Divide. From the moment Moses
gave the Great Commandment to the Israelites as their national
guide and ideal, their history and particularly their national
thought began to run in a radically different course from that
of any of the mélange of races around them. The discovery of
Moses was basic. It cut through the elaborate superstitions of
his time and reached the Absolute. So deep did he succeed in
driving this insight into the consciousness and the conscience
of Israel that all through the long centuries before the coming
of the Messiah—the centuries of violence and division, confusion and backsliding, of oppression, exile and desolation—the
flame never quite went out. When the nation's religious and
historical writings were edited and codified into the collection
of books we now call the Old Testament (1,000 to 150 B.C.),
the whole story was presented essentially from the standpoint

of the Great Commandment: one God, who alone should command the loyalties and deepest affections of man.

But this would not have been the case had it not been for
the prophets, spiritual seers who kept the conscience of Israel.
It was the vision of these great men that deepened and expanded the Hebrew concept of God, infused new meaning into
the Great Commandment, and showed its application more
broadly in human experience. It was the impact of their ideas
that stimulated the collection and rewriting of the ancient historical material and shaped its character. The illumination of
their teachings prepared the way for the coming of the Messiah.

Even before the Children of Israel had entered the Promised
Land, Moses had foreseen the temptations which would confront them there. In his farewell to them he spelled out plainly
what the divine law required of them. His words set the standard for a nation's history:

See, I have set before thee this day life and good, and death and
evil; In that I command thee this day to love the Lord thy God, to
walk in his ways, and to keep his commandments and his statutes
and his judgments, that thou mayest live and multiply: and the Lord
thy God shall bless thee in the land whither thou goest to possess it.
But if thine heart turn away, so that thou wilt not hear, but shalt be
drawn away, and worship other gods, and serve them; I denounce
unto you this day, that ye shall surely perish, and that ye shall not
prolong your days upon the land, whither thou passest over Jordan
to go to possess it. I call heaven and earth to record this day against
you, that I have set before you life and death, blessing and cursing:
therefore choose life, that both thou and thy seed may live (Deut.
30:15-19).

But despite Moses' warning, the tempting and enervating
worldliness of Canaan gradually seeped into the thinking of
Israel. After the Golden Age of David, climax of Israel's unity
and promise, the story is that of increasing deterioration. The
sense of national destiny, so dynamic in the time of Moses, became almost lost in the confusion and division of power politics.
The flame of true religion was nearly smothered in the trap-

pings of formalistic worship. The people drifted into idolatry; images and altars took the place of the living God. Yahweh became little more than a Canaanite Baal. From the Christian Scientist's point of view, we find here the prototypes of some of the problems we face today.

The glory of the prophets is that they put all this into the perspective of the Great Commandment. They held up the standard of one God alone. They related the pure spiritual discovery of Moses to the problems of a confused and beleaguered people, telling them that safety and strength lay solely in trust in God and the understanding of Him; and by so doing, they vastly expanded and clarified the implications of the monotheistic ideal.

Each in his own way, the prophets took the foundational teaching epitomized by the first commandment and set it alongside various kinds of human motives and actions, various states of human thought. The commandment was spiritual law; it was the measuring rod. In the light of this divine standard, human motives and actions are exposed for exactly what they are.

For example, Amos insisted a God of righteousness could be worshipped only by righteousness. He deplored the fatness and ease of material success and told his countrymen bluntly that they had turned from love of truth to love of money. Hosea showed that worship of one God meant *trust* in one God. In her efforts to save herself, Israel had turned everywhere but in the right direction for safety—to alliances with Egypt and Assyria, to her wealth, and to the false piety of elaborate altars and temple worship.

The theme of trust in one God alone, so beautifully stressed by the first Isaiah, later brought Jeremiah into bitter conflict with the priesthood and popular opinion of his time. He denounced the hypocrisy of outward sacrifice and worship while God had no place in the hearts of the people. He warned that the safety of besieged Jerusalem lay not in the presence there of the holy temple and the Ark of the Covenant, but solely in the understanding of God possessed by its inhabitants and their fidelity to His precepts. He showed that spiritual law makes demands on the individual as well as the nation. Let not the wise man glory in his wisdom, said Jeremiah, nor the mighty in his might, nor the rich in his riches, "but let him that glorieth glory in this, that he understandeth and knoweth me, that I am the Lord which exercise loving kindness, judgment, and righteousness, in the earth" (Jer. 9:24).

There is, of course, vastly more to the story of the Old Testament than these brief examples have indicated. But the towering message of the Great Commandment can be seen throughout. All through these turbulent centuries, the weaknesses and transgressions of Israel and Judah—both of rulers and of the people at large—provide a diversified catalogue of the follies of human nature and the pitfalls of human experience. The insights provided by the prophets enable the discerning reader to watch the various kinds of human thinking in action and to see where they lead. Always the measuring rod is the Great Commandment. Thus the nature of spiritual law is unfolded, and also its application to basic human problems.

The fact gradually emerges that there are many other kinds of false gods besides those represented in the fertility rites and sacred images of the Canaanites. There are what Ezekiel called idols in the heart. They are typified by such mental states as arrogance, hypocrisy, pride, smugness, hate, lust, greed, treachery, selfishness, dishonesty, covetousness, apathy, and dependence on material might. As the Scientist sees it, nothing could be more modern or practical than the lessons involved here.

The fact emerges, too, that punishment is not an unpredictable divine vengeance, but is inherent in idolatrous thoughts and actions. As the second Isaiah, of the Babylonian Exile, wrote: "Behold, the Lord's hand is not shortened, that it cannot save; neither his ear heavy, that it cannot hear: But your iniquities have separated between you and your God, and your sins have hid his face from you, that he will not hear" (Isa. 59:1,2).

Thus we are led back to the central truth discovered by Moses, a truth which the Isaiah of the Exile put in these words:

"There is no God else beside me; a just God and a Saviour.
. . . Look unto me, and be ye saved, all the ends of the earth:
for I am God, and there is none else" (Isa. 45:21,22).

Out of all the turmoil, cruelty, and desolation of Old Testament times, the truth contained in the Great Commandment
emerged indestructible. Like a beam of light stealing into the
inner reaches of a cave, it had penetrated the mental darkness
and primitive confusion of the Israelites in the desert. It had
given them the guide they needed: a separation from the idolatry and superstition surrounding them; a foundation for a stable ethical and legal system and for national cohesion; a sense
of national destiny.

If we follow the beam of light reaching into the recesses of
a cave, it grows stronger and leads all the way to full daylight.
The great seers of Israel followed the light of Moses' discovery
and contributed to it the insights of their own spiritual vision.
As a result the shining truth of the first commandment grew
clearer through the centuries and led to a progressively higher
idea of God. It made the ancient Hebrews a unique people; it
not only gave them a totally new viewpoint of their own history; it shaped that history.

But the simile of a beam of light does not fully convey the
character of this scriptural discovery. We are confronted here
with the inherent power of a profoundly dynamic and self-
revealing spiritual Truth. It produced the inspired upthrust and
majestic poetry of the prophetic age; but it went much further.
It continued to unfold and reveal itself, even when Israel was
desolate and Judah laid waste. The nation's long search for God
was a beginning and not an end. It was a preparation for the
coming of the greatest prophet of them all—the one who
showed forth perfectly, by the way he lived and triumphed,
what it means to know one God alone.

From the beginning of the ministry of Jesus to its triumphant climax, the law of absolute loyalty to one God alone
shines through his words and works. The Old Testament had
recorded the story of a people caught by their own iniquities in
the labyrinth of idolatry, and deaf to the inspired call of the

prophets; Jesus demonstrated the perfect and complete triumph that comes through perfect obedience to one absolute God, good. The Old Testament had served to draw a sharp line of demarcation between the standard of one God and the evils of the carnal mind; Jesus lived this divine standard, utterly and unreservedly, and thus he fulfilled the Great Commandment and showed the dominion this brings.

The Old Testament had stressed law, obedience, and punishment, and these had evolved in the hands of the priesthood into binding legalism and ritual. Jesus revealed a God of Love, whose law not only punishes sin but redeems and saves mankind. Jesus did not destroy the law of the mighty commandment; he illustrated its fulfillment through the riches of God's goodness and grace. As John said, "The law was given by Moses, but grace and truth came by Jesus Christ" (John 1:17).

At the very beginning of his ministry, when he was tempted in the wilderness, Jesus answered each temptation in terms illustrative of the Great Commandment: first, "Man shall not live by bread alone, but by every word that proceedeth out of the mouth of God"; second, "Thou shalt not tempt the Lord thy God"; and third, "Thou shalt worship the Lord thy God, and him only shalt thou serve" (Matt. 4:4,7,10).

He translated the Great Commandment into goals for human experience: "Lay not up for yourselves treasures upon earth, where moth and rust doth corrupt, and where thieves break through and steal: But lay up for yourselves treasures in heaven, where neither moth nor rust doth corrupt, and where thieves do not break through nor steal" (Matt. 6:19,20). "For what shall it profit a man, if he shall gain the whole world, and lose his own soul?" (Mark 8:36).

By word and deed Jesus elucidated the clear line of demarcation implied in the Great Commandment. He said bluntly: "No man can serve two masters. . . . Ye cannot serve God and mammon" (Matt. 6:24). "It is the spirit that quickeneth; the flesh profiteth nothing."

At no time did the Master honor any power apart from God. He did not bow to sin, storm, lack, distance, disease, persecution, or death itself. He overcame them all. His teachings involved a rejection of the evidence of the material senses: of the laws and might of matter, its temptations and limitations. They called for a complete mental rebirth, a new way of looking at the world, a new view of reality and of God and man. They called for a new way of life.

His teachings transcended the stern admonitions of "Thou shalt" and "Thou shalt not." The keynote of his Sermon on the Mount was "Blessed are ye. . . ." In showing the fulfillment of the law through grace and truth, Jesus also lifted up the human apprehension of the nature of man. Priestly law had dealt with men as though they were sinners, subject to guilt and condemnation. As the Scientist views it, Jesus showed forth the perfection and glory originally given to man in God's likeness, as recorded in the very first chapter of Genesis, where man is made in the image and likeness of God and "God saw every thing that he had made, and behold, it was very good." Jesus said, "The Father loveth the Son, and hath given all things into his hand. He that believeth on the Son hath everlasting life" (John 3:35:36).

The great seers of the Old Testament had gained gleams of the perfection of the Infinite. Amos and Isaiah had shown Him to be a God of righteousness, justice, and truth. Hosea and Jeremiah had taught that He was a God of love. The two Isaiahs had shown Him to be a universal God for all men and not an exclusive national deity. Christ Jesus, in the fulness of his inspired vision, gathered together all the various strands of the prophetic insights, defined God as Life and as Spirit, and revealed Him in vividness, realism, and full effulgence. By his mission he brought to its fruition the scriptural theme of man's original goodness and perfection.

In line with this revelation of the true nature of man, Jesus selected as basic two commandments from the 613 provisions of the Jewish Law. On these two commandments "hang all the law and the prophets," he said, and he made it clear that the two are essentially one:

"Thou shalt love the Lord thy God with all thy heart, and

with all thy soul, and with all thy mind. This is the first and great commandment. And the second is like unto it, Thou shalt love thy neighbour as thyself" (Matt. 22:37-39). Love for one's fellow man was the natural outcome of thinking of man not as a miserable sinner but as the child of God.

The Master did not stop with words. In his mission comes the full dynamic power of spiritual demonstration. At the last he submitted himself to the supreme and final test. He accepted the crucifixion. He made it clear that he submitted deliberately, for he said: "I lay down my life, that I might take it again. No man taketh it from me, but I lay it down of myself. I have power to lay it down, and I have power to take it again. This commandment have I received of my Father" (John 10:17,18).

By his mighty works and particularly by his final triumph over death, Jesus proved for all his followers in all time, the supremacy of eternal spiritual law over matter and material conditions. He did this through total and perfect obedience to the Great Commandment.

Thus he brought to light the original and eternal union of God and man. He said, "For as the Father hath life in himself; so hath he given to the Son to have life in himself" (John 5:26). Endeavoring to awaken the people to this underlying link of man with his Maker, he told them, "Behold, the kingdom of God is within you" (Luke 17:21). Jesus claimed no credit for himself as separated from God: "I can of mine own self do nothing . . . the Father that dwelleth in me, he doeth the works" (John 5:30, 14:10).

These were statements of eternal law—the law, or truth, of man's relationship to God. By his lifework Jesus proved this law to be demonstrable in human experience, in the exact measure that the Great Commandment is understood and obeyed. "With what measure ye mete, it shall be measured to you again" (Matt. 7:2). Thus he revealed the way of redemption by which men can learn to realize their at-one-ment with a loving, all-powerful Father, a God who is Spirit, Life, Truth, Love.

The Master said plainly that those who believed what he said would be able to do the works that he did. The deeds of the disciples after the resurrection corroborated this statement. Indeed, history records that for some three hundred years thereafter, these healing works were more or less widely performed by the Christians. But then the power to heal was lost sight of. As the career of Jesus receded into the centuries, the conclusion took hold that his spiritual power was a special dispensation from God, reserved only for him and a few of his immediate followers in the apostolic age. The radical teachings of the Christ were enshrined in elaborate tradition but their practical import seemed largely obscured.

It was to this problem that Mrs. Eddy brought the insights of a new spiritual discovery in the latter part of the nineteenth century. If there was an unchanging God, the eternal author of existence, then the truth concerning God must indeed have the character of unchanging law; and this truth, or law, must be everpresent in every age, capable of being demonstrated when understood. Furthermore, there must be spiritual rules by which human thinking could be brought into accord with this truth.

In other words, the practical religion demonstrated so unmistakably by Jesus and his early followers must have the character of Science, because it was based on divine Principle, or Truth, and was definable and demonstrable in terms of exact law.

Mrs. Eddy's discovery carried the first commandment to its logical conclusion, both in terms of the basic theology the commandment implies and in terms of the practical application it demands.

The basic premise of Science is precisely the one omnipotent God alone set forth in Scripture, and not the assumption that matter and mortality—whose supposedly immutable laws Jesus reversed—are real and fundamental. Working from the premise that God is one God, omnipotent and all-powerful, Isaiah had said, "there is none else." Mrs. Eddy's discovery revealed the full implication of this line of reasoning, namely, that since God, Spirit, is All-in-all, then matter, the exact opposite of Spirit, could have only a fraudulent and deceptive appearance of being. In absolute terms—those terms which go beyond the range of the physical senses—it must be literally nothing.

The logic is similar with regard to evil. Since God—defined by Jesus as Spirit, Life, Truth, Love—is All-in-all, then evil must also be deceptive and fraudulent, having no real validity nor power. In absolute terms evil must be literally nothing. It could not be found within the all-embracing God, for as it is written in the First Epistle of John, "God is light, and in him is no darkness at all" (I John 1:5).

The premise of one omnipotent God alone—infinite, good, and perfect—led also to the conclusion that despite all the sensory appearances, the real creation must express the character of its creator; it must be good and perfect, as is expressed in figurative terms in the first chapter of Genesis.

In her book *Miscellaneous Writings*, for example, Mrs. Eddy holds up the standard: "If God is All, and God is good, it follows that all must be good; and no other power, law, or intelligence can exist. On this proof rest premise and conclusion in Science, and the facts that disprove the evidence of the senses" (Misc. 101:26).

So far as the application of Science to human problems is concerned, its rules are really an elaboration of the first commandment from start to finish. They show how to separate real, godlike thoughts from false, idolatrous thoughts; reject wrong thoughts and cast them out by replacing them with the understanding of divine Truth.

In its application to healing, Science proceeds on the premise that sickness is foreign to the divine nature and no part of God's plan for His children; also that sickness is the outcome of fear, ignorance, or sin. Many of the rules given in *Science and Health* are very specific in showing how to cope with the root causes of sickness by obeying the first commandment. For example: "When the illusion of sickness or sin tempts you, cling steadfastly to God and His idea. Allow nothing but His likeness to abide in your thought" (S&H 495:14-16).

The goal which Science holds up for its adherents is strictly in line with the essence of the Great Commandment: "Every human thought must turn instinctively to the divine Mind as its sole center and intelligence. Until this be done, man will never be found harmonious and immortal" (Misc. 307:30).

This is the Great Commandment drawn to its logical conclusion. What Moses perceived at Mount Sinai, and what Jesus fulfilled in his mighty demonstration over all mortality, today is revealed in terms of an exact and practical Science.

Thus the Christian Scientist finds recorded in the Scriptures the unfolding in human thought of irresistibly dynamic spiritual Truth—a revelation that did not stop with the crucifixion, but whose continuing unfoldment of itself to humanity is illustrated today in the Science of Christianity.

Thus the Bible record is not fragmentary and contradictory. Its essential message is whole and coherent. Some may object to particular passages they think are obscure, just as one might object to certain details in an Oriental tapestry. But when the Bible is taken as a whole, and its spiritual import is seen, the pattern of Truth it contains emerges clearly; just as the design of a tapestry, when seen in its completeness, emerges in its full coherence and beauty.

For the Christian Scientist, the central meaning of the Bible is not and could not have been the product of the unaided human mind. It speaks of a realm that is hidden to unaided mortal vision but revealed to spiritual insight. It is the product of inspired thought derived from a divine source. Recognizing this, the Christian Scientist gladly accepts, as the very first tenet of his religion, these words written by Mrs. Eddy: "As adherents of Truth, we take the inspired Word of the Bible as our sufficient guide to eternal Life" (S&H 497:3).

2.

In modern times the Bible has come under more searching and critical scrutiny than ever before. For one thing, the last hundred years have witnessed the full impact of the scientific revolution on religious thought. Darwin's theory of evolution collided squarely with those structures of theology built upon literal interpretations of Genesis. The other sciences—geology, anthropology, astronomy, chemistry, and physics—all had information to offer which raised new challenges to traditional theology. Many felt that they called into question the correctness of the Scriptural record itself.

Concurrently the Bible was subjected for the first time to the sort of literary research, historical analysis, and archeological comparison applied to other ancient documents. Scholars working from an objective and sometimes highly critical point of view undertook exhaustive studies of the sources, authenticity, and authorship of scriptural material. Others examined in much detail the peculiarities of language, variations of ancient manuscripts, and inconsistencies of text.

These investigations upset a world which for centuries had been accustomed to viewing the Scriptures as sacrosanct, or to tolerating critical evaluation of them only within the limited framework of theological interpretations. For decades a spectacular controversy raged between the defenders of rigid traditional theology on the one hand and the proponents of the sciences and other academic disciplines on the other. The attackers went pretty far in destructive criticism of the Scriptures, and it is only in recent years that a saner re-evaluation has begun to emerge.

From the standpoint of the Christian Scientist, the work of careful and balanced Bible scholars is extremely useful. Knowledge of Bible history often serves to etch more sharply the significance of the scriptural teachings because it enables one to see them in their original setting.

It is exceedingly helpful to know, for example, that the two accounts of creation in Genesis emerged at different periods. It is useful to know that it was a custom of the ancient copyists simply to put divergent accounts side by side, often weaving the two together a few verses at a time, rather than attempting to rewrite or reconcile them. This fact throws much light not only on Genesis but also on many other portions of the Old Testament.

It is helpful to know, too, that while archeological discoveries have resulted in some emendations of the Bible text and thrown new light on scriptural origins, they have in the main confirmed the historical record the Bible contains. William Neil, in his book *The Rediscovery of the Bible,* takes note of this fact: "From all these finds the striking fact emerges that each new discovery tends to substantiate the general reliability of our Biblical text."

It is worthy of note, too, that some of the best Bible scholars have not been satisfied with merely humanistic interpretations of the mighty works of Jesus, including the resurrection. Close examination of what happened in the Holy Land some two millenniums ago seems to have shown beyond question that some exceedingly unusual events occurred—events that suddenly transformed the scattered disciples from despairing and frightened fugitives into joyful and courageous men willing to die for their faith. The most rigorous scholarship can only confirm the amazing power of Jesus' teachings to survive the oblivion of Calvary and to perpetuate themselves.

Many of the modern translations of the Scriptures are helpful in clarifying Biblical language and in bringing to the student the results of modern scholarship. However, the Christian Scientist in English-speaking countries finds the most useful to be the King James Version, whose incomparable language has the unique genius not only of defining thought but of liberating it, lifting one's gaze to the vision of things eternal.

In her published writings Mrs. Eddy draws from time to time on the work of various Bible translators. Always her purpose is to get at the spiritual meaning, the essence of the scriptural message. Her own perspective on textual questions is indicated by these words from *Science and Health:*

The decisions by vote of Church Councils as to what should and should not be considered Holy Writ; the manifest mistakes in the ancient versions; the thirty thousand different readings in the Old Testament, and the three hundred thousand in the New—these facts show how a mortal and material sense stole into the divine record, with its own hue darkening to some extent the inspired pages. But mistakes could neither wholly obscure the divine Science of the Scriptures seen from Genesis to Revelation, mar the demonstration of Jesus, nor annul the healing by the prophets, who forsaw that "the stone which the builders rejected" would become "the head of the corner" (S&H 139:15).

As the Christian Scientist sees it, little is to be gained by attempting to appraise the Bible solely by the criteria of ordinary literature. The insights of literary criticism are useful indeed but the essential character of the Scriptures outreaches any such framework. The prophets and Gospel writers were much more concerned with spiritual truth than with rationalist analysis or detailed explanations of historical background. What counts in the Scriptures is the transcendent spiritual message that leaps from the pages and outshines the literary setting.

Likewise, it is not very rewarding to attempt to appraise the Scriptures according to the criteria of the natural sciences. The sciences are designed to measure and evaluate material quantities and phenomena; the essential content of the Scriptures deals with spiritual realities. No conclusive appraisal can be reached by attempting, for example, to reconcile the healings of Jesus with physiological law, or his stilling of the storm with meteorology. The whole point of the Bible narrative is to show that the Master knew how to overrule laws of matter. It is generally acknowledged today that what we call the immutable laws of matter are but summaries of our physical observations as to the ways things usually happen. To the Christian Scientist, Christ Jesus furnished evidence of a much deeper and more powerful universal law that is truly immutable: the law of Spirit, which when understood overrules matter.

There is an obvious insistence all the way through the Bible and especially in the New Testament on the demonstrable superiority of spiritual power over material conditions. We find hints of this in the experiences of Abraham, Jacob, and Joseph and illustrations of it in the works of Elijah and Elisha. It was stressed by the prophets and most conspicuously demonstrated by the Master. This is certainly a leading fundamental of the scriptural message.

Many have attempted to prove the scriptural record to be exaggerated, and thus to explain away the healings and miracles. But these attempts have never been very successful. As the Scientist sees it, they never will be; the validity of miracles and healing does not actually depend upon issues of textual detail; it transcends them. Nor does it depend simply on doctrinal teachings. To the Scientist, the conclusiveness of the Bible record for our present age is confirmed by the demonstrable fact that such works are being repeated today, in the measure in which the scriptural teachings are understood and utilized.

Much evidence could be adduced for this statement. For example, a friend of mine was dying—someone on the hospital staff had even called an undertaker. But at the moment of crisis, she turned her thoughts to God and gained a new and deep insight into the words of Paul that neither life nor death nor things present nor things to come shall be able to separate us from the love of God (Rom. 8:38). Her restoration began at that moment of inspiration. Although she knew little of Christian Science at that time, she whispered to her husband to call a Christian Science practitioner for help, and he did. By morning she was well. Though the doctor who had attended her called her recovery a freakish thing and said she could never be normal again because so many chemical changes had taken place in her body, she is today the picture of blooming health. When one knows personally of verified instances such as this, it is not hard to believe that Jesus raised the daughter of Jairus from the dead.

It is unquestionably true that one's ability to understand the Bible and appreciate it depends upon his standpoint. Is he looking at it in material terms or in spiritual terms? *Science and Health* stresses the point that since the Science taught in the original language of the Scriptures came through inspiration, it needs inspiration to be understood. It would seem logical to view the Bible message in terms of its own basic elements. Two of these leading elements surely are the Great Commandment and the supremacy of spiritual power over material conditions.

When one adopts such a standpoint, it gives him a new perspective on the abundant use of figurative illustrations in the Bible. Everyone accepts the fact that metaphor and symbol are used in the Bible. Again and again the Master used homely illustrations to bring out spiritual truths—for example, the sower and the seed, the new patch sewn into an old garment, and the parables, such as that of the Good Samaritan. And in the Old Testament, figures of speech are used constantly. The statement of the Twenty-third Psalm, "He leadeth me beside the still waters," really has little to do with sheep or quiet watering places along the brook. The material meaning is of little importance; the spiritual meaning is all-important; and in this instance, of course, it refers to what Paul described literally as "the peace of God, which passeth all understanding" (Phil. 4:7).

The full beauty and depth of the scriptural figures of speech emerge only as one views them in terms of the fundamental elements of the whole scriptural message. For example, if we view materially Jesus' statement "It is easier for a camel to go through the eye of a needle, than for a rich man to enter into the kingdom of God" (Matt. 19:24), it might appear to be a denunciation of certain economic groups and a description of poverty as a virtue. Viewed in the light of the Great Commandment, however, it becomes an admonition that not only love of money but every false god must be given up. Love of money is certainly idolatry; but there are many other worldly treasures too often worshipped as false gods. We find them in the riches of pride, arrogance, selfishness, for instance.

While people have sometimes gone to excess in looking for allegorical meanings in the Bible, nevertheless it is a generally accepted fact that the Bible abounds in symbolism. The Apocalypse of St. John, for example, is incomprehensible as a literal narrative. But as an allegory, it teaches spiritual lessons of unsurpassed beauty and depth, as brought out in a chapter entitled "The Apocalypse" in *Science and Health*.

Whether or not one discerns the hidden meaning of an allegory depends upon one's viewpoint. To a child, Bunyan's *Pilgrim's Progress* is an adventure story. From an adult viewpoint, it is an allegorical description of a Christian-oriented concept of salvation.

So the symbolical teaching in the Bible takes on clearer and deeper perspective when viewed in terms of the central fundamentals of Scripture: the Great Commandment, the mastery of material conditions by spiritual power, and the reality of the things of the Spirit as contrasted with the futility and valuelessness of materialism and the flesh.

For the Christian Scientist, the unique character of the Bible is apparent also in another fundamental: the use of prophecy. In the true and broadest sense, prophecy refers to much more than the foretelling of future events. It means clear and deep insight into the nature of reality; spiritual discernment of Truth. The prophets had the clear vision of things eternal. All through the Bible the prophetic line consistently reveals new glimpses of the divine nature. All through the Bible is recorded the conflict of this revelation with the materialism of ritual and ceremony. The great light of the Christ was of course the scriptural culmination of this prophetic line, unfolding the nature of reality and of God.

But the validity of prophetic insight is to be found also in the foretelling of things to come. The Old Testament prophecies of the coming of the Messiah are well known and widely accepted among Christians of many faiths. The New Testament writers refer to them repeatedly and show how the events of Christ Jesus' career coincided with them. Truly these prophecies show a remarkable discernment of the manner in which truth would appear.

To the Christian Scientist it is significant that Christ Jesus himself indicated that spiritual truth would continue to unfold. His prophecy of the coming of the Comforter is recorded in considerable detail in the Gospel of John. The Master called it "the spirit of truth"; and for the Scientist, this "spirit of truth" is apparent in the Science of Christianity, which enables men today to fulfill the commandments of Jesus, and to understand, feel, live, and demonstrate the spiritual power he expressed.

Another leading element in the Bible is its central concern with the nature of thought. The book of Proverbs says of a man, "As he thinketh in his heart, so is he"; and the same point was very fully developed by Christ Jesus. The Christian Scientist attaches much importance to the significance of Bible characters as representing various kinds of thinking—qualities of thought and motive. When one looks beyond the literal record and examines the qualities of thinking personified by Bible figures, the whole narrative becomes richly illumined.

An example of this accepted by people of many faiths is the story of Naaman, who was healed of his leprosy when he swallowed his pride and bathed seven times in the river Jordan as instructed by Elisha. Seen in terms of the thinking involved, Naaman's story becomes a beautiful lesson in the healing influence of meekness, teachableness, humility, unselfishness.

To help the Scientist discern the significance of Bible narratives, *Science and Health* contains many references to Bible characters and, in the Glossary, a number of definitions indicating the spiritual meaning of certain scriptural words and names.

For example, the name Jacob is given two definitions: one picturing the patriarch's state of thought before his regeneration at Peniel, and the other describing the changed mental state he personified thereafter, as illustrated in his reconciliation with his brother Esau. The definition reads: "JACOB. A corporeal mortal embracing duplicity, repentance, sensualism. Inspiration; the revelation of Science, in which the so-called material senses yield to the spiritual sense of Life and Love" (S&H 589:5).

This brings us to a cardinal point regarding the nature of the history given in the Bible. While it is widely held among scholars that a sound historical basis underlies the main stream of scriptural narrative, it is also true that scriptural writers seldom included historical information for its own sake, but rather, they used it to bring out certain strongly held convictions. In other words they were not interested in history itself, but in the meaning of history. Consequently the historical narrative contained in the Bible is unlike any other history we know of. It consists of carefully selected incidents well adapted to bring out a spiritual meaning. As history, some of these incidents are comparatively trivial; but in terms of the moral and spiritual lesson they teach they are very important. Again and again the purpose is to bring out the point stressed by the prophets: that when the people obeyed the Great Commandment they prospered; when they disobeyed they paid the price.

As Mrs. Eddy writes in *Science and Health*: "In Egypt, it was Mind which saved the Israelites from belief in the plagues. In the wilderness, streams flowed from the rock, and manna fell from the sky. . . . In national prosperity, miracles attended the successes of the Hebrews; but when they departed from the true idea, their demoralization began" (S&H 133:8-15).

The secular approach to history usually involves showing the ways in which the environment and material circumstances of a people have determined their thinking and culture. The Bible does exactly the opposite. Its historical narrative is used to show how the thinking of the people, individually and collectively, determined the nature of their experiences—how it brought them into subjection to or dominion over their surroundings. The concern of the Bible is always with the nature of thought and where it leads, and particularly with the cardinal truth that a mental state in faithful obedience to the Great Commandment brings dominion over material conditions.

By elucidating the nature of good and its consequences, and exposing the nature of evil and its consequences, the Bible draws a sharp line of demarcation between good and evil. Thus it defines the law of God. Often the exposure of evil involves a dissection of it. This is decidedly valuable for humanity, since evil is inherently deceptive, masked, self-concealing.

In explaining the law of God—the truth which separates good from evil—the Bible brings out three fundamental aspects of it: that it acts as a law of blessing and preservation to all that is good; that it acts as a law of destruction to all that is evil;

and that it operates as a means of salvation to humanity. These are three separate and distinct aspects; often an apparent contradiction in Biblical statements regarding God's law is resolved when this fact is taken into account.

All the way through the Scriptures one can see also the yielding of primitive ideas of God and the gradual unfolding of a better concept, until the revelation reaches its zenith in the New Testament. To understand this also resolves many of the apparent contradictions in scriptural statements regarding the nature of God.

So vast and deep are the spiritual treasures of the Scriptures that much more could be said. Much more would be needed to convey fully and comprehensively what Christian Science derives from the Bible. Almost every page of *Science and Health* and of Mrs. Eddy's other writings contains references to scriptural teachings, either in direct quotation or in essence—and that, of course, is the place to turn for an authoritative appraisal of the Christian Science understanding of the Bible.

Every active Scientist makes the Bible a constant companion and draws daily inspiration from its pages. Viewed in the light of Science, the Bible is indeed a chart of life.

Chapter Five

Why Call It a Science?

The term "science" is subject to various definitions. The traditional view is reflected in Webster's description of it as "accumulated knowledge systematized and formulated with reference to the discovery of general truths and the operation of general laws." Another definition from the same dictionary speaks of science as "a branch of study concerned with observation and classification of facts, esp. with the establishment of verifiable general laws, chiefly by induction and hypotheses."

But such definitions hardly convey the approach of natural scientists. In the first place, they barely suggest the dynamics of an activity whose discoveries are swiftly transforming the world.

Furthermore, such words as "facts" and "truths" may lead the layman to infer that natural science provides final explanations of reality. Actually, scientific researchers today tend to avoid dogmatic conclusions and to describe scientific explanations as "highly provisional."

For example, one natural scientist writes: "Our science is not a collection of laws and facts, however accurate or however confirmed in observation and experience. It is not truth strewn about the fields of reality for us to pick up and store in a cabinet of curios. . . . The theories we propound are ways of organizing our experience and we recognize their lack of finality."

Most leading scientists object to a static definition of science. For example, James B. Conant maintains that information is important to science "chiefly as a basis for further operation." Here is his definition: "Science is an interconnected series of concepts and conceptual schemes that have developed as a result of experimentation and observation and are fruitful of further experimentation and observations."

Conant stresses the word "fruitful." He emphasizes that science is a dynamic "speculative enterprise." While the purpose of scientific research and experiment is to accumulate data, he makes it clear that scientists are a lot more interested in continuous exploration than in the achievement of any final certainty in an absolute sense.

So an important evolution has taken place in the meaning of the word "science." To use it in regard to religion may seem strange to some readers. Yet it would be difficult to find a better word to describe the unique character, scope, and operation of the system of Christian metaphysics discovered by Mrs. Eddy.

This is not to say that Christian Science conforms to any of the above definitions of science. Nor does it share a common basis with the natural sciences. It deals with a different realm. Yet parallels do exist which are highly illuminating.

Let us consider some of the parallels and some of the contrasts.

It might be said, first of all, that the purpose of the natural sciences is to enable men to understand their environment, and thus to gain control over it. Similarly, the aim of Christian Science is to give men an understanding of God, man, and the universe, and, through this understanding, to give them dominion over themselves and their surroundings.

Fundamental to the natural sciences are the concepts of universal law, cause and effect, systematic logic, discovery, and verification. The Christian Scientist feels at home with these concepts; they characterize the approach to fundamental questions which his religion inculcates.

One finds in Christian Science the concept of a universe wholly governed by law; but this universal law is not physical but spiritual. When one begins with God as immutable Principle, unchanging Truth, it becomes logical to conclude that the divine Being operates invariably through law and can be rationally understood. From this basis one also can conclude that there is, in reality, no irrational element in the correct explanation of things.

Many religious systems of East and West have put forward concepts of the deity or deities as being basically irrational —that is, as bestowing special favors, imposing capricious punishments, intervening in certain human situations, performing miracles at particular times or places. Indeed, traditional Christian thought interprets the mission and the works of Christ Jesus as constituting miracles, or exceptions to law.

On the other hand, in Christian Science one views the mission and works of Jesus as providing evidence of fundamental spiritual law—law which is impartial, unchanging, universal, deeper than what appears to human sight as law. To the Christian Scientist, the pure teachings of Christianity are expressive of this foundational law, and therefore understandable as Science.

Thus one finds in this religion an answer to the dilemma of those who have felt that they could accept Christianity as poetry or as a source of inspiration and moral uplift, but could never accept dogmas that assume infractions of law, alias miracles. To the Christian Scientist, what are known as the miracles of the Bible are evidence of God's laws brought to light. As Mrs. Eddy writes: "Miracles are no infraction of God's laws; on the contrary, they fulfil His laws; for they are the signs following Christianity, whereby matter is proven powerless and subordinate to Mind" (Misc. 29:27).

We have said that Christian Science deals with a realm dif-

ferent from that of the natural sciences. The framework of the
natural sciences is the universe of space, time, matter, physical
energy, which is accepted as fundamental. Here scientists search
for the interrelationships of cause and effect, and for explanations of natural mechanisms and processes in terms of law. They
confine their field of exploration to phenomena that are materially observable and measurable. Rarely do they look beyond
the physical universe. Schneer says frankly that physical scientists are "not seekers after truth in a metaphysical sense,"
and others in the scientific community have expressed similar
views.

On the other hand, Christian Science, being a religion, has a
special concern with the ultimate problems of existence. It deals
with the question of primal causation. Its subject matter has
to do with the nature of God and His universe—its structure,
laws, forces, substance, and action. This Science does not
accept the physical universe as fundamental or even as real in
an absolute sense. It deals with that which lies beyond the sensory universe. It is concerned with causative Mind, or Spirit,
and its phenomena. Its basic propositions have to do with the
nature of ultimate reality.

For example, the proposition that Spirit is the real and eternal
and that matter is unreal, temporal, deals with a question of
ultimate truth. Likewise, to hold that Mind creates the universe
leaves no room for anything more basic. Such a statement is
concerned with the nature of absolute truth.

Some may question whether it is valid to attach the name
"Science" to that knowledge which is apart from the universe
of matter and is not materially measurable. But a better criterion
might be the test of whether such knowledge is rational, systematic, demonstrable; whether it expresses a universal Principle
and is provable in conformity with law.

In this connection it is worth repeating that natural scientists
rarely think of their physical conclusions in terms of finality.
They are much less dogmatic today than a few decades ago, so
revolutionary have been modern discoveries and so drastic the
overturning of some long-respected theories. Natural scientists

often point out that the sciences consist of humanly contrived explanations of objective phenomena. In other words, the theories, laws, and processes of the sciences are human conceptions, or explanations, of what can be physically or mathematically observed of mankind's surroundings. Alfred North Whitehead was fond of reminding his students that the sciences are "abstractions from reality." Others have called the sciences the noblest edifice constructed by the human mind. C. P. Snow speaks of "the scientific edifice of the physical world" as being "in its intellectual depth, complexity, and articulation, the most beautiful and wonderful collective work of the mind of man."

Schneer illustrates this point when he writes that the old mechanical view of solid atoms, which would have reduced all phenomena to particles and the void, "was a mechanism of idea. It was a human mental construct."

He goes even further—further, in fact, than most physicists would care to go with him. He writes, in describing the difficulties of observing electrons, mesons, and other particles currently believed to make up the atom: "These particles are not real particles in the sense that grains of dust or marbles or tennis balls are real particles. These particles are instead constructs, ideas, schemes for the organization in mathematical law of a tangle of experimental complexity. They elude the sight and the touch as any idea must elude the sight and touch."

Such statements—which one encounters not infrequently in current literature on scientific subjects—do not mean that scientists are saying that matter is essentially mental or that it is nonexistent. Usually they do mean that natural scientists are describing scientific knowledge as made up of conceptions formulated by the human mind to explain objective phenomena —formulated on the basis of physical observations.

But the Christian Scientist would ask: Do such conceptions hold the answers to basic scientific questions? Can one safely assume that the essential mysteries of the universe and life and man, which the natural sciences seek to unravel, can be fathomed within the framework of physical investigation? Who can say that the final scientific answers don't lie elsewhere? Who can say that they do not lie in what the anthropologist Loren Eiseley calls "that mysterious shadow world beyond nature, that final world which contains—if anything contains—the explanation of men and catfish and green leaves"?

In his book *Of Stars and Men* Harlow Shapley hints at the existence of truth beyond the materially measurable. He outlines certain epochal adjustments which have already taken place in mankind's outlook upon the human environment: first, from ancient man's self-centered awareness of himself and his immediate surroundings to the belief that the earth was the center of the universe; from this view to the recognition that the earth was tributary to the sun and the assumption that the sun was the center of the universe; from this heliocentric theory to the realization that our solar system is but a tiny way station near the edge of one galaxy in a universe of millions of galaxies; and finally, to the growing belief that there are hundreds of millions of planets in the physical universe where material life may exist, perhaps in much higher forms than our own.

These four historic adjustments of mental outlook present a panoramic sweep for pondering. Yet Dr. Shapley ventures the speculation that "a fifth adjustment might be in the psychological realm, or in the 'negative matter' world, or in one of those fanciful existences where our metagalaxy is only an atom in some superuniverse, or in the equally droll (and equally possible) existence where our electrons are the galaxies in some microcosmic universe that is below our measures and our knowing."

But does the next adjustment really lie in such directions? Does it lie in the physical mysteries of the very large or the very small or even of the in-between? May it not lie in a totally new direction, wholly distinct from a matter universe—namely, in the dawning of the Science of Mind, the Science of Spirit, which shows matter to be only a misconception or illusion? To the Christian Scientist, this is not idle speculation. He thinks of basic reality as omnipresent Spirit and its manifestation, *instead of matter*.

In line with this view, he thinks of divine Science as conscious truth derived directly from God—absolute, complete, immutable, eternal: divine Mind's own knowledge of itself and its phenomena. In other words, as identical with the laws of God and their perpetual action.

At this point it may be useful to point out an important distinction. In its deepest sense the word "Science"—especially as used in the phrase "divine Science"—means the laws which express the dynamics of the Creator Himself and govern what He creates. It means the laws of divine Principle controlling the universe; the unchanging spiritual relationship of Creator and creation, and of God's ideas one to the other. In this ultimate sense, divine Science is both absolute and final.

Its nature is metaphorically described in these words of Mrs. Eddy: "It is God's right hand grasping the universe—all time, space, immortality, thought, extension, cause, and effect; constituting and governing all identity, individuality, law, and power" (Misc. 364:13-17). This is the divine order of things, of which Mrs. Eddy also writes in *Science and Health*: "Human language can repeat only an infinitesimal part of what exists" (S&H 520:5-7). This is the ultimate reality which the Christian Scientist feels Mrs. Eddy discerned in her spiritual discovery.

On the other hand, the term "Christian Science" refers in a specific sense to the truths of Science as reduced to human apprehension and comprised in a demonstrable metaphysical system. As such, its statements are expressive of divine reality, but they also include the practical rules for its demonstration in the overcoming of material discords. Its categories of reasoning range from the greatest of universal truths to the simplest application. Its basic propositions offer inexhaustible fields for exploration; yet they are so simple that a child can in some measure lay hold of them and experience their benefits.

From all that has been said it will be evident that while Christian Science and the natural sciences parallel one another in some respects, they are poles apart in basic standpoint. The natural sciences deal with the universe of matter; Christian Science deals with the universe of Spirit.

We can carry the point a step further. The natural sciences assume that the material universe and all its physical phenomena are objective reality, and that mind is a derivative of matter, through processes of biological evolution. Matter and physical law are considered fundamental; consciousness and thought are therefore but a product of matter.

Christian Science takes an opposite position. Mind, or Spirit, is fundamental. The universe to which it introduces the learner is a universe of infinite spiritual consciousness. One gains from it a new view of matter, as an illusory concept of creation held in a limited and false mortal mind, which is a suppositional inversion of Mind and has no real existence. All material phenomena and material laws are described as modes of this false so-called consciousness. As Mrs. Eddy writes in *Science and Health:* "Science shows that what is termed *matter* is but the subjective state of what is termed by the author *mortal mind*" (S&H 114:29).

Modern science holds that matter is convertible into energy—in effect, that matter is energy in another form. But one is led into new territory in Christian Science. This energy is seen to be a phenomenon of mortal mind; thus one resolves matter into a mental state, and finds this mental state to be an illusion since real Mind is Spirit. While, generally speaking, physical scientists hold to the standpoint that matter and physical law are fundamental, it is interesting to note that occasionally an outstanding scientist has voiced a speculative hunch as to something deeper. For example, Sir James Jeans wrote more than a generation ago: "The universe begins to look more like a great thought than a great machine. Mind no longer appears as an accidental intruder into the realm of matter; we are beginning to suspect that we ought rather to hail it as the creator and governor of the realm of matter."

Mind is fundamental, not matter; Mind is primal, original, causative. It is interesting to contemplate what would happen if natural scientists were to accept this basic proposition as true. The scope and character of scientific investigation would be turned in a new direction. The fact would be acknowledged that what is really basic for man's understanding of himself and his environment is not the science of matter but the Science of mental action. But this Science goes much deeper than any study of the human psyche. It deals with infinite Mind and its infinite manifestation, because Mind is the sole source of all real consciousness, intelligence, and thought.

There are other contrasts between the science of matter and the Science of Mind. The natural sciences deal with that which is intrinsically finite and limited; Christian Science deals with the measureless and inexhaustible. The physical sciences deal with measurement; they are fundamentally quantitative; and the quantitative approach has strongly influenced the behavioral sciences, too. On the other hand, Christian Science has to do with the allness of boundless Spirit and the inexhaustible character of spiritual ideas ranging from the infinitesimal to the infinite. This Science lays great stress on qualities of thought, but consciousness is neither qualitative nor quantitative in the sense in which physical scientists use these words.

The physical sciences deal with measurement, mass, velocity, probability. But the laws governing thoughts are quite different from the laws of physics. How can one measure a thought? What is the velocity of love? What is the mass of kindness? What laws of motion or of probability govern an inspired awareness of absolute Truth? The simple illustration is often cited of the curious difference between a thought and a doughnut. If I give you a doughnut, you have it and I don't. But if I give you a thought, we both have it and in a sense the thought has spontaneously multiplied itself.

Let us consider another comparison.

One outstanding characteristic of the scientific revolution has been the courage and imagination with which researchers have altered their long-held views when new evidence showed these not to give a consistent explanation of all the known facts. Great qualities of insight are often required here. As a result of scientific investigation, the pushing back of frontiers of earthly knowledge has been spectacular. In exploring the unknown, researchers have been willing to examine any promising hypothesis, however surprising it may be, and to test it out.

For instance, up to the end of the nineteenth century, atoms were believed to be solid and indivisible. Then J. J. Thomson discovered that much smaller particles, electrons, could be extracted from atoms. Further, the discovery of radioactivity in the closing years of that century was soon crowned by Rutherford and Soddy's hypothesis that radioactivity is a spontaneous disintegration of atoms, smaller particles being shot out. Thus the old concepts of the atom were changed.

Again, the theory of relativity arose from the observation that the speed of light is the same no matter in which direction the earth is moving, thus invalidating the then-prevalent view that light was carried in an immaterial ocean of ether through which the earth was supposed to move in its revolutions around the sun.

As a result of modern discoveries, the material universe itself is now supposed to be continually expanding; space must be presumed curved to explain gravitation; and the X-rays which so easily penetrate matter opaque to ordinary light are now known to be similar to ordinary light but of much shorter wave length.

It is a characteristic of all the sciences to look beyond the outward appearance of things, to investigate more profoundly, and to revise long-enthroned beliefs.

Somewhat parallel has been the approach of Christian Science to fundamental questions, such as the nature of life, substance, causation, reality. When Mrs. Eddy embarked upon the exploration of this Science, she looked deeper than the traditional ways of approaching, for example, the question of reality: ways which had produced centuries of honest frustration. Working on the hypothesis that God, Spirit, is actually infinite, supreme, and good—in the full meaning of these words —she challenged the time-honored assumption that evil and matter are real and powerful. Reasoning from the basis of an infinitely good God, who is Spirit, she drew the conclusion that evil and matter are mistaken concepts of things, having the nature of a fraud or lie which disappears when the truth becomes known. She subjected her hypothesis to practical test in terms of healing, and found that the evidence abundantly confirmed the hypothesis.

Admittedly such an hypothesis runs counter to popular conceptions. But scientific researchers habitually look beyond outward appearances to find explanations of phenomena not previously understood. In the same spirit, one may agree that the basic propositions of Christian Science deserve consideration, even though they are unconventional. Some of mankind's most remarkable discoveries have come from the most unorthodox lines of exploration.

According to Conant the work of modern science includes these essential elements: (1) speculative general ideas which lead to working hypotheses, (2) deductive reasoning, and (3) experimentation. There is a parallel (and a contrast) between these three elements and the essential processes by which Christian Science is humanly apprehended—namely, revelation, reason, and demonstration. All three steps are indispensable to a satisfactory grasp of this Science.

Some readers may balk at use of the word "revelation" on the ground that it carries us beyond the ramparts of reason into the mystical. But to the Christian Scientist revelation does not imply a supernatural phenomenon; it means the profound and sudden insight of discovery—the discovery of dynamic, self-revealing Truth.

Even in the physical sciences clarity of insight is of crucial importance. Conant makes this striking statement: "The great working hypotheses in the past have often originated in the minds of the pioneers as a result of mental processes which can best be described by such words as 'inspired guess,' 'intuitive hunch,' or 'brilliant flash of imagination.' Rarely if ever do they seem to have been the product of a careful examination of all the facts and a logical analysis of various ways of formulating a new principle."

While Conant obviously did not have in mind the discovery of metaphysical truth, the fact remains that throughout history there have been inspired thinkers who have gained luminous views of the primal reality which lies beyond matter. They have experienced flashes of insight so deep and clear as to produce instantaneous physical healing, the sudden transformation of a character, or other mighty works transcending material explanations.

So the starting point for the Christian Scientist is the eternal Principle, or God, which unfolds to humanity through revelation. Many thinkers in many epochs have caught glimpses of truth proceeding from this divine source. To the Christian Scientist, the record of such revelation of God's nature is contained in Scripture—from the lessons of Abraham and the Commandments of Moses, through the centuries to the matchless words and works of Christ Jesus—and this unfoldment has culminated in modern times in the discovery of Christian Science. In her autobiography, *Retrospection and Introspection*, Mrs. Eddy wrote: "All Science is a revelation. Its Principle is divine, not human, reaching higher than the stars of heaven" (28:25).

Revelation, reason, demonstration; the thinker in Christian Science begins with the universal supremacy of the divine Principle, or God. He begins with acknowledgment of the primordial truth contained in the scriptural dictum "I am the Lord, and there is none else, there is no God beside me: I girded thee, though thou hast not known me" (Isa. 45:5).

Again, to quote Mrs. Eddy: "The starting-point of divine Science is that God, Spirit, is All-in-all, and that there is no other might nor Mind—that God is Love, and therefore He is divine Principle. To grasp the reality and order of being in its Science, you must begin by reckoning God as the divine Principle of all that really is" (S&H 275:6).

To borrow the terminology of modern science, this is the working hypothesis on a grand scale. From this basis the Scientist deduces scientific rules and truths, which he applies in concrete situations. Demonstration follows, and thus he confirms the validity of the teachings by practical proof.

Like the natural scientist, the Christian Scientist thinks in terms of research and exploration, discovery and proof. For Science as he knows it is much more than a catalogue of facts, though facts are important; it is a spiritual discovery continuously unfolding to him a whole new universe. He feels that primal Truth irresistibly reveals itself; that it can be humanly discerned, and made the basis of thought and reasoning and demonstration.

To the Christian Scientist, this Science of Christian metaphysics contains the spiritual dynamics to transform human society. It is utterly different from conventional systems of thought. It challenges long-entrenched convictions; calls for bold and accurate, yet humble, thinkers, and invites them to enter vast new realms of ideas.

When the Christian Scientist contemplates the range of this Science of God and man and universe, he feels a profound sense of humility—even as an astronomer contemplating the silent grandeur of the deeps of space. He feels humble indeed when he views the very limited degree to which men have thus far learned to utilize its truths. We of today have not yet advanced very far in exploring its revolutionary propositions and plumbing its reaches. But at least a start is being made.

We come now to another contrast between Christian Science and the natural sciences.

The natural sciences have not discovered any single principle governing the totality of experience. In fact, none of the sciences considers the totality of experience to be its concern. Each has its own realm. Each has become more and more specialized as scientific knowledge has become deeper and more diversified. Each has developed its own structures of laws and principles. But no underlying unifying principle to which these can all be traced—embracing all experience and explaining all phenomena—has ever come to light.

In fact, the tendency toward specialization is familiar to practically everyone in modern society, from the worker on an assembly line to the scientific researcher. As one goes more deeply into the realm of material knowledge, he often finds his field of understanding, in a sense, growing narrower. From a comprehensive study of biology, for example, he may go to a specialized study of insects; from there to research on a single species; and from there to study of one subgroup of the species. It is a little like an ant climbing the trunk of a tree and onto smaller and smaller branches. I suppose this is what accounts for the old joke about learning more and more about less and less until one knows everything about nothing!

It is true, of course, that exploration in the natural sciences has brought to light, from time to time, physical laws which tend to draw together a whole range of data in a new synthesis. Then, too, there certainly are many interesting patterns of similarity in nature which exploration has disclosed—a fact illustrated, perhaps, by the spinning of electrons and the rotating of planets.

But still no unifying principle comes to light. Einstein searched for a unified field theory. But this related only to physical phenomena, into which the relativity and quantum phenomena theories introduced radically new conceptions. If discovered, such a theory might provide a unified explanation of matter, energy, and the basic processes of the material universe. But even then it would not be designed to embrace the totality of experience; many disciplines and many realms of thought would be left outside.

In contrast, the whole range of concepts and ideas and forces in divine Science rests upon one Principle alone. This Principle embraces all things and is infinite in its manifestations; it is one only, and without an equal. As explained in this Science, all phenomena converge toward this infinite Principle, or God. They proceed from it, point to it, bear witness to its nature. This Principle embraces the totality of experience, the explanation of all things. The more one pursues any line of study in this Science, the more deeply he is exploring this one universal Principle, which might be termed the Principle of cosmic unity. It is infinitely diverse in its manifestations.

The discoveries of modern science have shaken to their foundations many systems of intellectual, philosophic and religious thought. One might ask what bearing these discoveries have on the propositions of Christian Science.

It is worth noting that modern scientific discoveries do not in any way disprove the metaphysical teachings of Christian Science, as these teachings are grounded in a different realm, the realm of Spirit. It is interesting to observe, however, that certain of the modern insights of the natural sciences come somewhat closer to its propositions than do older theories and long-accepted dogmas.

For example, current theories that mortal man is a biochemical organism, his brain a complex of electrical patterns and impulses wherein no divine element can be found, only call to mind this perceptive statement of Mrs. Eddy: "The material and mortal body or mind is not the man" (S&H 209:8-9). The Scientist does not think of mortal man as the image and likeness of God. He thinks of man as the spiritual phenomenon of Mind, its individualized expression, held in Mind as idea. To discern his own real self, he looks deeply into Mind, for he thinks of man as the spiritual embodiment of Mind's qualities.

Modern science has unveiled the immensity of the cosmos and given new weight to the possibility of life on other planets scattered throughout the universe. But the Scientist thinks in terms of the infinite; his textbook speaks of the teeming universe of Mind; this universe is filled with spiritual ideas evolved by God; their identity is forever unfolding; and they are obedient to the will of their Maker.

The vastness of the cosmos has raised new questions for some religious groups regarding the nature of heaven and hell. The Christian Scientist, however, does not think of heaven and hell as physical locations, but as states of thought. He does not have a one-planet deity. The Science he endeavors to fathom and demonstrate is neither man-centered nor earth-centered: it is God-centered, for the universal God, divine Principle, is both the center and the circumference of being.

The evolving conceptions of the physical sciences develop within the accepted terms of a material universe. The propositions of Christian Science relate to a universe beyond matter, which is governed by unchangeable, harmonious, divine laws, and is eternal.

2.

We have spoken of the real universe as the phenomenon of Mind, or Spirit. Let us consider this spiritual universe.

Religious literature includes certain poetic or symbolic descriptions of the universe of God's creation. Students of the Bible will think of the first chapter of Genesis, and portions of the Apocalypse. But it remained for Christian Science to describe this universe in scientific terms—in terms of divine cause and effect; Principle and law; spiritual substance, action, force, energy, evolution, and so on.

This presentation is not at variance with scriptural revelation but an exposition of it. For the Christian Scientist, it resolves the apparent conflict between the symbolic, pictorial idiom of the Scriptures and the exacting standards of the scientific investigator.

Mrs. Eddy's writings contain hundreds of passages dealing with the nature of the spiritual universe. We could not hope to summarize them adequately in this brief survey, but a few may be noted.

In exploring the nature of the real universe, the Christian Scientist begins, as we have seen, with the understanding that God is One and All. Adopting this as her starting point, Mrs. Eddy concludes: "Then whatever is real must proceed from God, from Mind, and is His reflection and Science. Man and the universe coexist with God in Science, and they reflect God and nothing else" (Message for 1900, p. 4).

This statement calls to mind words from the Gospel of John: "All things were made by him; and without him was not any thing made that was made" (John 1:3).

In line with this, the Scientist finds the spiritual universe reflecting the character of perfect Mind. It is a universe of infinite consciousness, illumined by supreme intelligence. It is orderly, complete, harmonious, indestructible, perfect, as the outcome of Spirit. One reaches the conclusion that everything in it manifests law, for it is governed by immutable Science. He learns, too, that the laws of divine Principle never produce any evil effect, directly or indirectly, because this Principle is Love.

Does a description of God's universe as perfect suggest a motionless state of affairs? On the contrary, this universe expresses the dynamics of inexhaustible Life, the diversity of all-embracing intelligence perpetually expressing itself.

Time and space once were deemed independent measurements in the physical universe. But Einstein proved that time and space are relative to each other. In the Science of Mind, one discovers that the whole framework becomes irrelevant. Time cannot measure ideas; space does not form the dimensions of Mind.

The physics of today describes the time-space universe as comprising vast fields of force—gravitation, magnetic attraction, macrocosmic and microcosmic electrical forces. This calls to mind the words of Mrs. Eddy written many years ago: "We tread on forces. Withdraw them, and creation must collapse. Human knowledge calls them forces of matter; but divine Science declares that they belong wholly to divine Mind, are inherent in this Mind, and so restores them to their rightful home and classification" (S&H 124:26).

As one explores further this universe of Spirit, he begins to realize that the forces of Love exert absolute authority and control over Mind's infinite systems of ideas. These divine forces are moral and spiritual, the resources of Spirit sustaining all creation. They are not the blind forces of matter. All that God creates proceeds from and converges toward the one infinite Mind, which is Love. The properties of Mind include the only power of attraction, adhesion, and cohesion.

Light is considered fundamental to the physical universe; the speed of light is an absolute for measurement. In divine Science one finds that God is the source of inexhaustible light—

but this light is not the radiant energy associated with matter. Radiation is the shining forth of omniscient intelligence. It needs no transmission because it is already there. The Bible says: "God is light, and in him is no darkness at all" (I John 1:5). In Science, energy is the omnipresent power of God in action.

Shapley speaks of the "fortunate 'cooperation of charm and countercharm' (as an ancient Chinese saying puts it) that permitted natural laws to provide for the existence of the cohesive atomic nucleus." He adds the remark "I am reminded that a famous physicist who explores the nature of atomic nuclei once confided that it is only by a narrow squeak that matter exists at all."

In Christian Science one takes a different view of primal law: law expresses Spirit. It is shown in the cohesion of a spiritual idea. Matter is not its outcome. In Science the material atom is described as an outlined falsity of consciousness. The "atoms" of God's universe are formed of the elements of Mind. They embody the forces of God and they are harmless. They express the substance of Spirit, in accord with the law of Spirit. "Atomic action is Mind, not matter," writes Mrs. Eddy in *Miscellaneous Writings*.

The concept of law expressing Spirit is not necessarily in total conflict with the thinking of natural scientists. The geologist Kirtley Mather, for instance, once referred to the regularities of the material universe, the orderliness of motion, called "natural law," and then went on to emphasize "the extremely high probability that spiritual forces and spiritual entities, whatever they may prove to be, are also orderly in their operation and that there is spiritual law in the natural world."

Astronomers tell us that in the categories of material systems, ranging from subatomic particles to the galaxies, everything is in motion. Again, translating the material appearance back into Spirit, *Science and Health* says: "Mind is perpetual motion. Its symbol is the sphere. The rotations and revolutions of the universe of Mind go on eternally" (S&H 240:14). In Mind's universe, all action expresses the divine law of harmony.

In Christian Science one often draws figures of speech from the planets, stars, and earth. But Mrs. Eddy makes clear: "The universe, including man, is not a result of atomic action, material force or energy; it is not organized dust" (Misc. 23:20). It is the reflection of pure Spirit.

Nor is this universe a vacant cosmos. The Scientist finds the understanding dawning upon him that it teems with individual, conscious, spiritual beings—God's ideas expressing all the diversity and order, perfection and beauty, of an infinite cause. As understood by the Christian Scientist, this whole universe is embraced within the one infinite Mind, or God; and this Mind is reflected in the intelligent compound idea, image, or likeness, called man—man, who is the climax of creation. Man forever shows forth the radiant glory of his intelligent divine Principle, Love.

All this is a far cry from the material theory of man as evolved from ooze. Biological science defines evolution as the gradual emergence of organic life from primeval marshes. The Christian Scientist thinks of life as evolved from Mind. One notes in the diversity and progression of material species a hint of the infinite variety and endless unfoldment of God's creation. Earthly progress dimly echoes the dynamics of Spirit. But to the Christian Scientist, the real life, identity, and evolution of man and the universe will never be pinned down in matter because they never were there. As Mrs. Eddy writes: "The true theory of the universe, including man, is not in material history but in spiritual development" (S&H 547:25).

The reader may ask if the material universe, with all its apparent beauty, diversity, and grandeur, is to be summarily dismissed as nothing. Discussing this question, Mrs. Eddy writes:

Even the human conception of beauty, grandeur and utility is something that defies a sneer. . . . It is next to divine beauty and the grandeur of Spirit. It lives with our earth-life, and is the subjective state of high thoughts. . . . To take all earth's beauty into one gulp of vacuity and label beauty nothing, is ignorantly to caricature God's creation, which is unjust to human sense and to the divine realism. In our immature sense of spiritual things, let us say of the beauties of the sensuous universe: "I love your promise; and shall know, some time, the spiritual reality and substance of form, light and color, of what I now through you discern dimly; and knowing this, I shall be satisfied" (Misc. 86:22-26, 87:3-11).

3.

To the natural scientist, systematic knowledge and reasoning are only part of the picture. Their validity depends upon practical proof. Test and verification are not only fundamental but often the most exciting aspect of science.

Conant says: "The activity we associate with the word 'science' is the sum total of the potential findings of the workers in the laboratories; it is their plans, hopes, ambitions in the process of realization, week after week, year after year, that is the essence of modern science."

The Christian Scientist also lays great stress on test and proof, a topic we must now examine. The Science of Spirit is set forth in the Bible and *Science and Health;* but it is the demonstrations, the findings, the verifications, worked out by the individual student in practice that give this Science its practical meaning for him and for mankind. The progress of the Christian Scientist is measured not by how much theory he knows but by how successfully he is able to put it into practice.

Mrs. Eddy refers to Science as "the infinite calculus defining the line, plane, space, and fourth dimension of Spirit" (Misc. 22:11). But she also writes bluntly: "If Christian Science lacked the proof of its goodness and utility, it would destroy itself; for it rests alone on demonstration" (Misc. 365:10).

Throughout her writings it is made plain that this demonstration consists of the destruction of sin, sickness, and death through the power of Spirit.

This is the realm which engages the attention of the student. Practical demonstration is emphasized throughout *Science and Health,* and throughout the literature produced by the church. This demonstration is still in its infancy, so vast are the implications of Science and so involved are human needs. Even the most advanced Scientists feel that they have merely scratched the surface of what can be accomplished. But the measure of verification and proof gained thus far in healings seems to them to confirm the validity and utility of the teachings. From small beginnings one gains stronger evidence of the existence of God. This in turn leads to stronger proofs and increased basis for faith. As Mrs. Eddy writes in *Science and Health*: "Christian Science must be accepted at this period by induction. We admit the whole, because a part is proved and that part illustrates and proves the entire Principle" (S&H 461:4-7).

Of course, effectual prayer is not the exclusive property of any sect or denomination. If one surveys the range of religious history, he encounters numerous examples of answered prayer; but it would be difficult to find any system really comparable to Christian Science. In this Science, answered prayer is considered not an exception, or miracle, but the natural, consistent, impartial result of universal spiritual law when properly utilized.

As one explores the fields of philosophy or ethics, religion or psychology, he will find many illuminating insights and glimpses of truth in various contexts; and he will encounter concepts bearing more or less resemblance to certain aspects of Christian Science. But this Science is unique in maintaining that the allness and goodness of God, Spirit, and the nothingness of evil can be demonstrated in actual practice.

Answering the question "What is the cardinal point of difference in my metaphysical system?" Mrs. Eddy replies:

This: that *by knowing the unreality of disease, sin, and death,* you demonstrate the allness of God. This difference wholly separates my system from all others. The reality of these so-called existences I deny, because they are not to be found in God, and this system is built on Him as the sole cause. It would be difficult to name any previous teachers, save Jesus and his apostles, who have thus taught (Un. 9:27).

Thus Christian Science could not be described as a synthesis of ideas from philosophical thinkers. In the light of its essential teaching, familiar ethical ideas become transformed. They appear in a new prespective—the radical perspective of a Science which is both absolute and demonstrable.

It would be beyond the scope of this book to attempt a full explanation of the method of demonstrating Christian Science. That properly belongs to *Science and Health* itself, to class teaching, and to the realm of practical experience. But it should be emphasized that the practical proof, or demonstration, comes through utilizing the teachings *as Science*; hence it will be helpful to our discussion of Christian Science as Science to note here a few of the fundamentals of demonstration.

One fundamental is this: Even though a problem such as illness appears to consist of physical conditions, it is seen in Christian Science as wholly a mental phenomenon. But in this sense the word "mental" means a great deal more than what we ordinarily think of as the conscious thought of a person.

The behavioral sciences, going deeper than conscious thought, picture the individual as including drives and conflicts, anxieties and tensions, at various levels of the unconscious. Numerous aspects of conscious experience—including both bodily health and the proneness to accident—are now being linked to deep-seated emotional and psychological causes.

But as seen from the standpoint of Christian Science, the body itself is a phenomenon of thought, a subjective condition of mortal mind, its unconscious substratum. According to *Science and Health* it is constructed of mortal mind's own mortal materials.

And speaking of bodily conditions: "The mental state is called a material state. Whatever is cherished in mortal mind as the physical condition is imaged forth on the body" (S&H 411:23).

So in Science one is led to resolve physical conditions—including the body itself—into the mental constituents. In the light of this Science, one begins to see that, fundamentally, all experience takes place within consciousness. Once the fact is grasped that a physical discord is essentially a condition of thought, so-called physical laws lose their finality. Bodily conditions become subject to change through a deep-seated change of thought.

But to resolve disease into its mental elements—fear, guilt, hate, lust, bitterness, greed and so on—is only one step in the right direction. If matters were left at this point, the sufferer would be left to wander in a maze of confusion, the victim of his own wrong thoughts or of generally accepted fears and impulses. The growing concern for mental health today indicates that it is not enough to uncover the latent demons within the human mind. To probe its perversities is one thing; but to destroy psychological, emotional, and physical disorders is quite another thing.

The insights which Christian Science brings to this problem stem from its foundational teaching: the all-inclusiveness of God, Mind; the inviolable individuality of man as the spiritual image of God; and the nothingness of evil.

The demonstration of this Science in healing consists of utilizing the laws, or truths, of Mind to bring fear and similar mental states under control and destroy them, replacing them with a consciousness of the presence of divine Life, Truth, and Love. This consciousness is realized increasingly in such mental states as integrity, compassion, courage, meekness, trust in God. Mrs. Eddy writes that "God's preparations for the sick are potions of His own qualities" (Misc. 268:22-23).

The understanding of man's relationship to God provides an unchanging point of reference for reducing to nothingness the mental elements that cause discord. Whatever denies man's perfect likeness to God is illusory. Because this is true the Scientist gains increasingly clear evidence that before the resistless forces of Truth, the destructive and limiting conditions of mortal existence yield up their authority. Paul refers to these moral and spiritual forces when he writes that we do not war after the flesh, and that the weapons of our warfare are not carnal, "but mighty through God to the pulling down of strong holds; Casting down imaginations, and every high thing that exalteth itself against the knowledge of God, and *bringing into captivity every thought to the obedience of Christ"* (II Cor. 10:4,5. italics added).

At every footstep in this work, the student finds practical guidance in the teachings of Science. For example, all prayer, or treatment, in Christian Science finds its guide in the Mosaic commandment "Thou shalt have no other gods before me" (Ex. 20:3). To the Christian Scientist, this calls for acknowledging and declaring what is true of God and what is true of man as His likeness. It means denying, as unreal, whatever is opposed to God: fear, pain, sin, mortality. It means rejecting everything that is not a postulate of the one divine Principle, God. These mental affirmations and denials can be very specific, in accord with the needs of the case—"bringing into captivity every thought to the obedience of Christ."

To enable the student to follow this scientific standard of prayer faithfully, *Science and Health* gives many exact rules, for example: "Mentally contradict every complaint from the body, and rise to the true consciousness of Life as Love—as all that is pure, and bearing the fruits of Spirit" (S&H 391:29-32).

To enable him to follow such rules, the Christian Scientist often uses reasoning and mental argument. What counts, however, is not the argument but the depth of inspiration and the clarity of spiritual conviction. It should be emphasized that Christian Science treatment is not an exercise in intellectual gymnastics. At times it may consist of the simplest declarations of truth, or even of the consciousness without words of God's omnipresence.

But whatever its form, scientific prayer means something much deeper than surface thoughts. The Scientist finds that he cannot really obey the Great Commandment while the heart goes unredeemed. Christ Jesus emphasized this when he used this phrasing of the first commandment: "Thou shalt love the Lord thy God with all thy heart, and with all thy soul, and with all thy mind, and with all thy strength," and when he added, as the second Great Commandment: "Thou shalt love thy neighbor as thyself" (Mark 12:30,31).

Further emphasizing this fundamental point, Mrs. Eddy

writes: "To have one God and avail yourself of the power of Spirit, you must love God supremely" (S&H 167:17). Love for God and man needs to be the polar magnet of one's being. Successful prayer must be lived.

All this is to stress the consistency and deep-running scientific obedience to spiritual law which form the standard of restorative prayer in Christian Science. Such prayer is not a question of emotion. It is not a pleading for special favor. It is not a shallow effusion of lofty sentiments. But for all its scientific exactness, it must be winged with the power of humility, love, faith, and purity, and its sentiments must come straight from the heart.

It is sometimes assumed that this healing method bears some relation to hypnotism, which seems to be gaining increasing importance today in psychotherapeutic techniques. But this is not the case.

Hypnotism operates wholly on the levels of the conscious and unconscious fleshly mind. This so-called mind is not a healing factor in Christian Science. The method of this Science is to bring to human consciousness the truths of divine Mind.

Hypnotism works on the assumption of one material mind influencing another. Christian Science works on the assurance that there is only one Mind, or Spirit, and that man is tributary to this Mind, his real consciousness subject alone to its laws.

Hypnotism plays upon the weaknesses of the human mind in order to control it. Christian Science shows how to surrender the weaknesses of this so-called mind, and lay hold of the strengthening truths of Spirit.

The essence of hypnotism is suggestion. The method of Christian Science is rational reasoning from the basis of one Mind, which is supreme intelligence. In fact, Christian Science provides a changeless spiritual framework of scientific truth which, when adhered to, makes one impervious to suggestion.

While hypnotism involves the temporary loss of critical faculties, the study of Christian Science involves a sharpening of the perceptions and a strengthening of intellectual powers. The workings of hypnotism would deprive one of his individuality, at least temporarily; while in contrast, the effect of Christian Science is to bring out more of one's inviolable God-given individuality characterized by intelligence and freedom.

Nor does Christian Science involve any element of autosug-gestion—any more than does the learning of mathematical truths. Rational reasoning and suggestion are opposites; one tends to exclude the other. Christian Science embraces the for-mer and shows one how to defend himself against the latter.

In Christian Science, prayer does not consist of willing the sick to be well. It consists of acknowledging the will of perfect Love, the all-power of Spirit, and the complete obedience of man to his Maker.

Nor does this scientific method consist of merely shutting one's eyes to human suffering and drifting off into ethereal realms of theorizing. On the contrary, it involves coming directly to grips with the elements of evil in human thought, from the standpoint of God's omnipotence. It means wiping out destructive mental elements such as fear, malice, selfishness, ig-norance, and sensuality, through the inspired understanding of the Christ, Truth.

Perhaps a simple example will illustrate. A Christian Scientist I know fell ill with influenza one night and could not go to work next morning. He endeavored to pray for him-self, but was so ill that clear thinking seemed next to impossible. Finally in midafternoon, he turned again to the Christian Sci-ence Lesson-Sermon for that week. Slowly and painfully he tried to read each statement and absorb its meaning.

He came to a section dealing with the story of Christ Jesus' coming. As he read the Bible account he began to think: "Here is startling evidence of the power of divine Truth and Love! Christ Jesus came into a cruel and evil world. Human thought was dark, gross, hostile, murderous. Yet, through the power of Truth and Love, made manifest as the Christ, Jesus was em-powered to accomplish his mission. He found receptive hearers. His pure teachings have survived every conceivable attempt of the carnal mind to blot them out. The power to which he bore witness was irresistible. He revealed the Christ.

"Now," the man thought, "this same Truth which Jesus expressed is always true. This same Love is always present. The eternal Christ—as the power of Truth and Love made manifest to humanity—is always just as triumphant as when Jesus demonstrated it. It must be so, right here and now!

"If this is true," he reasoned, "then the Christ, the power of Truth and Love, must be able to penetrate this fog of pain and suffering, just as it did for those whom Jesus healed. It must have irresistible power to overrule the so-called laws of matter, dispel the sickness, and waken me to my God-given dominion as the child of God."

As he pondered these thoughts, he literally felt the congestion and fever recede. Soon he was well. He returned to work the next morning.

Now what had happened? It was simply a matter of scientific rules and their results. He had followed the rule to "rise to the true consciousness of Life as Love—as all that is pure, and bearing the fruits of Spirit" (S&H 391:30). He had deeply acknowledged, with firmness and conviction, Mind's absolute government and Love's power and everpresence. Worship of other gods —fear, pain, suffering—fell before the simple acknowledgment of the omnipotence of God. His consciousness was transformed, by the Christ-power, from a hypnotic preoccupation with sensations of sickness to an awareness of the presence of God. And with this change of consciousness, the body was healed.

It should be kept in mind that Christian Science healing, like any other therapeutic practice, is an art. If one turns to the literature of medicine, for example, one finds great stress laid on the fact that the practice of medicine is not an exact science but a highly demanding art. To be sure, medical theories have their foundations in the sciences—physics, chemistry, and mathematics—as well as in biology and physiology. But their application to the cure of disease requires skill and experience. No two cases are ever exactly alike to the last detail, and all of them require the exercise of insight, experience, judgment.

The same is true of Christian Science. While Science itself

is exact in Principle and rules, nevertheless the practice of Christian Science healing by human beings is unquestionably an art of the highest order. It is thoroughly mastered only through assiduous study and experience. It requires, among other things, an unusually keen capacity to discern the underlying motives, hidden fears, and unconscious beliefs which may be responsible for physical discord. While it is true that a child can utilize its restorative powers, the capacity to heal the sick can be fully developed only through spiritual growth and actual experience in the healing work.

This is a point which deserves to be dwelt upon. It helps to answer the question sometimes raised: What about the case that is not quickly healed—the stoic sufferer who must continue to endure even though treatment is prolonged? The limited degree to which a practitioner and patient have mastered the art of utilizing spiritual law and power may have a bearing on the outcome of a case; but this would tell comparatively little about the validity of the power of Science itself.

It is sometimes asked, in regard to long-continued cases, whether Christian Scientists do resort, or should resort, to medical help. Here some careful distinctions need to be noted, since they help to make clear the nature of scientific healing practice.

No church rule exists prohibiting a Christian Scientist from choosing whatever type of help he wishes. He is not under any compulsion: he is free to make his own choice. At the same time, Christian Scientists recognize that under ordinary circumstances it is useless to try to combine medical methods and Christian Science treatment; it doesn't work. This applies not only to treatment but to diagnosis. Medical diagnosis deals with physical conditions and usually calls for physical treatment. The diagnostic procedure of Christian Science is mental and spiritual, and calls for spiritual restoration and remedy. There is a sharp line between medical methods and those of Christian Science; neither can ever cross the line.

On the other hand, the present degree of Christian Science demonstration is such that its adherents sometimes go to physicians for help of a more or less mechanical nature. This might include the pulling of a tooth, the setting of a broken bone, the taking of stitches, or the delivery of a baby. Such aid is referred to in these words: "Until the advancing age admits the efficacy and supremacy of Mind, it is better for Christian Scientists to leave surgery and the adjustment of broken bones and dislocations to the fingers of a surgeon, while the mental healer confines himself chiefly to mental reconstruction and to the prevention of inflammation" (S&H 401:27).

It should be added, however, that many instances have occurred where a fractured bone has been perfectly set and quickly healed entirely through prayer; where a severe wound has been closed without stitches and healed without scars; and where other structural or organic conditions ordinarily considered amenable only to surgery have been entirely cured by spiritual means alone.

Of course, one can narrow down the question to the point where it is hard to draw a line: whether, for example, to have an abscessed tooth pulled or to rely on spiritual means alone for its restoration. No categorical answer can be given to such hypothetical questions. The individual would do the best he could under the circumstances, in the light of his own spiritual growth and understanding. But it needs to be recognized that resorting to medical methods is incompatible with Christian Science.

It is true that students of Christian Science sometimes, under stress of circumstances, have turned from reliance on their religion to medical aid as a temporary expedient. But it is also true that many Christian Scientists, through courageous and steadfast reliance on God alone, supported by intelligent and systematic prayer, have experienced truly wonderful healings. Sometimes such healings have come only after a strong and unyielding stand in the face of alarming conditions, and sometimes only after long-continued treatment. When such a healing has finally come, it has sometimes come quickly and suddenly.

Each individual has the opportunity to make his own choice, keeping in mind that a sharp line exists between material medicine and Christian Science, and that as Christ Jesus taught, it is not wise to try to serve two masters. While criticism has sometimes been directed at Christian Scientists for continued reliance on spiritual treatment in cases of prolonged illness, the same point could be made with equal fairness in regard to continued reliance on other healing systems when Christian Science might bring a recovery. It works both ways. A fair conclusion would be that Christian Scientists, like doctors, are doing the best they can, at their present stage of progress, to relieve the sufferings of mankind. It is a fact beyond question that uncounted multitudes have been rescued from nightmares of suffering and restored to normal health when they turned to Christian Science for help.

The healing method of Christian Science is designed to bring the thinking of the individual into harmony with spiritual law, the law of Life and love. In the degree to which this is accomplished, the healing qualities of divine Love flow into human consciousness and wipe out the mental elements which produce sickness and discord. The result is beneficial to both mind and body.

4.

This is an age of skepticism. Modern thought is saturated with it. The faith of an earlier era is hardly the spirit of these times. So far has swung the pendulum today that whoever dares to argue for the availability of final answers to the deepest questions of man and universe is apt to encounter a frosty reception —not only in the halls of scientific learning but in citadels of religion itself.

This is hardly surprising. It was the rebellion of skepticism against entrenched religious dogmatism that made possible this modern age of science. It is skepticism, the wholly free play of inquiry and analysis, which repeatedly has led modern scientists to look deeper than the obvious and to make incredible discoveries.

There are other reasons for skepticism. Traditional religious teachings have suffered blow after blow as new scientific findings have come to light. Discoveries in organic evolution have called into question the literal interpretation of the story of Adam and Eve. Development of massive computers—with the science of cybernetics promising to duplicate in electronic machines the functions of the human brain—have raised questions as to whether any soul, or spirit, dwells in mortal man.

In the sciences themselves, long-held concepts have been discarded: for example, the phlogiston theory and the concept of matter as made of solid particles. The beliefs that Euclidean geometry and Newtonian mechanics furnished final and complete explanations of things have been outgrown.

Medieval man rested his hopes for meaning and value upon the religious doctrines of his time. Modern man has long pinned his aspirations for a sense of mastery and meaning upon the wondrous developments of the sciences. But in an age of hydrogen bombs and concealed microphones, the belief that the natural sciences will solve all our problems is being undermined by disillusionment and skepticism.

In the face of this mounting doubt is there any room left for faith in an unseen God? Is religious certainty possible for informed people in the modern world, without the sacrifice of their critical faculties? How can one believe in the supremacy of Spirit when the wonders of matter are so elaborately developed?

Can religion really answer the hard questions of a scientifically sophisticated age?

Religion will need to face these questions. A generation steeped in modern knowledge will not settle for less. A world facing ultimate dangers dare not settle for less.

The Christian Scientist is profoundly convinced that religious teaching can answer the hard questions. By the logic of demonstration he concludes that the answers are to be found in the revolutionary thought-patterns of Science.

So long as skepticism means free inquiry and analysis, the Scientist welcomes its examination of religion. So long as skepticism does not deteriorate into a mere dogmatism of doubt, he feels that its demands can be reconciled with new Christian insights.

Indeed, from the viewpoint of Christian Science, skepticism may even be the ally of religion when it begins to question the long-accepted premises of a material world. The rapid advances in the physical sciences, the increasing awareness of realms beyond the range of our present observation—these and many other present-day developments seem to augur new trends in the direction of thought. Human thinking may be coming somewhat nearer to contemplation of the radical Christian proposition that the only absolute reality is pure Spirit.

But the challenge of relating this religious insight to modern needs calls for more than a traditionally theological approach. It calls for more than honest faith and conviction. It calls for demonstration and proof. And more, too: it calls for a perceptive grasp of the underlying concepts and assumptions that are shaping the thinking of the present age, and a discernment of how the truths of Spirit apply to them. This is indeed a time for thinkers.

Even the proofs are sometimes subjected to question. Many people frankly doubt the healings through Christian power. But there is a steadily growing body of evidence: healings accomplished solely through prayer under circumstances where no other explanation can be reasonably given. Beyond question these include numerous cases where the patient, before turning to Christian Science, was attended by many doctors; the condition thoroughly tested and diagnosed in consulation; every available remedy tried; the patient given up to die; and then, as a last resort, Christian Science help enlisted, and the patient permanently healed. In one such instance, the woman told me how, when she was desperately ill with tuberculosis of the bone, no less than seven consulting doctors stood around her bed while her own physician urged her to permit one more operation. Without it, she was told, she could not live more than three months. But instead she turned to Christian Science, and today she is well and normally active.

But the modern seeker after truth still may demur. Granted

that wonderful healings do take place through prayer alone: what do they mean? The value of any scientific test depends upon proper evaluation of the data. Do the healings prove the validity of the Christian Science teachings regarding God, man, reality, matter, evil, and so on? Or are they some sort of psychological phenomenon which the physical sciences will eventually explain? Are the healings clear evidence of basic Truth?

The same question may be put in a somewhat different form. Granted that Christian Science offers a logical explanation of reality. One may contend that the same is true of the natural sciences: they start with a given basis (the physical universe); they follow fixed rules; they arrive at logical and demonstrable results.

Which are we to accept as true? A system based on matter, or a system based on Mind?

It is perfectly true that even after the healing evidence is duly surveyed, after the logic of Science is thoroughly examined, still there remains one element necessary for a fair and conclusive estimate of this metaphysical system. What is it?

The Christian Scientist would call it spiritual sense. And he would agree that without it, a convincing grasp of the teachings of Science is impossible. Mrs. Eddy writes frankly that only through the illumination of the spiritual sense can Christian Science be understood.

Only from the standpoint of awakened spiritual sense do the healings stand out in their proper context and significance. Only from this standpoint does the logic of Science take on meaning. Only with spiritual sense can one discern the realism of Science, and see it with the vividness of a mountain climber who gazes at an emerald lake in the wilderness below him and exclaims, "Of course, there it is!"

Spiritual sense enables one to discern that which lies beyond the range of the five physical senses, beyond the range even of the instruments mortal man is using to probe the dim reaches and inner secrets of the physical universe. Spiritual sense enables one to plunge deeper than the physical realm and to apprehend the reality which lies beyond matter.

Many natural scientists have developed a humbling skepticism regarding the adequacy of the five physical senses to grasp ultimate reality. Shapley says frankly: "Many realities may lie beyond the comprehension of human terrestrials, simply because our outfitting with sense organs is limited." In *Of Stars and Men* he describes the physical senses as rather primitive, limited in number, in range, in effectiveness.

Our eyes, for example, are sensitive to only about one octave of the electromagnetic spectrum. Yet by various means, including the use of gamma-ray detectors, X-ray and optical spectrometers, and receivers of a wide range of radio waves, we can now detect radiation whose wave length ranges over more than 50 octaves!

Shapley further states that "sense receptors, in quality quite unknown to us and in fact hardly imaginable, which record phenomena of which we are totally ignorant, may easily exist among the higher sentient organisms of other planets."

Lecomte du Nouy in *Human Destiny* remarked, in commenting upon the views of the rationalist: "The image he has built up of the universe rests upon reactions determined in him by a minute fraction (less than 1 per thousand billions, or 0.000,-000,000.001 per cent) of the vibrations surrounding him and which go through him without leaving a trace in his consciousness."

Such statements call attention to the limited range of the physical senses in grasping even the phenomena of the physical universe. Christian Science goes a step further and calls attention to the need of exercising spiritual sense in order to grasp spiritual reality at all. This spiritual sense is defined as a conscious capacity to understand God. Mrs. Eddy writes: "The physical senses can obtain no proof of God. They can neither see Spirit through the eye nor hear it through the ear, nor can they feel, taste, or smell Spirit" (S&H 284:21-23). But elsewhere she stresses that what appears real to the material senses is not more distinct nor vivid than are the realities of God's creation to spiritual sense.

Almost from the hour of birth our material senses are

educated and elaborately developed. They gain keenness through use. Our faith in them grows prodigiously with experience. But what about our spiritual sense—this capacity to understand God, this intuitive power to think spiritually, this ability to lay hold of spiritual ideas and qualities and express them?

Jesus referred to the need for development of the spiritual sense when the disciples asked him why he spoke to the people in parables. He commented:

In them is fulfilled the prophecy of Esaias, which saith, By hearing ye shall hear, and shall not understand; and seeing ye shall see, and shall not perceive: For this people's heart is waxed gross, and their ears are dull of hearing, and their eyes they have closed; lest at any time they should see with their eyes, and hear with their ears, and should understand with their heart, and should be converted, and I should heal them (Matt. 13:14,15).

All that truly goes by the name of revelation can be attributed to the perceptive power of highly developed spiritual sense. The propositions of Christian Science can be understood only as one exercises this God-given capacity. The healing spirit of Christ cannot be measured in a test tube or detected by a geiger counter. Those values which partake of absolute Spirit can only be known as one develops a sensitivity to spiritual things.

There is nothing unusual about this. One who understands baseball will see much more at a big-league game than a tyro. An archeologist will immediately perceive many things about an Egyptian frieze that escape the eyes of laymen.

So it is with the Science of Spirit. It can be evaluated properly only through spiritual sense. And spiritual sense can be developed only through assiduous efforts to understand God.

Christian Science admittedly calls for acceptance of propositions beyond the power of human eye to see or of conventional materialistic reasoning to understand. But has not this been the story of human enlightenment and advancement since the dawn of history? Copernicus was persecuted for refuting the obvious "fact" that the sun revolves around a stationary earth.

Even the young Einstein encountered the hostility of other physicists when he announced his special theory of relativity. It seemed outrageous for an unknown young clerk in the Swiss patent office to upset the assumptions drawn from Newtonian mechanics and insist that a meter was longer or shorter and a pound greater or lesser, depending upon your own relative motion!

But the opposition to Einstein soon faded away, and nobody any longer questions the view held by Copernicus. The incredible of yesterday has become the axiom of today.

May it not be that the day will yet come when the strange proposition of Mary Baker Eddy—"There is no life, truth, intelligence, nor substance in matter. All is infinite Mind and its infinite manifestation, for God is All-in-all" (S&H 468:9-11) —will also be recognized as a profoundly valid scientific insight, a step beyond the long-entrenched assumptions of her time?

Chapter Six

A Great Discovery

Today there are many who feel that Christian Science has opened to them new fields for thought. But there was a time when its radical propositions were unexplored. The thought-systems of mankind offered little or no hint of the existence of such a Science; there was little that pointed in its direction except the inspired insights of the Bible.

The experiences which marked the discovery of Christian Science centered in 1866, when Mrs. Eddy was about forty-five years old and at the midpoint of her long life. But it will be worth while to note briefly her life prior to that time, since this helps to explain how she came to discover this Science.

She was born on a farm in Bow, New Hampshire, in 1821, the youngest of six children. It was a time when life in rural New England was still characterized by stern religion, simple pleasures, Puritan conscience. Devotion to religion was deeply ingrained in both sides of her family. Her mother was gentle, prayerful, wisely patient, a woman of deep Christian faith and unselfishness. Her father was strict, unbending, profoundly religious, relentless in his theological views. Daily prayer, frequent Bible-reading, and Sundays devoted mostly to church activities characterized the home. It was a cultural context in which religion largely shaped the way of life. The children early learned the Westminster Catechism and recited it every Sunday; around the family hearth they heard frequent theological discussions.

From early childhood Mary showed an interest in divine things that was exceptional even in that deeply religious era. Though she was high-spirited and full of fun, she studied the Bible by herself and wrote prayers patterned after the Psalms. Throughout her life she wrote poetry, and even in childhood it often had a religious theme. A compilation published many years later includes five poems composed in girlhood, all of which have a religious note. Some of her letters and also a journal written between 1835 and 1843 are still extant. They show a normal range of girlhood interests, but they also contain evidence of her religious inclinations.

During her teens a warm friendship sprang up between her and the Rev. Enoch Corser, congregational minister at Tilton (at that time Sanbornton Bridge) New Hampshire where the family then lived and attended church. The two had many long talks on deeply religious subjects. Years later the minister's son recalled:

As Mrs. Eddy's pastor—and for a time teacher—my father held her in the highest esteem; in fact he considered her, even at an early age, superior both intellectually and spiritually to any other woman in Tilton, and greatly enjoyed talking with her. It was in 1837 when, if I remember rightly, Mrs. Eddy was about fifteen, that I first knew her, she being several years younger than myself.

He adds that during these years he frequently heard comments regarding "her superior abilities and scholarship, her depth and independence of thought, and not least, spiritual-mindedness." (This letter is quoted in part in *Historical Sketches* by Clifford P. Smith.)

Her independence of thought led to what was perhaps the most meaningful religious experience of her girlhood. It will be recalled that at this period much of American Protestantism still was committed to the gloomy Calvinistic doctrine of predestination. This was the accepted creed of her church, and it was vehemently espoused by her father and his friends. A sensitive and affectionate child, she was deeply disturbed to think that if she joined the church (as she wished to do) she might be saved while her brothers and sisters—none of whom had yet been "converted"—might be eternally banished from God's presence. It was a doctrine at which she rebelled.

Her father, alarmed at her heretical views, tried to talk her out of them by picturing vividly the horrors of eternal damnation. She would not budge. The clash was prolonged and tempestuous. It culminated in an argument one day after which Mary was put to bed with a high fever and her father had to go for the doctor. Her mother, always the gentle peacemaker, bathed her inflamed temples and counseled her to pray for God's guidance and rest in His love. She did so and was immediately healed. After that, the grim doctrine lost its power to frighten her.

Later she applied for church membership. This required her to go before a church meeting to answer the questions put by the minister. When she was asked about the teaching of predestination, she steadfastly insisted she could never accept it, and that she would rather take her chances on spiritual safety with her brothers and sisters even if the church refused her membership. Her plea was so earnest and moving that the members decided to accept her into the church in spite of her theological doubts.

She was seventeen when she joined the church. From that time until her discovery of Christian Science many years later, her life was essentially a period of searching for the answers to the deepest questions of human life. The search was intensified by the overwhelming succession of tragedies that came into her experience.

The first of these took place in 1841, when she was twenty. Her brother Albert, a brilliant young lawyer then running for Congress, died after a brief illness. The two had always been particularly close; it was he who had encouraged her love of books and had tutored her during his vacations from college.

In 1843 she was married to George Glover, who took her to Charleston, South Carolina, to live. But only seven months later he died of yellow fever in Wilmington, North Carolina, where the young couple had gone on business. During his illness she prayed ceaselessly for him, and the doctor said her prayers had prolonged his life. This awful bereavement increased her questions and her searching.

The deep yearning that characterized these years of tragedy is described in these words: "From my very childhood I was impelled, by a hunger and thirst after divine things—a desire for something higher and better than matter, and apart from it —to seek diligently for the knowledge of God as the one great and everpresent relief from human woe" (Ret. 31:9-13).

Pursuing this search she read and studied the Bible assiduously, and particularly in the decade which immediately preceded her discovery of Christian Science. Throughout successive trials it is evident that she never accepted disaster as final or as representing the divine will; deep within her was something that rebelled at the limitations of matter and, in fact, at the whole human condition.

Following the death of George Glover, she returned to the family home in New Hampshire. For twenty years after that her search was not only for spiritual surcease from woe, but also for physical health. Her health had always been frail. After the birth of her son, two months following her return, she was unable to take care of him. It was many long months before she showed any improvement. Eventually, however, she was able to have her child with her for a period.

But in 1849 came the bitterest sorrow of all; her mother, to whom she had been deeply devoted, passed away. The next year her widowed father brought a new wife into the home, as a result of which Mrs. Glover and her child felt compelled to leave. This involved another separation: Mrs. Glover went to live with her sister Abigail; but Abigail would not have the child, and against Mrs. Glover's wishes he was sent to live with his former nurse, who had married and now lived in North Groton, forty miles away.

During this period Mrs. Glover's health deteriorated, with increasing weakness and the aggravation of a debilitating spinal condition, together with severe attacks of nervous prostration. Her condition during the latter half of the 1850's was such that she was confined to bed much of the time.

These were the years when she groped in a lonely wilderness. She explored every trail that might lead in a right direction in her search for a better way of life. But even in the midst of severe misfortunes, there remained a deep intuitive sense that somehow divine help offered the solution to human suffering. For instance, she wrote in a poem called "Prayer" in the *I.O.O.F. Covenant* in 1847:

> What is the Christian's balm for grief,
> When pain and wo invade?
> A holy calm, a sweet relief,
> In prayer to God.

As early as 1846 she had begun trying to trace physical effects back to a mental cause. She tried medical treatment, diets, various hygienic methods—but all without result. Finding allopathic remedies of no avail and having been helped by a homeopathic doctor on one occasion, she finally decided to investigate homeopathy, which was then attracting wide attention.

It was about this time that Daniel Patterson, a dentist, asked her to marry him. He promised to establish a home, where she could have her son, now eight years old, with her. They were married in June, 1853. But her hopes were doomed to disappointment. Dr. Patterson, though a kind and gregarious individual, was also a Micawberish and highly unreliable type of person. Before very long it became clear that he had no intention of bringing the child to live with them.

Years of poverty and unhappiness followed. At first the Pattersons lived in Franklin, New Hampshire; then in 1855 they moved to the mountain village of North Groton, where her child was staying. This proved to be the darkest period of all. Mrs. Patterson was ill most of the time. Without telling her, Dr. Patterson soon agreed with the foster parents for her child to go with them to Minnesota to live. It was not until 1879, when he was thirty-five years old, that Mrs. Patterson saw her son again.

Her closest investigation of homeopathy took place during the North Groton period. This system, employing as it did very highly attenuated doses of drugs, gave encouragement to her intuitive interest in mental causation. In fact, the founder of homeopathy himself, Hahnemann, had asserted that the healing factor in his system was mental.

Mrs. Patterson's success with homeopathy was promising enough so that for a time she herself began to help patients. Her experiments with extremely high attenuations brought results strikingly similar to those of some of the modern medical experiments with placebos, undertaken within the last ten or twenty years.

On one occasion, for example, she treated a case of dropsy which had been given up by the doctors. She prescribed high attenuations of a certain drug, only to learn that this same prescription had been previously used. Fearing an aggravation of the symptoms from continued use of the medicine, she asked the patient to give it up. But the patient was afraid, whereupon it occurred to Mrs. Patterson to substitute unmedicated pellets and watch the result. The patient improved and finally said she could do without the medicine. After three days, however, she relapsed, whereupon Mrs. Patterson again began giving her unmedicated pellets. The patient promptly began to improve again, and use of the placebos was continued until she was entirely cured.

This and other such experiences served to deepen Mrs. Patterson's feeling that it was the patient's faith in drugs, and not the drugs themselves, that brought healing. But still this all seemed only a hint; it left unanswered the basic questions of mental causation, of mind and matter.

In the early 1850's she had begun exploring other realms in her search for enlightenment on these questions. This was the period in New England history when practically all literate people were talking about the claims of spiritualism and mesmerism and investigating them. She found it impossible to believe in spiritualism, and later included a vigorous and comprehensive denunciation of its teachings in the first edition of *Science and Health*. Her investigation of mental healing methods of that era, however, culminated in her study of the method practiced by Phineas P. Quimby, a drugless healer of Portland, Maine.

The Patterson's sojourn in North Groton had ended in 1860, when the mortgage on their home had been foreclosed. The couple then moved to Rumney. But soon the Civil War broke out, and the always itinerant Dr. Patterson embarked upon a mission to Washington for the Governor of New Hampshire. While there he paid a visit to the battlefield at Bull Run and was captured by Confederate forces, who sent him to Libby Prison.

For a time after his departure for Washington, Mrs. Patterson remained at their home, in Rumney. Then she spent a period with her sister Abigail, who arranged for her to go to Vail's Hydropathic Institute in New Hampshire. But the treatment at Vail's was unsuccessful.

Mrs. Patterson had heard of Dr. Quimby of Portland some time previously, and for a number of months had wanted to visit him. In the summer of 1862, while at Vail's, she met someone who had been cured by Dr. Quimby of a supposedly incurable condition. She determined to go and see him. Though vigorously opposed by Abigail, and almost too weak and ill to make the trip, she managed to get to Portland.

She found that Quimby practiced a type of mind-cure which included dipping his hands in water and then rubbing the patient's head. He told her that her ailments—and all diseases—

were traceable to causes in the invisible world of the mind; that mental factors produced powerful changes in the fluids and processes of the body; and that he was able, by some sort of electrical transference, to take his patient's ills upon himself and destroy them. While at this period he did not consider himself a mesmerist, the methods he used would today be considered a form of mental suggestion.

Strangely enough, Mrs. Patterson was benefited quickly and radically by his treatments. Within a week she was able to walk up the 180 steps to the dome of the Portland City Hall. It looked as if her long search for health finally had been successful. She felt better than she had for years. Her gratitude to Quimby was unbounded. Having long sought the explanation of how Christ Jesus and his disciples had healed the sick, and now deeply impressed by Quimby's explanations of mental causation, she concluded—inaccurately, as it proved—that he had rediscovered the Master's healing method.

This initial encounter was the beginning of a period during which Mrs. Patterson made several visits to Portland to see Quimby, exchange ideas with him, read some of his manuscripts, do some writing herself, and attempt to help fellow patients when they called on her. But the benefits she had experienced did not prove permanent; the old ailments returned, and she sought Quimby's help from time to time virtually until his death in January, 1866.

Meantime, Dr. Patterson had escaped from prison and come home in late 1862. But he was even more restive and irresponsible than before. There was a period during which the couple were unsettled, moving from one place to another. In 1864 they moved to Lynn, Mass., where he was to set up a new dental practice. But soon he became involved in adultery. Their life together was marked by repeated faithlessness on his part, as well as poverty, until he finally deserted her in the summer of 1866. She did not divorce him, however, until 1873.

Thus the early part of 1866 marked the culmination of years of suffering, heartache, and tragedy. The world was dark; there was nothing to inspire hope. Quimby, on whom she had placed such faith, was gone. Her health was still poor. Other means of healing had been tried and proved unavailing. Her relatives were estranged for various reasons, including her unorthodox views. Her home life was disintegrating into wreckage.

This was the situation when the discovery of Christian Science came. On Thursday evening, February 1, 1866, Mrs. Patterson slipped and fell heavily on the ice in Lynn and was taken to a nearby house in an insensible condition. A doctor was called, and found her condition so critical that he made an additional visit during the night, prescribing medicines to be given her every few minutes. Her husband, in New Hampshire on business, was summoned by telegram.

Despite intense suffering and apparent spinal injury, she insisted on being taken to her home, in nearby Swampscott, next day. There she was nursed by friends. On Sunday she was still helpless and her condition filled her friends with misgivings. They sent word for the minister to come.

But that same day the sick woman asked for her Bible. She turned to the account in Matthew, Chapter 9, of the healing by Christ Jesus of a palsied man, and she turned to God in prayer.

Like a shaft of light when the sun flashes briefly through black and heavy clouds, there came in this hour of suffering a spiritual illumination. It was a clear view of Life totally apart from earthly scenes, wholly separate from matter and material living, a new world of spiritual consciousness.

Mrs. Eddy herself describes it in *Miscellaneous Writings*: "That short experience included a glimpse of the great fact that I have since tried to make plain to others, namely, Life in and of Spirit; this Life being the sole reality of existence" (24:14-18). In the radiance of this new consciousness she was immediately healed.

This was the awakening that broke through the mists of mortal views and revealed to her the Absolute. It was the vision of reality that gave her an entirely new basis of thought, a new starting point for reasoning and deduction.

In its initial dawning, this revelation came without words, without patterns of logic or structure of reasoning. It was a pure sense of at-one-ment with God, of His immediate and palpable presence—clear, unmistakable, utterly apart from theories based on a material universe, profoundly different from accepted human processes of thought. It was an awareness brought by the incorporeal Christ. It transcended words and called for searching and pondering. At the time, as Mrs. Eddy herself indicates in her autobiography, she did not know how she had been healed; she only knew that the divine Spirit had "wrought the miracle." It was only later, as a result of much further searching and exploration, that she came to grasp the divine law of healing, which her recovery illustrated, and to understand the universe of Spirit, which she had glimpsed.

She had had previous intimations of spiritual reality. There had been her intuitive feeling, going back to her youth and expressed in various ways, that a reality existed which was higher and more genuine than matter. During the 1850's she had once restored sight to a blind baby through prayer. Her experiences with homeopathy and with Quimby had confirmed to her the power of thought to work changes in the body.

But the experience of 1866 set her inquiring thoughts to work in new and deeper directions. It caused her to study with redoubled diligence the record of spiritual healing in the Scriptures. As she pondered the meaning of her experience she found it opening new realms of insight. She later spoke of it as revealing a fresh universe, a new world filled with light and Life. This brought new vantage points for further discovery and original thought. As she puts it, "Frozen fountains were unsealed" (Ret. 31:28).

She did not fully grasp its implications for some time after it happened, and for some years the old views of things mingled somewhat with the new; they had to be sifted out. But gradually they disappeared and the new revelation became clearer. She saw plainly that this deep experience put everything in a new light. It marked the beginning of a forty-five-year period during which she became known to the world as the Discoverer and Founder of Christian Science. It was a chapter which nobody, examining her life up to that time, could possibly have foreseen or predicted.

Yet in retrospect it is possible now to see a certain logical unfoldment at work here. For one thing, the moral and spiritual climate of mid-nineteenth-century New England had been unusually conducive. This was a period of eager inquiry and revitalized faith in the goodness of God and man. New England offered little foothold to ancient despotisms. Mental shackles were being struck off; new intellectual frontiers beckoned. It was an atmosphere ripe for spiritual discovery.

The very tragedies were part of her preparation. Along with her innate spiritual intuition and insight, they had helped to evolve a profound change in her whole outlook. They brought her to a mental standpoint where she was utterly willing to relinquish matter and material loyalties as a basis of thought. She speaks of how she learned the "frailty of mortal anticipations"; how the illusion was thoroughly shattered that material living could offer any true or abiding rest; how she realized that even "exultant hope, if tinged with earthliness, is crushed as the moth" (Ret. 32:9).

She summed it up in her autobiography: "The heavenly intent of earth's shadows is to chasten the affections, to rebuke human consciousness and *turn it gladly from a material, false sense of life and happiness, to spiritual joy and true estimate of being*" (Ret. 21:17-20, italics added).

By these footsteps she came to a mental and spiritual standpoint extremely rare in human history. It was characterized by a total willingness to relinquish all the most entrenched assumptions of the human mind; to think differently from material systems of thought. It was a willingness to give up hopes of finding happiness, health, life, by dependence on matter or material power, and to think patiently and persistently from a purely spiritual basis—the basis of an infinitely good and all-powerful God. It was a willingness to sacrifice mortal self, to be born again, lay hold of the true spiritual capacities of man.

This receptivity opened the way for a clarity of vision that reached absolute Truth. It liberated those spiritual capacities which all the pain and heartache of merciless years could not kill. It brought the fruition of those intuitive qualities of thought which most deeply characterized her nature. The English historian H.A.L. Fisher referred to these when he wrote:

Prayer, meditation, eager and puzzled interrogation of the Bible, had claimed from childhood much of her energy, so that those who met her in later times were conscious of a certain quiet exaltation, such as may come to a woman nursing a secret spiritual advantage. . . . The great ideas of God, of immortality, of the soul, of a life penetrated by Christianity, were never far from her mind.

2.

Great composers like Beethoven and Mozart have gained their inspiration by dwelling in a thought-world of which the rest of us are oblivious. So Mrs. Eddy, attuned through spiritual sense to divine reality, listened and caught visions of Truth from a realm which to material sense is unknown. Having turned her gaze from earthly views, she discovered a new world of ideas, a new Science.

For three years after her healing she studied the Bible to the exclusion of practically all else. She gained new light on the Scriptures. Their spiritual significance became illumined; she discerned in them a thread of demonstrable Science. She saw fresh meaning in the words and works of Jesus.

A new trust in God and a profound humility pervaded her thoughts; she saw as never before that thought must be spiritualized in order to understand the realm of Spirit. As the understanding of God unfolded to her, she began to perceive the vastness of Christian Science, comprising the laws and truths of His illimitable creation. She also gazed into the utter vacuity of evil.

A good deal of Christendom accepted theoretically the view that God is incorporeal Spirit, or Mind; that He is infinite good, a God of Love. But until Mrs. Eddy's discovery, no one had ever adopted this basis—wholly, unreservedly, totally—and then followed it through rigorously to its logical scientific conclusion.

She found that when she adopted this basis and then sought to deduce the character of man, law, and universe, she was led to the Science of infinite good—*i.e.*, the allness of God and the nothingness of evil; the allness of Spirit and the nothingness of matter; the spiritual character and perfection of God's creation; and the demonstrable possibilities of these propositions as fundamental Truth.

This was unfamiliar ground. Some of the best intellects of the centuries had become engrossed in a thicket of involved explanations which were intended to reconcile a material world of pain, suffering, and injustice with the divine order of things. The stubborn human assumption that evil and matter are real invariably got in the way. But when she turned with pure insight to the nature of God as omnipotent Love, absolute and all-embracing Mind, or Spirit, she found therein no consciousness nor element of evil or matter.

In the latter part of 1866 she reached the scientific certainty that all causation rests with Mind, and that every effect is a mental phenomenon. It was much longer before she was able to express clearly in words the implications of these revolutionary ideas. Years later, however, she summed up these early explorations in this way: "My discovery, that erring, mortal, misnamed *mind* produces all the organism and action of the mortal body, set my thoughts to work in new channels, and led up to my demonstration of the proposition that Mind is All and matter is naught as the leading factor in Mind-science" (S&H 108:30).

The process of exploring this new realm of thought involved patient scientific reasoning, without deviation, from the basis of one infinite Mind, God. She had to work out the line of demarcation between the errors of the human mind and the pure consciousness of Spirit: between mesmerism, suggestion, mental science and the pure Science of immortal Mind as practiced and lived by the Master.

The years from 1866 to 1875, when the first edition of *Science and Health* was published, were a period of hard work testing her discovery in its application to healing, and of ceaseless struggle to convey to others by spoken and written word the meaning of Science. In teaching the few students who would listen to her radical ideas, she faced the question, as she later phrased it: "If a divine Principle alone heals, what is the human modus for demonstrating this—in short, how can sinful mortals prove that a divine Principle heals the sick, as well as governs the universe, time, space, immortality, man?" (Misc. 380:2).

At that time the idea of treating the sick exclusively by mental and spiritual means, through prayer and without material applications, was virtually unknown. Her students could not grasp it; they sought a material sign that something was being done for the patient. For a time she permitted them to manipulate the patient by such means as rubbing the head (though she herself did not use any material method). This was the technique Quimby had used and which other practitioners of drugless healing in that era had adopted.

But in the early 1870's she came to see plainly that such methods were basically contrary to the Science she taught. They led to dependence on matter instead of Spirit; on suggestion instead of on divine power; on the will of the practitioner instead of on God; in a word, to mesmerism instead of to Christ.

This realization led her into a deep and thorough exploration of the profound gulf which separates the essentially Christian metaphysics of Christian Science from the practice of mesmerism. It forced her to investigate the modes of mental malpractice for the purpose of exposing them and providing the method of spiritual defense. She was compelled to explore and expose the nature of evil as intrinsically hypnotic: deceptive and delusive, aggressive and malicious—but actually nothingness, with no mind to create or support it, though seeming so real to mortal sense.

She set forth the fruits of her discovery and practice in the first edition of *Science and Health*. This volume elucidated the absolute propositions of Science, the rules for their application to healing the sick, and the spiritual method which overcomes the suggestions of evil.

By these steps there was inaugurated a basic conflict between Christian Science and mental evil; between a Christian mental practice and mesmeric suggestion; between scientific use of spiritual power and those destructive elements of the carnal mind which have loosed so much confusion and horror upon the modern world.

This was essentially a cosmic battle, though it was fought out first of all in her own consciousness. It explains much of the turmoil which attended the growth of the Christian Science movement. Naturally it centered around the leader, and already it has made her one of the most controversial figures in history. It is a tribute to the omnipotent power of Truth, and to her utter devotion, discernment, and spiritual strength, that she endured to the end in this pioneering work and succeeded in founding her church and movement.

Today this same battle against mental evil still goes on, but now it is a battle in which all men are more and more obviously engaged, in their wrestlings with thought-manipulation, mass hypnosis, and the devious attempts of ruthless systems to invade and dominate men's minds.

It was the separating of pure Science from materially mental methods—through steadily unfolding revelation, reason, and demonstration—that cost Mrs. Eddy so much struggle in the years following her initial discovery. The many-faceted significance of this work is illustrated by the numerous unsuccessful attempts over the years, by writers who have not understood Christian Science, to trace its origins to certain materially mental systems or to various philosophies.

It has been alleged, for example, that Mrs. Eddy drew her basic ideas from the German philosopher Hegel. This assertion, put forward on the basis of alleged "documents," was thoroughly discredited in 1955, when a detailed examination of the subject by the religious historian Conrad Henry Moehlman was published under the title *Ordeal by Concordance*.

Again it was asserted that some of Mrs. Eddy's ideas could be traced to various other German or English Idealist philosophers, or to Oriental religions—if not directly through study of her

own, then indirectly through Emerson and the Transcendental-
ists.

But there is no historical evidence that Mrs. Eddy made any
study of European or Oriental philosophers, or that she looked
very deeply into transcendentalism before *Science and Health*
was published; nor does the theorctical idealism of the Tran-
scendentalists bear much resemblance to the practical metaphysics of Christian Science, so notable for demonstration in
healing.

A comprehensive scholarly analysis of the contrasts between
Christian Science and transcendentalism—both historically
and ideologically—was published in 1958 in *Christian
Science: Its Encounter with American Culture* by Robert Peel.

There are those who have asserted that the Science she put
forward in *Science and Health* was drawn from Quimby. Actually, the two are basically different, in both origin and content,
and it is precisely these differences which mark the road Mrs.
Eddy had to travel in those crucial years after the first light of
discovery.

It will be worth our while to note briefly some of these differences from Quimbyism. For one thing, this will help to show
the nature of Mrs. Eddy's exploratory work, in defining and
elucidating the Science she had discovered, in the eventful period from 1866 to the 1870's and on into the 1880's. For
another, this will help to clarify the sharp differences between
Christian Science and certain modern systems of mental healing—notably New Thought—with which it is often mis-
takenly confused. More than any one individual, Quimby is
considered the founder of the New Thought movement, which
is represented today by various cults belonging to the International New Thought Alliance as well as by Unity. Too often
it has been assumed that Christian Science is a derivative of this
thoughtstream.

But a careful comparison of the fundamentals of Christian
Science with Quimby's writings brings to light a clear and unmistakable line of demarcation, the sharp line Mrs. Eddy
explored, step by step, in the years and decades after her dis-

covery. It shows the differences to be not superficial, but of the essence. While Quimby's manuscripts contain some positive ideas and occasional flashes of exceptional insight, he never made the all-important distinction between humanly mental methods and the Science of divine Mind. Quimby never attempted to teach students his healing method nor did he ever publish any explanations of it.*

To be sure, there are certain superficial resemblances between Christian Science and Quimbyism in certain limited directions (*e.g.*, that there is no intelligence in matter) and also an occasional similarity of terminology (*e.g.*, that sickness is "error" or "belief"). But the meaning of the terms is radically different in Christian Science. In the Science Mrs. Eddy discovered, ideas and terms become completely transfigured, because of the absolute foundation to which they are referred—the allness of Spirit and the total nothingness of matter. This basis was not shared by Quimby, nor is it accepted by New Thought and Unity. The gulf is fundamental, and it sharpens every specific point of comparison or contrast.

One important contrast is that Christian Science is a religion devoted to the worship of God, while Quimby's writings are not essentially religious in focus or character, even though he often refers to the healing work of Jesus. The whole focus of Christian Science, both in theory and in practice, is the understanding of the nature of God and man's relationship to Him; it is through this understanding that sickness and discord are dispelled. On the other hand, the essential focus of Quimby's explanations was on the power of human thought to produce physical effects. As Dresser comments of Quimby in

---

* However, he did write notes and manuscripts and a collection of them was published, in edited form, long after his death, under the title *The Quimby Manuscripts,* edited by Horatio W. Dresser, New York: Thomas Y. Crowell Company, 1921. The quotations from Quimby cited in this chapter are taken from this volume.

For citations from Mrs. Eddy's letters and other documents reflecting this period of exploration, see *Mary Baker Eddy: A Life-Size Portrait,* by Lyman P. Powell, Boston: The Christian Science Publishing Society, 1950. Further contrasts between Christian Science and Quimbyism are shown in *Christian Science and its Discoverer,* by E. Mary Ramsay, Boston: The Christian Science Publishing Society, 1935.

his "Editor's Summary": "He is always tracing a patient's trouble to the particular beliefs, religious, social, medical, which have been accepted in place of realities. Thus his main interest seems to be to disclose the power of adverse suggestion, fear, error, ill-founded belief."

This contrast between the two approaches is reflected in dealing with a patient. We find Quimby saying, "So it is with the sick, each must have his case explained to himself." He writes to a patient:

Of course you get very tired, and this would cause the heat to affect the surface as your head was affected, the heat would affect the fluids, and when the heat came in contact with the cold it would chill the surface. This change you call "a cold." But the same would come about in another way. Every word I said to you is like yeast. This went into your system like food and came in contact with the food of your old bread or belief. Mine was like a purgative, and acted like an emetic on your mind, so that it would keep up a war with your devils, and they will not leave a person, when they have so good a hold as they have on you, without making some resistance.

Such a statement is totally foreign to the language and method of Christian Science. The instruction of Mrs. Eddy, as given in the chapter on "Christian Science Practice" in *Science and Health,* is to deal with patients as follows: "Turn their thoughts away from their bodies to higher objects. Teach them that their being is sustained by Spirit, not by matter, and that they find health, peace, and harmony in God, divine Love" (S&H 416:30).

This instruction epitomizes the procedure of Christian Science practice as it is carried on today. A patient with a physical problem visiting a Christian Science practitioner may be surprised to find that the practitioner will make little or no inquiry about symptoms, and will, in fact, avoid any detailed discussion of them, turning the patient's thought away from the body to a discussion of the nature of God and man in His likeness.

In Christian Science the central emphasis is strongly Christian and regenerative. Its healing is not only physical but moral.

Mrs. Eddy writes: "Hatred, envy, dishonesty, fear, and so forth, make a man sick, and neither material medicine nor Mind can help him permanently, even in body, unless it makes him better mentally, and so delivers him from his destroyers." Throughout her writings there is repeated stress on the necessity of regeneration, reformation, purification of thought and life, in accord with the precepts of the Master.

In contrast, Dresser says of Quimby's approach:

Naturally enough Quimby is not interested in the question of sin, and he hardly ever uses the word "evil." For him it is all a question of ignorance or error. There is neither ignorance nor error in Science, hence no sin or evil. The problem of evil differs in no way from that of disease. Therefore Quimby says nothing about repentance and regeneration.

This same contrast is evident in the teachings on prayer. While Quimby wrote that the desire to know God is prayer, and that real prayer means to "act rightly and honestly," the tone of what he says seems essentially negative; it is largely a denunciation of the petitionary prayer espoused by the churches. This is a far cry from the emphasis on deep and fervent scientific prayer in Christian Science, as in the opening chapter of *Science and Health*: "The prayer that reforms the sinner and heals the sick is an absolute faith that all things are possible to God—a spiritual understanding of Him, an unselfed love" (S&H 1:1-4).

There is a fundamental contrast in the mental standpoint required of the healer. Quimby writes that the healer must take the burdens of his patient upon himself and his editor summarizes: "So he was in the habit of entering the thought-world of all his patients, to see how the situation appeared to the patient."

But in contrast, the Christian Science textbook says in so many words that sympathy with error should disappear. Mrs. Eddy counsels compassion, kindness, understanding, the tender word and gentle patience with the fears of the sick, but she writes:

To the Christian Science healer, sickness is a dream from which the patient needs to be awakened. Disease should not appear real to the physician, since it is demonstrable that the way to cure the patient is to make disease unreal to him. To do this, the physician must understand the unreality of disease in Science (S&H 417:20).

The deepest contrast, of course, comes on the issue of what is real. This is the point which separates Christian Science from virtually all other systems; and it was Mrs. Eddy's clear revelation on this subject that enabled her to find her way through a wilderness of human concepts and elucidate the pure Science of Spirit.

As Dresser puts it: "Quimby never denied the existence of the natural world, although sometimes referring to it as a mere shadow, and contending that matter contains no intelligence." But Quimby's explanation of it as "shadow" is somewhat comparable to the modern explanation of matter as energy; this explanation says matter is not what it appears to be, but does not deny its existence. Nowhere does Quimby deny utterly the reality of matter.

All of this is in sharp contrast to the underlying premise of Christian Science, which is that, as Mrs. Eddy writes, "matter disappears under the microscope of Spirit" (S&H 264:21). "All is infinite Mind and its infinite manifestation, for God is All-in-all" (S&H 468:10).

It is comparatively easy to lay the finished fruit of Mrs. Eddy's labors alongside the views of Quimby or other systems and to note the differences—if the meaning of the teachings is accurately understood. But she had no such easy opportunity. Guided only by sheer inspiration from on high and a new perspective on the Bible teachings, she had to fight her way through a maze of confusing and conflicting views, discern the scientific rules of mental practice, find the terminology to communicate her discovery, and then embark upon the herculean task—in a hostile and uncomprehending world—of establishing a church organization which would preserve, protect, and promulgate her revelation.

Her governing desire was to bring to all mankind the clear,

transcendent vision of absolute Truth which she herself had gained, and the spiritually scientific means by which this Truth could be taught, learned, and practiced, and thus made to benefit others. That she succeeded in accomplishing this mighty task—a task she herself shrank from because it looked as if it would take centuries of spiritual growth—is nothing less than a miracle.

3.

The complete and authoritative statement of Mrs. Eddy's discovery is contained in the textbook *Science and Health*. As H.A.L. Fisher commented, "In the development of Christian Science that book, and that book only, has been of decisive importance." And it is today of decisive importance in the Christian Science way of life.

To bring the textbook to its final form, Mrs. Eddy worked for more than thirty-five years—writing, editing, revising, condensing, clarifying. Begun in 1872 and first published in 1875, it went through more than four hundred printings, some of which comprised major revisions, before reaching its final wording in 1910. Mrs. Eddy's own copies, now in the archives of the Mother Church, are filled with her penciled editing and interlineations, sometimes covering the margins and flyleaves.

Always she sought to give clearer expression to her revelation. Her pencilings reflect her own spiritual growth and experience through the eventful years when the Christian Science movement was being launched and given its present worldwide momentum.

Her own growth was prodigious, and so was that of her movement. From a handful of students in Lynn, Massachusetts, in 1875, the movement grew through many trials and crises to be an international religious denomination of some 1200 churches at the time of Mrs. Eddy's passing in 1910. In contrast to her former years of near-invalidism, she lived a life of unusual activity and manifold responsibilities practically throughout this period. Her work of teaching had begun with one student in 1867. During the 1870's and 1880's she taught large numbers of students and began sending others out to teach, healed the sick, lectured, wrote some short books and pamphlets, organized her church (1879), served as its pastor, set up new headquarters in Boston, established the Massachusetts Metaphysical College (1881), launched *The Christian Science Journal* (1883), edited it, and defended her budding movement from the onslaughts of its critics and the schisms created by disloyal followers.

For almost six years (1877-1882) she had the help and support of her husband, Asa Gilbert Eddy, who was the first to advertise himself publicly as a Christian Science practitioner and the first to conduct a Christian Science Sunday School. But from the time of his passing in 1882 she carried on alone.

From the perspective of today, however, these steps in the 1870's and 1880's were but the laying of foundations for greater achievements. In 1889 Mrs. Eddy disbanded her church, dissolved the Massachusetts Metaphysical College at the height of its prosperity, and retired to Concord, New Hampshire, to prepare a revision of *Science and Health* and to give thought to the deeper problems of her movement.

Thus began the last two decades of her life. They were marked by a series of achievements which gave the Christian Science movement its present scope and structure.

The fiftieth edition of *Science and Health*—a major revision that brought it much nearer its present-day form—was issued in 1891. In 1892 she organized her church on its present foundation. Three years later the original edifice of The Mother Church was built in Boston—the huge-domed extension was added ten years after that (1903-06). In 1895 she ordained the Bible and *Science and Health* as the pastor of the Mother Church and its branches. That same year she published the first edition of the *Manual of The Mother Church*.

The year 1898 brought a number of important steps: establishment of the Board of Lectureship, the Committee on Publication, the trusteeship of the Publishing Society and the Board of Education (for training teachers); also the initiating of the present plan of Lesson-Sermon subjects in the *Quarterly*; the launching of the *Christian Science Weekly*, later called the *Sentinel*; and, in November, the teaching, in Concord, of Mrs. Eddy's last class.

Succeeding years brought additional progress, culminating in her last great organizational move, the establishing of *The Christian Science Monitor* in 1908. In preparation for this step, Mrs. Eddy moved from Pleasant View, Concord, New Hampshire, to her last home, in Chestnut Hill, near Boston.

During all this period branch churches were springing up all over the United States and in various other parts of the world. It was a period of tremendous growth and multiplied responsibilities. But through all of it, Mrs. Eddy found time not only to actively guide her church but also to write additional books, articles, and messages on Christian Science, and to bring the textbook to its final form.

The massive growth of the Christian Science movement during these years has often been attributed to Mrs. Eddy's organizational genius. In a sense this is correct; but it is also an oversimplification, because at the heart of the movement then, as now, was the book which contained the teachings, *Science and Health*.

This was the book to which, with the Bible, every student turned daily for inspiration and guidance. It was the book which then, as now, gave morale, impetus, courage, strength, spiritual vitality, and healing power to the movement.

It is sometimes asked how intelligent people can read, over and over again, day after day through many years, the same book. The answer is that from the Christian Scientist's point of view, *Science and Health* is quite unlike any other volume that one is apt to think of.

It is a rare thing, for example, for a book to be so constructed that you can select from it sentences, paragraphs, passages, arranging them in innumerable patterns and thus forming coherent discussions of the infinite topics it contains, still preserving clearly the fundamental teaching of the whole volume.

This is outstandingly true, of course, of the Bible—so much so that the King James Version and many other translations divide the material into verses which can easily be selected and arranged in differing combinations for reading.

This is rare in other volumes; yet it is done all the time with *Science and Health,* as well as with the Bible, in the preparation of the Lesson-Sermons and by every First Reader when preparing for a Wednesday meeting.

In fact, Christian Scientists study *Science and Health* in terms of short passages on a given topic more frequently than they read it consecutively. Often they use a concordance. The lines on each page are numbered in the margin to facilitate ready reference. One gains some especially rich insights and perspectives by reading the book through consecutively but its message can be gained quite thoroughly by other methods of study.

As the Scientist sees it, one of the outstanding and highly rewarding characteristics of this textbook is that a given passage, used over and over again through the years, will continue to yield new inspiration and to open new and sometimes totally unexpected vistas of spiritual understanding. Many times a single word or phrase, carefully pondered, pours forth new inspiration like a spring which continually gives forth fresh water. The statements go on unfolding because they deal with ideas that are intrinsically illimitable. There is no end to what can be said, or written, or discovered within the scope of its teachings. Mrs. Eddy herself wrote, "Truth cannot be stereotyped; it unfoldeth forever" (No. 45:27).

The essential nature of *Science and Health* is that, while defining thought with the accuracy of spiritual law and Science, its statements at the same time liberate thought and lift it to the exploration of new realms. This is a quality which cannot be found in writing that conveys the limited, finite thoughts derived from the human mind, but is found in writing that points toward the infinite.

There are those who have asserted that *Science and Health* is "filled with contradictions." It is easy to see how this might appear to be the case. For example, we find the statement "A sick body is evolved from sick thoughts" (S&H 260:20), and a few pages farther on, "Spirit and its formations are the only realities of being" (S&H 264:20). What is needed, however, is to recall that the textbook is concerned with making clear two things: the nature of absolute Truth, or reality; the application of this Truth to proving the unreality of matter and evil, which seem so real to misguided mortal sense. The latter sentence just quoted, for example, is a statement of what is regarded as absolute Truth. The first is one example of many to be found through the textbook which resolve material phenomena into their mental elements; the next essential step after that, also explained in passages throughout, is to exchange these erroneous mental elements—inherently empty, deceptive, illusory, unreal —for the solid and substantial ideas and qualities, that is, the consciousness, which reflects immortal Mind, God.

Sometimes it has been objected that it is basically illogical for a book to maintain that Spirit is all and matter is nothing, and then devote pages to showing how a material body can be healed and human woes overcome. There is, indeed, an element of utter illogic involved here—but the illogicality lies in the illusion of matter and evil itself. The book shows this illusion to be totally illogical. It is enigmatic and erratic. It cannot be deduced from the premise of one infinite God, Good, any more than mistakes can be logically deduced from mathematical reasoning. The textbook sticks to its point throughout that matter and evil therefore are utterly without foundation or reality, and its pages are devoted to making clear consistently and logically the allness and supremacy of God, good. This is what the Scientist devotes his prayers to demonstrating. The point is summarized in these words from *Science and Health*:

All reality is in God and His creation, harmonious and eternal. That which He creates is good, and He makes all that is made. Therefore the only reality of sin, sickness, or death is the awful fact that unrealities seem real to human, erring belief, until God strips off their disguise. They are not true, because they are not of God (S&H 472:24-30).

The exercise of spiritual sense is needed in order to understand *Science and Health*. But this is not to imply that even the most experienced Christian Scientist feels he fully understands the book. Far from it. In fact, Mrs. Eddy herself wrote, late in her life, that she had been learning the higher meaning of the book since writing it. She expressed the view—with which the most advanced Christian Scientist would heartily and humbly agree—that it would take centuries for the vast topics of *Science and Health* to be sufficiently understood in order for its statements to be fully demonstrated.

This is the case because the fundamentals set forth in the book deal with the nature of infinite Truth. As a discoverer, Mrs. Eddy herself continued throughout her years to explore the fresh universe of Life which Science reveals; and those who study deeply her textbook find that it contains a spiritual discovery whose possibilities for development, in individual and collective experience, are without limit.

Chapter Seven

Religion for the Space Age

Modern man stands at the threshold of the stars but lives in an earthly atmosphere of deepening unrest and danger. Our astronauts have pierced the frontiers of space and our technology promises increasing traffic across the deeps that lead to distant worlds. But here on earth the delicate edifice of civilization shudders under the upheavals of social struggle and the peril of total destruction.

A man may walk across the fields at night and gaze with a certain knowing thrill at the majestic wheel of the galaxy, across which range the planets men expect some day to visit. But millions wonder whether the human race will survive to reach the stars. There is a danger the whole structure of civilization may come crashing down into a heap of ashes.

It is not the hydrogen bomb alone that makes the world of the 1960's a scene of turmoil. Free men everywhere are under siege by a militant philosophy of total subjugation whose purpose it is to subvert the dignity of the individual and to invert the structure of society as we know it. Racial tensions have currently heightened the pressures operating in domestic and world affairs. While many binding taboos and superstitions have been abolished, the established systems of morality have suffered severely under the impact of war and social change.

Our civilization is being transformed before our eyes, mechanized, urbanized, automated. While technological change has brought a tremendous liberation to the average man, human society has become so complex as to be in some ways almost unmanageable. Greater changes have taken place in the last few decades than in all the rest of recorded history. The accelerating pace imposes new and unfamiliar stresses on individuals and institutions.

All this brings new challenges to religion. Many present-day thinkers are concerned that religious teachings and the world seem to have lost contact with one another. Traditional theology seems outmoded to many people, especially the younger generation; the world of the 1960's talks a new language and thinks in new concepts. Some careful religious observers question the depth and substance of the celebrated "religious revival"; they feel the estrangement between religious teachings and the practical world is increasing in America and is especially serious in Europe.

Yet the parched inadequacy of secularism is obvious. Despite the comforts and amenities of material abundance, we are told this is an age of anxiety; that men are plagued by inner doubts; that they lack a clear sense of meaning in life, a condition which heightens the uncertainty of national purpose; that they are robbed of a sense of peace by a pervasive atmosphere of disillusionment and selfishness. These problems, we are told, become apparent in tangible conditions: personal frustrations, prevalent crime, national perplexities, international discord.

Our period is characterized by profound restlessness and unparalleled opportunities. It is a period of marvelous progress yet incredible dangers, of vastly expanding knowledge yet deepening doubts. It is a time of magnificent achievements, yet of massive assault on man's confidence in himself.

From the Christian Scientist's point of view, however, one finds the real significance of this turbulent era not so much in the thunder of turmoil and cataclysm as in the silent influence of revealed Truth, powerfully at work in the deep recesses of human consciousness.

There are many signs that mankind is gradually emerging into light, and perhaps more rapidly now than foretold by the long slow struggle of the past. There is a growing recognition, spurred by technological and economic progress, that poverty and filth are not necessary; that slavery is not legitimate; that mankind no longer need bow to subjection as an inevitable victim of the material environment.

Men have outgrown a great deal of ignorance and intolerance. Barriers of provincialism and race prejudice are beginning to come down. There is a dawning perception, however dim as yet, of the dignity of each and all as human beings; of inherent human rights; and of the underlying oneness of man. All this finds expression in heartening steps, however faltering, toward the establishment of a more just and stable world order, rooted in the recognition of universal human rights. Despite all the nihilistic influences and present-day tides of reaction, still it is true that a growing sense of humanity has found its way into organized society.

To the Christian Scientist, all this is evidence of something profoundly dynamic at work. It is evidence of a new concept of man emerging—a concept of man loosed from material chains—man made in the image of his Creator, richly endowed out of the resources of an infinite Mind, which is illimitable good. It points to man's immortal birthright of freedom and dominion over all the earth. It is evidence of the presence, here and now, of a higher law than the barriers of ignorance or the fetters of matter: the law of Spirit, which is demonstrable among men when understood in its Science.

These signs of progress the Scientist does not attribute merely to the evolution of material conditions. He traces them to an eternal source, to that irresistible Truth and Love whose healing touch is again transforming human lives as in the days of Christ Jesus—and whose power can remake the earth, however severe the birth pangs may be.

To the Christian Scientist this growing spiritual enlightenment is the wave of the future. It holds the destiny of mankind. Because of his conviction that all good is of God, and that good is indestructible, and that man's relationship to God is unbroken and eternal oneness, and that these facts are dawning in human thought—because he deeply believes all these things, the Scientist is convinced that this is not the age of doom but the springtime of humanity.

2.

I suppose there is no more profound need among men today than the need for a sense of spiritual certainty. Some would call it a need for a sense of direction, a sense of purpose, a sense of individual worth, or a sense that life does have meaning. But all of these, it seems to me, go back to something much deeper. They go back to an underlying lack of spiritual certainty: the certainty of an individual relationship to the eternal Truth, which is the origin and explanation of all things. If one studies deeply the problems afflicting men in our era, one finds this lack of spiritual certainty emerging as a common denominator.

There is not much comfort to be gained from scientific explorations of the nature of man. Evolution describes him as a biochemical organism emerging from aeons of slow and unthinking growth. Behaviorist psychology pictures him as a neural mechanism operating through conditioned responses and irrational impulses of his own "unconscious." The natural sciences have pictured the span of the human race as an inconsequential interval somewhere between the steaming swamps of a newly born planet and what Eiseley calls "our final freezing battle with the void." From all this arises the question of whether man is anything more than a biological incident in a meaningless universe.

Deep in his heart many a person wonders: What is my identity, anyway? Is man merely an aimless offshoot of hereditary and environmental conditions? Can the individual find any link to the Eternal? Does any such link exist?

The doubts on such questions are pervasive in present-day thinking. They lie at the root of much personal anxiety and insecurity, and they contribute profoundly to social confusion.

The social and mental upheavals of the present-day world call for something more than religious formalism. Faith without works is not enough. Unless religion can offer an understanding of demonstrable spiritual law, how can it hope to answer the questions of an age steeped in the empiricism of the sciences? Unless it can show plainly man's spiritual link with divine reality, may it not become merely a well-intentioned expedient to promote group living? Unless it can provide the individual the means to defend himself against the mental and social pressures of a mass civilization, and thus enable him to preserve his sense of individuality, can religion meet his deepest needs?

So far as the Christian Scientist is concerned, he is convinced that the practical truths of revealed Christianity can answer this modern challenge. He feels that religion does indeed have a vital message for the present-day world, a message that is abreast of the times and vibrant with meaning. As he sees it, a sense of spiritual certainty is indeed possible; an abiding sense of absolute faith and conviction, grounded in a perception of the nature of God and man and the relationship between them. He finds this faith vastly reinforced by the evidence that the Truth of God and man is provable here and now.

The Scientist is convinced that certain great thinkers through the centuries have caught gleams of an absolute reality deeper than the material universe; that this primordial Truth is unfolded in the Scriptures and was demonstrated by Christ Jesus; and that it is abundantly revealed today in a practical spiritual Science.

As the Scientist sees it, the light of this absolute Truth is becoming more and more apparent to humanity. To him this present age harbors unusual promise (as well as unusual dangers): the promise of a kinder and more deeply spiritual order among men. For even in the confusion of human struggles we can lay hold of Truth through Science, know its illumination, come to understand it. When one does so, he has a changeless guide and standard amid the quicksands of human experience. He finds in this Truth an explanation of man which reassures him of his spiritual identity as the child of God. This explanation is radically different from material theories about man and infinitely more comforting.

In other words, this underlying Truth is not remote from us, even in the human condition. We can plunge deeper than the frailties of the human personality and find the real man whose link to his Maker is unbroken. When Truth is understood in Science, it supplies to the individual a sense of purpose and of individual worth. It answers the deepest cravings of the individual in an anxiety-ridden age. It gives him a perception that his real identity survives the power of death because man is the indestructible expression of Life eternal, forever held in his God-defined orbit by spiritual law.

This understanding brings a sense of absolute spiritual certainty, a sense of man's relationship to God. It provides a practical way of life, for in it one gains courage and a sense of direction for coping with the challenges of the modern world.

3.

Let us explore more thoroughly the need for a sense of meaning, so plain in both individual and collective affairs.

So far as the collective aspects are concerned, some of the most thoughtful leaders in America have called attention in recent years to the lack of a clear and positive sense of national purpose. In their view the materially abundant American commonwealth acts as if it had "arrived" and no other commanding national goals remained to be achieved. Certainly the Western nations have not succeeded in conveying a sense of dynamic idealism to emergent peoples of the world. And it is unquestionably true that the negative purpose of resisting communism is not enough for greatness; by itself this hardly could be the road to national fulfillment.

But to the extent that any national aimlessness may exist, is not this a reflection of a profound sense of individual aimlessness? The aspirations of a free nation can only reflect the deepest purposes to which its individual citizens commit their lives. It is on the individual level that the need for a sense of meaning is most obvious today.

This need is recognizable in the sense of emptiness and restlessness that characterizes so many people's lives. It is dramatized by the problems of the *new leisure,* which is widespread today and may be more so tomorrow through automation. For the first time in history the question is a vital social concern: What goals remain after the individual is fed, clothed, housed, transported, educated, and entertained?

More people have more of the ingredients of the "good life" than ever before: high wages, laborsaving gadgets, planned recreation, cars, pensions, leisure, rich food, and free mobility. Yet we still have appallingly prevalent tensions, domestic discord, high rates of psychosomatic illness, and the greatest per capita boredom on earth. Such problems call to mind the words of the Master: "What shall it profit a man, if he shall gain the whole world, and lose his own soul?" (Mark 8:36).

"The average man of today seems to be haunted by a feeling of the meaninglessness of life," writes Viktor E. Frankl, a prominent European psychiatrist, in *From Death Camp to Existentialism.*

What we can observe in the majority of people is not so much the feeling of being less valuable than others, but the feeling that life no longer has any meaning. . . . How does it manifest itself? In the state of boredom. . . . In actual fact, boredom is now causing us—and certainly us psychiatrists, too—more problems than is distress. . . .

Let us think only of the Sunday neurosis—that kind of depression which afflicts people who become aware of the lack of content in their lives when the rush of a busy week is over and the void within them becomes manifest. Not a few cases of suicide could be traced back to this existential vacuum, this lack of a goal. . . .

We know the various masks and guises under which existential frustration appears: juvenile delinquency, alcoholism, the crisis of pensioners and aging people, and the like. . . . What the old scholars used to call the *horror vacui* exists, not only in the realm of physics, but apparently also in that of psychology: man is afraid of his inner void. . . .

Tillich analyzes this strange lack in modern life and speaks of the "lost dimension in religion." His view is that men in this period of history have largely lost an answer to the deep religious questions relating to the ultimate meaning of life—and that they have almost ceased to ask these questions. This he calls "the decisive element in the predicament of Western man in our period."

He appraises the "lost dimension" thus: "It means that man has lost an answer to the question: What is the meaning of life? Where do we come from, where do we go to? What shall we do, what should we become in the short stretch between birth and death?"

Whether or not one accepts these particular interpretations, it is true that quite aside from the scientific curiosity that leads men to explore the mysteries of the cosmos and the living cell, there persists a yearning, on a deeper level than the material, for a sense of meaning. All the magnificence of scientific knowledge has not quenched that yearning. Technological triumph over our environment cannot assuage it and may, in fact, only increase it. It is a spiritual hunger, and no answer will ever be found in materialism.

But the Christian Scientist feels it is possible for one to gain an answer here and now, because the light of Spirit, the rays of Truth, shine even in the dimness of human wandering. One can realize the answer when he turns unreservedly away from the calculating of his life-prospects on a material basis, and bases his conception of man wholly on the reality of Spirit. This gives him a totally new view of himself. He learns that man exists as the reflection of Spirit; that he does have a divinely established purpose, namely, to be the living witness of his Maker.

Through this approach, the Christian Scientist gains an abiding sense of man's inviolable spiritual individuality, empowered with Spirit's own inexhaustible energies. Such a view transcends physical personality. It awakens one to the fact that, as Mrs. Eddy says, man outlives finite mortal definitions of himself. One begins to grasp the fact that the horizons of man's being are without limit, for as the expression of God he bears witness to the nature and possibilities of inexhaustible good.

This understanding begins to shape the Scientist's whole practical outlook on life and to give him his goals. In the degree that he understands the teachings of Science and follows them, he finds restlessness giving way to the firm purpose of demonstrating more of divine Truth, which includes all harmony. As he gains a sense of spiritual enrichment, the feeling of the emptiness of life tends to fade away. Boredom gives way to a living desire to bless others, self-indulgence to the satisfaction that comes from unselfishness. He gains a more positive sense of meaning in life.

The rationale of this way of life has a significance not only for the individual but also for national stability. There is a serious question whether a popular mood of uncertainty, doubt, and expediency would be strong enough to cope with the fanatical purposefulness of communism. Can these conditions of thought galvanize the free world into concerted action and an unyielding stand against totalitarian encroachments? Can they win the allegiance of the uncommitted peoples?

We face in the Communist movement a philosophy which deals in absolutes, of a sort. As a fully developed system of scientific materialism, it purports to be strictly scientific in its analysis of man, social progress, and the laws of nature. With implacable fanaticism it rules out every vestige of spiritual values, every trace of objective moral law. On the basis of its absolute tenets of sheer and unrelieved materialism, the Communist world has embarked with grim determination on a program of conditioning its own people and trying to impose its system on the rest of mankind. It has made considerable headway among the uncommitted peoples of the earth—and probably not so much by physical force, or even intrigue, as by the naked force of its radical ideas. When ideas with a definite aim are propelled into a mental atmosphere of frustration and confusion, apathy and doubt, they are apt to have a tremendous impact even when they are wrong.

In the face of such a challenge we are finding that material defenses are not enough. We have rallied vast resources of money, technology, diplomacy. But these have not ended the menace of communism's crusade, particularly among uncommitted peoples. The deepest issues are in the realm of ideas.

It is the force of ideas deeply felt that makes men willing to sacrifice for a cause. Only a sense of meaning in life can rally the full resources of the human spirit. It is deep convictions regarding the nature of man, of truth, of the origin of human rights and the nature of human destiny that move men and nations to superhuman achievements. To interpret the great victories of the past as motivated simply by greed or poverty, ambition or self-preservation or economic pressures, would be to misread history.

And so today, a sense of meaning, based on spiritual certainty, can help to galvanize the free world with direction and purpose. This can come only through deep and awakening insights into that eternal Truth, whose influence has lifted the Western world out of the sludge of endless poverty and ignorance. The human values of freedom and justice, duty and honor, self-discipline and respect for the integrity of individual man, have their ultimate source in absolute Truth.

As the Christian Scientist sees it, the immortal purpose of man is to bear witness to his Maker: to show forth the nature of Life, Truth, and Love, thus demonstrating through spiritual power man's God-given dominion over all things. The Scientist feels that the understanding of man's spiritual status and relationship to God illumines one's life with new possibilities. It brings a new sense of meaning in life—and it can inspire a nation.

4.

On all sides the individual today is pressured by forces which would tell him what to think, how to act, what he wants, what kind of person he should be. This is an age of mass influences: mass culture, mass conformity, mass hysteria, mass opinions, mass trends. Like breakers washing the beach, demolishing the sand fortress shaped by a child's hands, the currents of mass thought claim the power to demolish the fortress of individual mental privacy.

The language of our day is studded with terms referring to invasion of the individual's mental home and the manipulation of his thoughts: hidden persuaders, motivational research, conditioning of thought, climate of consent, thought-control techniques, power of suggestion.

The model teenager who suddenly kills somebody, the housewife tortured by unexplainable chronic terror, the nation lulled into apathy and a hazy sense of security in the midst of mortal danger—all of these may reflect influences in the general atmosphere of human thought of which the victims are scarcely aware. There is just as much need today for the individual to know how to defend himself from harmful mental influences as there is for defense of the body against the contagion of a plague.

More than the average person realizes, his tastes, interests, and outlook are shaped by tides of public thought. Techniques for influencing thought have found their way into the fields of advertising, public relations, and propaganda. Like the infant who unthinkingly swallows the Pablum spooned into his mouth, many young people and adults unconsciously accept the standards set for them by the mass media and by other group pressures in our civilization. Though much of advertising and public relations activity is constructive, nevertheless it is also true that people today are subjected to incessant suggestion on behalf of self-indulgence, sex, status-seeking, greed, tawdry morals. Millions of people, saturated with this atmosphere, scarcely dream that things could be any other way and hardly know what it would be like to get a breath of the fresh air of spiritual beauty, pure affection, clear inspiration, genuine peace.

In a world equipped for rapid communication, drawn together by social pressures, swept by massive crosscurrents of thought, how can the individual preserve his mental integrity and freedom? What are his means of defense from thought-manipulation?

For an answer the Christian Scientist turns to the understanding of man's real individuality, which is derived from God and cannot be invaded, as it is defended and upheld by spiritual law. This law is the divine will, or force, which holds man's real self in proper relationship to divine Mind, its source. Through Science, one learns how it is possible to avail himself of this law and thus to defend himself from the silent mental influences so prevalent today. He avails himself of this law through prayer.

The Scientist bases such prayer on the great fundamentals which underlie all prayer in Christian Science. These include: the everpresence and all-power of God, perfect Mind; the consequent nothingness of evil in any guise; the perfection of man's individual consciousness as God's spiritual likeness; the fact that in all-inclusive divine Mind there is no transfer of evil thoughts or motives, and that such thoughts have no real power, attraction or control over man.

These are fundamentals. But it may be helpful to be a little more specific.

One finds that an essential element of those particular forms of mental influence described above, for example, is that they seek to appeal to something within the individual. This is especially evident in those types of advertising which are based on psychological research. Often the effort is to appeal to greed, vanity, fear, competitiveness, jealousy, desire for prestige, or repressed urges in the potential customer.

Back of such appeals is the widely accepted theory of Freudian psychologists that most of human thought is unconscious; that below the surface of human personality is a substratum of fears, drives, desires, instincts; and that the individual is largely responsive to impulses which arise in this unconscious, or subconscious, realm. Consequently these appeals are designed to manipulate unconscious emotions and desires.

In this connection it is interesting to note that Mrs. Eddy long ago applied the phrase *animal magnetism,* as a generic term, to all the myriad forms of aggressive mental influence. In view of some of the techniques of influence being used today, her use of the term was strangely prophetic; for these techniques are designed to exert a magnetic attraction on certain animal elements commonly attributed to human nature.

The point involved here is fundamental in the Christian Scientist's defense against mental invasion. While aggressive mental influences may appeal to unconscious (or conscious) material desires and motives, one learns through exploring Science that the real individuality of man includes no animal elements but is purely spiritual. He finds also that pernicious influences or temptations cannot touch those qualities of thinking which have their source in Spirit, God, Mind. Consequently one's defense lies in becoming aware of man's real individuality, and in bringing one's thoughts into harmony with it. Since the real individuality of man is derived from Spirit, not matter, its basic elements can only be spiritual and not material or animal. Man's real self, the image of God, is not the servant of unconscious desires and instincts; man truly has dominion over himself because his whole being is governed by spiritual law. His native attraction is to Spirit, not matter.

On the basis of this understanding, one can learn to reject as actually unreal and illusory such motives as greed, fear, pride, and so on—however real they may seem to human knowledge —and to replace them with unselfishness, expectancy of good, and a standard of values in which pride and jealousy have no place. This method of defense involves cultivating the spiritual qualities, which constitute man's immortal God-given nature: love, joy, truthfulness, purity, intelligence, honesty, and other qualities exemplified by Christ Jesus. It calls for examining one's thoughts and motives, analyzing them, to see where they come from, what is their nature, and where they lead. Whatever is deceptive, dishonest, or lustful is to be rejected as inherently worthless and powerless; whatever tends to bring to light man's spiritual nature, and to turn one's thoughts toward God as the source of all good, is to be accepted and cultivated as real and valid.

To illustrate, let us take a very simple example. Much of the liquor advertising today suggests that drinking brings social prestige and business success, relaxation and fellowship—to name just a few of the appeals. Often the suggestion is subtle and indirect. A pretty girl and her escort may be shown by a waterfall or in some other scene suggesting refreshment and leisure. Persons may be shown drinking in the setting of a swanky business men's club, or on the terrace of a rich suburban home. The effort is to create an "image" of drinking as refreshing, smart, socially respectable.

The Scientist would tend to view such an advertisement with much skepticism. To begin with, it is contradicted by the whole system of spiritual values to which he gives his allegiance. He considers legitimate prestige and success to be the outcome of genuine worth of character, and this he finds to be inherent in the spiritual nature of man. For refreshment and fellowship his religion admonishes him to look to the graces of Spirit: inspiration, spontaneity, unselfishness, a genuine interest in others—spiritual freedom. From his point of view, the commercialized appeal of drinking is essentially deceptive, and he would reject it.

This is not to imply that all advertising is suggestive. Nor is it to imply that a Christian Scientist feels he would automatically be able to spot any hidden appeal contained in any ad or elsewhere. But it does mean that one actively studying this religion—practicing the scientific method of reliance on divine law, learning how to weigh thoughts and motives, striving to cultivate spiritual desires in place of greed, vanity, fear, selfishness, or animality—has available to him an effective method of defense against deceptive appeals. His only need is to use it intelligently and conscientiously. To the extent that he genuinely replaces greed with unselfishness, vanity with humility, fear with confidence, animality with spirituality—utilizing the laws of Science—he finds he can avail himself of a mental fortress impregnable to the enticements of hidden persuaders.

Present-day practices also impose on the individual a great need for mental and spiritual defense in regard to his health and well-being. Aggressive "health" propaganda, too often purveying sheer and unadulterated fear, depicts various maladies and dins into the ears of the citizen, "You may be next!" Vivid pictures of disease—painted in words in popular magazines, broadcast over the airwaves, or thrown on the screen in movies for schoolchildren—tend to promote the consciousness of disease and thus cultivate the mental soil in which fear and disease flourish. As the Christian Scientist sees it, an effective spiritual defense calls for a recognition of man's true nature in the image of God, sustained and protected by the divine Life, in which there is no disease nor death. Here one finds the possibility of gaining a scientific consciousness of health and Life, which antidotes fear and disease.

There are many forms of mental influence at work in modern society more serious and more subtle than those cited above. But these relatively familiar examples serve to illustrate some of the more obvious techniques being used for getting past one's guard, and to indicate something of the Christian Scientist's method of defense through spiritualization of thought.

While it is true that no mental force can manipulate one's thoughts except as he allows it to enter, this question is not always decided at the level of conscious thought. Hence the need for the discernment that spiritual sense alone can give. As everyone knows, it is possible for one to take in, more or less unconsciously, a catch phrase or a tune; and the point is that it is also possible for him to take in a thought or a conclusion, if his mental home remains spiritually unguarded.

In utilizing the method of spiritual defense the Scientist endeavors to adopt the standard of the first commandment in accepting or rejecting the thoughts that come to his mental door. When one looks to God as the source of all good—refreshment, freedom, beauty, companionship, satisfaction, abundance, peace—he has a basis for testing the thoughts and motives that come to him, and he is not so likely to be duped. Insofar as the consciousness of the individual is filled with an awareness of man's real individuality as the image of God, it cannot be manipulated. What ensures protection to the individual is scientific reliance on divine law, as distinguished from merely well-intentioned good thoughts. Jesus referred to the fortress of spiritual consciousness when he said, shortly before his crucifixion, "The prince of this world cometh, and hath nothing in me" (John 14:30).

As the Scientist sees it, this method of spiritual defense has an application to the fraudulent ideological propaganda currently being used to sway the convictions of whole nations and peoples. The problem is generally recognized, in its more blatant aspects, but much more remains to be done before it is thoroughly dealt with. From the Christian Scientist's point of view, half the battle lies in being awake to what is going on, since apathy regarding such influences subjects one to their control.

The other half lies in actively using the techniques of spiritual defense. The telltale earmarks of aggressive mental suggestion—deception, dishonesty, appeals to selfishness, fear or hate—are apt to be noticeable wherever found. While correct information is necessary, and much more is involved in complete defense than anyone has yet achieved in demonstration, the Scientist is convinced that much protection for mankind is available in the insights which come through utilizing spiritual power scientifically.

Unquestionably there is a great deal to be done in order to neutralize the injustice and crime, fear and dishonesty which too often control the thinking of men. The Christian Scientist feels the effectual remedy goes back inevitably to religion. Materialistic theories of man have exposed human weaknesses, but have not provided the answer to them. The need is to go deeper than the frail human personality and find refuge in man's spiritual self, which is never the medium of evil thoughts. This real self, like the image in the mirror, reflects without deviation the exact nature of its source, God.

The power of spiritual resources in defending one's thinking was tested to a limited extent in the brain-washing of American prisoners of war held by the Chinese Communists in Korea. According to subsequent testimony by a number of witnesses before a Congressional committee, those soldiers who had a deep religious faith weathered the test better than those who did not.

It is interesting to note that the ingredients of spiritual defense are indicated in the Scriptures, as illustrated in this passage from Ephesians:

Take unto you the whole armour of God, that ye may be able to withstand in the evil day, and having done all, to stand. Stand therefore, having your loins girt about with truth, and having on the breastplate of righteousness; And your feet shod with the preparation of the gospel of peace; Above all, taking the shield of faith, wherewith ye shall be able to quench all the fiery darts of the wicked. And take the helmet of salvation, and the sword of the Spirit, which is the word of God (Eph. 6:13-17).

5.

A tremendous amount of attention is being given today to the dissection and analysis of the human personality. While more time and talent are being devoted to mental health than ever before, the prevalence of mental and emotional distress bears witness to the multiplied pressures of present-day living and the great need for effective relief.

From the viewpoint of the Christian Scientist, the problem of mental health, like so many others characteristic of our era, comes back to religion. Often the patient yearns for something higher, deeper, purer, and more powerful than the resources of the unaided human personality. The deepest troubles of the human heart can best be removed by the healing balm derived from divine Love. These yield to the strengthening and enlightening awareness of God's nature and presence as Love, and of man's relationship to Him, as healings in Christian Science amply prove.

There is a profound and striking contrast between the fundamental assumptions of psychiatry and those of Christian Science in approaching the problems of mental health, a contrast so fundamental it is worth pointing out.

Psychiatry accepts the view that the human personality is rooted in brain and body, and largely composed of unconscious mental elements. Very briefly and broadly speaking, the method employed in psychotherapy is that of analyzing the patient's statements and behavior in an effort to identify the elements in the subterranean recesses of his mind—those fears, desires, drives, and conflicts which are causing trouble. While it is sometimes deemed possible to remove them, more often the aim is simply to bring them under control. The underlying assumption often is that they are and will remain part of the patient's nature. Often the therapy involves explaining their presence to the patient, helping him to accept them as part of himself, and then guiding and counseling him so as to help him rebuild his personality and outlook around them in terms that bring a more satisfactory adjustment. The center of attention is frequently the abnormality. In fact, psychologists themselves have sometimes complained that too much attention is given by their profession to investigating the abnormal and too little to the normal.

The approach of the Christian Scientist is quite different. As is true even from the viewpoint of psychiatry, it is often the deficiencies of the human personality that bring trouble: its lacks, cravings, fears, frustrations, inadequacies, feelings of inferiority, or what the theologian might term the inner void of mortal man. The approach of the Christian Scientist is that what fills the void is the recognition of man's spiritual status as the upright, complete, whole, abundantly blessed beneficiary of divine Love.

The Christian Scientist always starts with the goodness and all-power of God and the perfection of man as His likeness, no less in the case of psychic distress than in instances of physical illness. From his viewpoint traumatic experiences, fears, obsessions, conflicts, are no real part of man's genuine individuality.

The therapy employed in Science therefore consists of finding out what belongs to the patient's true and genuine God-given nature. Science stresses what is divinely right with him, not what is wrong. Thus the Scientist strives to bring to light the integrity, strength, purity, goodness, and perfection of man's real individuality as the reflection of God. He endeavors to understand these and make them uppermost in his living and thinking. He finds that these God-given elements of character have power, since they are derived from God and express spiritual law; and he reasons that therefore the negative and trouble-causing elements of the carnal mind have no genuine power over him. His aim is to demonstrate the fact that these negative elements cannot control him when he identifies himself with the divine Mind as its idea, utilizes demonstrable spiritual law, and thus relies scientifically on God.

The Christian Scientist shares with many others, including many in psychotherapy, the emphasis on love as a healing influence. But he would not think of love as only a human emotion. He would seek to trace human expressions of compassion and love to their pure, divine source, divine Love, and would view them as embodying a healing influence insofar as they mirror this Love. Since the power of divine Love is irresistible, he would attribute vast possibilities to the scientific understanding and utilization of this spiritual power, and the expression of it in compassion, comfort, a genuine interest in and valuing of the individual.

The Scientist also would endeavor to see deeper than the perversities of mortal personality and to gain a conscious awareness of the individual's real selfhood: satisfied, complete, at peace, governed harmoniously, motivated by Love, untouched by frustration, trauma, conflict, thwarted desires, or feelings of inferiority.

The experience thus far in dealing with problems of mental health through Christian Science confirms the fact that this approach tends to develop and strengthen whatever is good in one's human makeup and to dissipate whatever is bad.

Let us take a very rudimentary example. The contrast in basic approach between Christian Science and psychiatry is illustrated by the case of a college student in which both methods had an opportunity to play their respective parts.

The girl was a freshman at a state teachers' training college, serving a populous area, whose student body had presented numerous moral problems of various kinds. Though her past misdeeds were unknown to the college authorities, this particular girl had been found guilty of thefts during her senior year in high school, and subsequently had been expelled for stealing from the summer camp where she was serving as a counselor.

From the start of her freshman year at college, thefts began taking place in the dormitory where she lived. The thefts of money followed a pattern: a student's wallet would disappear; suddenly it would turn up on a staircase or coffee table, robbed of its contents. The incidents grew more flagrant and frequent until they were occurring two or three times a week.

Circumstances pointed toward this girl as the culprit, but the college authorities were unable to get any positive evidence of her guilt. This was a severe handicap: the state laws governing the college were such that the authorities dared not confront a student with a direct accusation in the absence of convincing evidence. To have done so would have made them liable to lawsuit by the parents. As a result of this situation, it had been a very rare thing for any student ever to confess to stealing, though numerous thefts had occurred over the years and had been probed by local and state police.

The girl was interviewed by a faculty member who was a registered psychiatrist. He tried everything he could think of to find a soft spot in her implacable resistance but he was unsuccessful. She stuck defiantly to her alibis.

Meantime a new housemother had taken over the dormitory; a young woman in her first year in this kind of work, whose responsibility covered three hundred girls. She was untrained in psychology, but she was a Christian Scientist. While naturally she could not pray for the girl without the latter's consent, she could and did pray for herself and for the welfare of the dormitory as a whole. In working with the girl she sought divine direction and relied upon the insights and intuition gained through her religion.

The situation came to a head the night before Thanksgiving, when a student's sweater disappeared. Again the circumstances pointed toward the girl, but nothing could be proved: the sweater was located by an investigating student counselor in the bottom of the guilty girl's suitcase, but while the counselor was downstairs reporting this to the housemother, the girl, who had come back to her room and evidently sensed danger, removed it and left it hanging innocently in the community bathroom.

Learning that it had been found there, the housemother called the girl to her office and asked if there was anything worrying her that she wanted to tell. For some fifteen minutes the housemother talked to her, necessarily avoiding any accusation, direct or implied, but the girl refused to talk. At last the housemother fell quiet and began praying silently. Finally it came to her to tell the girl that she knew a sweater had been stolen, that she had a pretty good idea where it had been, and that her motive in talking with her was not to stand in judgment or to get her thrown out of school, but simply to help her to become a teacher. But the girl still sat mute and defiant.

At this point the housemother unavoidably had to leave to attend a meeting. As she did so she was impelled to ask the girl if she felt honesty was a quality necessary for a schoolteacher. Still no reply. Then the housemother said: "I want you to do something for me. I want you to go to your room and write down for me everything you know about honesty—what your concept of honesty is. If you think it is important for a school-teacher, I want you to write down why. I'll be back in an hour and I want you to bring me your notes."

The girl obeyed and filled two sheets of paper, which she then brought to the housemother. The housemother read what she had written, and they discussed it point by point. Then she asked the girl again if there was anything she wanted to tell. At this point the girl suddenly broke down. She confessed to stealing the sweater, and gave a complete catalogue of her other thefts. A long conversation followed, in which the girl told the housemother about her background, her family, why she wanted to be a teacher, and so on. The housemother was able to help her in connection with problems in her relationship with her parents, and to discuss with her the various qualities, including honesty, which are necessary for success as a teacher. She did not reproach the girl, but—as the girl herself later acknowledged—she made it clear that she had genuine confidence in the girl's innate character, and that she felt she was a worth-while individual.

While it would be too much to say there was perfect reformation at once, there was a drastic change in the girl's whole attitude and outlook. When she returned to school after the holiday, she brought the housemother a sum of money covering all her thefts from the dormitory. Her conduct improved so radically that she was able to continue attending the college. She became cooperative and worked closely with the housemother. She began developing new interests and new life; she was a changed girl. Many months later, after the housemother had left to go to Europe, the girl wrote her a note, which the house-mother described as "the most wonderful letter I ever had from anyone." The girl expressed her appreciation for all the help given her, and especially for the understanding approach of the housemother. She stressed that what meant so much to her was that the housemother had expected good of her.

Now, the telling of this incident is not to suggest that the girl's reformation was accomplished through Christian Science treatment, since she knew nothing of Science and was not having such treatment. But what broke the impasse was the housemother's appeal to her innate sense of honesty. All efforts based on centering attention on her stealing encountered defiant resistance; it was only when her thoughts were turned away from dishonesty to the contemplation of what honesty is that the problem was resolved and the girl reformed.

Of course a somewhat similar approach might have been used by a therapist of some other school of thought. Yet this simple example does serve to illustrate a basic point in the Christian Science approach: not to center attention on the aberration, but to bring to light the qualities belonging to the patient's genuine and properly integrated individuality as the offspring of deific Mind.

The Scientist proceeds on the basis that man's pure spiritual individuality is good because God is good; that it manifests not disorder but the perfect order of divine law; that it is not composed of negative traits or of conflicting elements to be described by such terms as "superego" and "id," but is the image of God—whole, complete, its integrity forever intact because it expresses divine Truth.

6.

The way in which the housemother dealt with this problem gives a hint of the approach which Christian Science brings to moral questions.

Many religions have set forth moral standards and called on people to observe them. The failure of mankind to meet the standards often has evoked moral judgments and led to a view of men as basically sinners. The resultant burden of guilt and fear in human thought has often been heavy.

Today we are witnessing a strong reaction: skepticism has undermined the authority given religion; people have tended to rebel against established ethical standards. Some thinkers in the social sciences—notably in psychology, sociology, and anthropology—have questioned the existence of objective ethical values and tended to picture moral codes as the product of social environment, custom, and group living.

From the viewpoint of the Christian Scientist, however, the solution does not lie either in viewing men as sinners or in reducing moral standards to a merely relative level. It lies in showing the individual that he can meet the demands of honesty, humanity, compassion, temperance, because it is in accord with his real nature to do so. This involves freeing him, through prayer, from the hypnotic domination of dishonesty, hate, lust, fear, or whatever form depravity may take. As the Scientist sees it, the basis for doing this is the spiritual perception and understanding that man, as God's image or expression, is not fundamentally a sinner; his real nature, though faintly seen by mortals, is characterized by purity, wisdom, uprightness, spiritual power, spiritual goodness. In other words, the solution as seen in Christian Science lies in healing: regeneration of character through spiritual power.

In the last analysis, one's concept of morality goes back to his concept of man, as well as of God. In a rigidly materialistic view of man, the concept of objective right and wrong becomes largely irrelevant; conscience becomes simply a set of acquired inhibitions and man himself is interpreted as a product of processes of matter which are basically amoral. The acceptance of such a concept of man tends to rob human beings of any sense of a relationship to God. In the resulting vacuum of faith, many have been left without authority, without moral commitment, and without any basis for a system of morals except social expediency.

Many have deplored the present condition of our moral climate. For example, Dean Robert E. Fitch of the Pacific School of Religion in Berkeley, California, wrote in *Christianity and Crisis*:

We live in an age when ethics is becoming obsolete. It is superseded by science, deleted by psychology, dismissed as emotive by philosophy: it is drowned in compassion, evaporated into aesthetics and retreats before relativism. . . . The usual moral distinctions are simply drowned in a maudlin emotion in which we have more feeling for the murderer than for the murdered, for the adulterer than for the betrayed, and in which we gradually begin to believe that the really guilty party, the one who somehow caused it all, is the victim, not the perpetrator, of the crime.

Many factors enter the moral fuzziness Dr. Fitch is talking about. But in some measure is it not traceable to the moral relativism which inevitably stems from materialistic theories of man? The logical conclusion to which relativism leads is indicated in the following words of Mortimer J. Adler, director of the Institute for Philosophical Research in San Francisco:

Our college students are taught in anthropology or sociology—most professors of social science are moral skeptics—that there are no objective principles in morality, that there is no way to establish what is right or wrong. If a tribe practices cannibalism, it is wrong by *our* standards, but not by the tribe's standards. So they leave college with the view that all morals are a matter of opinion.

The end result of this moral relativism tends to be pure subjectivism: nothing to worship and cherish and satisfy but the self. This underlying approach is often reflected unconsciously by the politician or businessman who subordinates honesty to the question "What's in it for me?" and in the too-common excuse for dishonest practices "Well, everybody's doing it."

It is a question whether an anarchic moral climate can provide a solid-enough foundation for a free society seeking to endure the rigors of the modern world. A moral order based on selfishness or on mere accommodation for group living hardly would provide a dynamic system of ethics for a free people.

But from the viewpoint of the Christian Scientist, materialistic explanations of man do not tell the whole story of human experience. Plainly, experience includes much that cannot be traced to matter-processes. As the Scientist sees it, human experience is the point where the true spiritual nature of man, and its exact reverse—the carnal mind's misconception of man—

seem (to mortal view) to be conjoined as the consciousness of the individual.

A sharp line of demarcation actually exists between the two: one never becomes the other. But like the tares and wheat of which Christ Jesus spoke, the two *appear* to mingle "until the harvest"—that is, until the *nothingness* of the mortal elements is recognized and the unbroken wholeness of man's God-given individuality, forever intact and untainted, is demonstrated.

It may be freely admitted that according to a materialistic view, man is largely irrational, amoral, influenced by unconscious impulses. But all Christians would agree that such a definition of man is far too narrow to describe human nature. Human beings hear, however dimly, the promptings of spiritual Truth. Intuition, inspiration, aspiration, moral courage, self-sacrifice, compassion, honesty, purity, love, and spiritual understanding all bear witness to this fact.

There is a divine impulsion at work in human consciousness, which the Scientist understands to be the everpresent and incorporeal Christ, Truth. To this divine influence, as he sees it, can be traced the strength of moral fiber, the ingredients of awakened conscience, which make civilized society possible. It is a divine impulsion, however misunderstood or faintly felt, which leads a human being to a higher sense of what is morally right and makes him want to obey it. It is a divine influence which lifts human thought above the sod and awakens the individual to discern man's real self, which is spiritual.

So far as Christendom is concerned, this divine influence is articulated in the basic guides for human conduct given in the Bible: the Ten Commandments and the Sermon on the Mount, including the two commandments on which Christ Jesus said hang all the law and the prophets—to love the one God with all one's heart and soul and mind and strength, and to love one's neighbor as oneself.

The unique insight of Christian Science is that it shows that these great rules belong intrinsically to a spiritual Science; and that consequently they are demonstrable in human experience, in the degree that this Science is understood. While complete fulfillment of the high moral demands of Christ Jesus may be beyond our immediate human capacities, this Science shows that exact conformity to God's nature is natural to man's spiritual individuality. As one recognizes and understands this Truth, the irrational impulses of the carnal mind little by little drop away, and the real spiritual individuality of man shines through.

In other words, the Scientist finds here a basis for human goals and human conduct—hence, for morality—diametrically opposed to material premises. He views the underlying nature of man not as animal but as spiritual; not as organism but as conscious idea; not as amoral but as expressing the divine character.

In the view of the Christian Scientist, human consciousness needs to be spiritualized through the worship of one infinite God, good, and a deepening understanding of Him. This brings to human apprehension the concept of universal spiritual law. As the Scientist sees it, the possibilities for human progress are unlimited when a correct understanding of the universal God, Spirit, is made the basis of thought and action.

In the words of Mrs. Eddy:

One infinite God, good, unifies men and nations; constitutes the brotherhood of man; ends wars; fulfills the Scripture "Love thy neighbor as thyself"; annihilates pagan and Christian idolatry— whatever is wrong in social, civil, criminal, political, and religious codes; equalizes the sexes; annuls the curse on man, and leaves nothing that can sin, suffer, be punished or destroyed (S&H 340:23- 29).

7.

The thinking of mankind has been saturated for thousands of years with a sense of guilt. But the teachings of Christ, as interpreted by the Science of Christianity, bring the liberating revelation of man's pure innocence as the likeness of God.

Guilt and shame are the essence of the story of Adam and

Eve, for it is thus that the Bible depicts in allegory these deep-rooted elements in the nature of mortals. Traditional theological interpretations have centered quite largely around this theme; but despite the modern rebellion against them, the sense of guilt persists in old and new forms.

Some feel a sense of guilt because of the hideous weapons of mass destruction we have fashioned and the manifest danger we will use them; some because of inflamed racial hatreds; others because of prevalent or personal transgressions of morals. There is a sense of guilt some feel because they do not know what life means or what is expected of them. Guilt feeds on individual frustrations and collective failures. It is a deep-seated part of the mess the world is in.

But one finds in the Science of Christianity a new appraisal of the tragedy of the human condition, based on the Christian revelation of man's spiritual birthright of innocence and his unbroken relationship to his Maker. This explanation removes the barrier between men and their eternal Father and ends the estrangement. Thus it provides a new insight in religion.

It also provides a new standpoint for the psychologist. Comparing the asceticism of the Protestant ethic with the approach of modern psychiatry, the sociologist Philip Rieff has written: "The task of the clergy was to make the sinner hopefully aware of his sin; the task of the analyst is to make the neurotic therapeutically aware of his neurosis." It might be added that the task of Christian Science is to make the individual scientifically aware of his real self, in which there is neither sin nor neurosis, as the son of God, and thus lift him out of his bondage.

The lesson is epitomized in the greatest of parables, Christ Jesus' story of the Prodigal Son.

> *The younger son gathered all together, and took his journey into a far country, and there wasted his substance with riotous living* (Luke 15:13).

The scene of the transgressions was not his native land. It was a "far country" where he never really belonged.

One learns in the Science of Spirit that the flesh was never man's native land. The material conception of man, the mortal delusion or dream, appears to stand side by side in human consciousness with the genuine selfhood of man, and to hide it. But the flesh is only a "far country." The carnal mind's misconception of man as fleshly, sinful, guilty is never genuine.

Paul referred to the perishable material concept, and to the eternal reality of man, when he said: "For we know that if our earthly house of this tabernacle were dissolved, we have a building of God, an house not made with hands, eternal in the heavens" (II Cor. 5:1).

As the Christian Scientist sees it, the Biblical fall of man is but a means of depicting the carnal mind's misconception of man, which was an illusion from the beginning. It never really happened to the real man, our own true nature, the pure and innocent image of God.

> When he came to himself, he said, . . . I will arise
> and go to my father. . . . (Luke 15:17,18)

The very phrase implies an awakening from a deluded mental state: he *came to himself*. He turned from sin, tired of its punishment. He arose: lifted up his thinking, and turned again to his Father.

Every human being needs to come to himself: to repudiate the delusive mortal misconception which masquerades as man—to remember his divine origin, see that his true self never was sunken in the sins of the flesh, to recognize as his own real self the true man, the sinless and unfallen image of his Maker. Then he can assert his freedom in the name of Almighty God.

This is the Christian warfare of putting off the old man and putting on the new. It is being "born again."

> When he was yet a great way off, his father saw him,
> and had compassion, and ran, and fell on his neck, and
> kissed him (Luke 15:20).

There are some who feel so keenly a sense of guilt that they conclude they are not worthy of God's grace; that they merit only punishment and not His goodness. Some feel that since they have long ignored Him, they cannot justly expect His help, or even ask it, in time of trouble.

The Prodigal had to take the first step: to turn away from the husks and swine. But then the father saw him, *when he was yet a great way off,* and ran to meet him.

The revelation of Christ came to a world "a great way off" from spiritual things. Humanity was caught in the toils of sin and hate. But Christ's radiant message of Love outshone the evil in the world. All through the Bible the promise of redemption is given to the wayward nation, the lost sheep, those whose sins are as scarlet but who are willing to turn again to the Father.

The redeeming power of Christ is for all humanity—and for the humblest sinner. It is universal law and universal in its Science. It is not merely for some kinds of transgressions while excluding others; it is not just for some colors of skin while excluding others; not for some social classes while excluding others. It comes to awaken every repentant and receptive heart—however guilty, however wounded—to the purity and glory of man's real being. It is as universal as divine Love itself, and its rays of light steal into the very dungeons of human experience. We have only to open our eyes and let in the light.

The Prodigal's deliverance was not delayed. The father *ran* to meet him. There is no delay in the redeeming action of divine Love. There is no endless wait for a final Day of Judgment; the day of judgment comes each hour and each moment, with each thought and act. God's compassionate love awaits only our willingness to turn away from the riotous living and husks and swine, turn from the fleshly misconception of man which never really was the "I" or the "you." God's love for man perpetually invites us to enter into our heritage as the sons of God.

Even in the depths of mortal guilt we can awaken and feel the presence of the redeeming Christ. Mrs. Eddy writes: "Remember, thou canst be brought into no condition, be it ever so severe, where Love has not been before thee and where its tender lesson is not awaiting thee. Therefore despair not nor mur-

mur, for that which seeketh to save, to heal, and to deliver, will guide thee, if thou seekest this guidance" (My. 149:31-34).

The parable tells us that the son was repentant:

> Father, I have sinned against heaven, and in thy sight, and am no more worthy to be called thy son (Luke 15:21).

But his statement of guilt did not find the confirmation he expected. The father did not view him as a sinner; he called for "the best robe," a ring for his hand, and shoes for his feet. "Let us eat, and be merry: For this my son was dead, and is alive again; he was lost, and is found" (Luke 15:23,24).

It was the son who had come home; the false self, that which had gone into a "far country" and sinned, had perished in the repentance and suffering when the son "came to himself." It had been left with the abandoned husks and swine.

The parable does not end with the son's confession of guilt. If it ended there, or with a confirmation of the guilt by the father, the whole point of the story would be different. But the father repudiates the condemnation and guilt. Here is the affirmation that our heavenly Father looks upon us as sons, and that we should awaken to this true concept of ourselves, right here and right now.

Sin never touched the real self, the man of God's creating, our own real individuality and being. It is spotless, guiltless, blameless. How could the true likeness of a perfect Father be a wayward sinner? How could infinite widom and Love so lose control of its own creation as to permit man to sin and thus be lost?

To the unillumined human view, the tares and wheat grow together until harvest. But Christ Jesus said the harvest is not in the future but now. It is whenever we are ready to repudiate the misconception, which God never made, reject it as unreal, and enter into the recognition and acknowledgment of man's pure, innocent, faultless selfhood in the image of God.

In the words of Mrs. Eddy: "There are not two realities of being, two opposite states of existence. One should appear real to us, and the other unreal, or we lose the Science of being."

And on the same page: "The more I understand true human-hood, the more I see it to be sinless—as ignorant of sin as is the perfect Maker" (Un. 49:17).

Through this revelation of perfect God and perfect spiritual man in His likeness, Christian Science sheds new light on the problems of humanity and brings new hope and faith to human hearts.

A Christian Scientist's Life

By *Erwin D. Canham*

I. A MAINE CHILDHOOD

The only purpose of these autobiographical pages is to tell something of what Christian Science can mean to an individual. I must apologize for the "I's." In candor, and in hope of helping others, I am engaging in a degree of self-exposure which I find more than a little uncomfortable. I hope the reader understands the motive.

My life has been very happy. Childhood environment, educational opportunities, job, family—these things seem to me, at least, to have fitted together into a pattern of significance, fulfillment, utility. I am intensely grateful for all the life experiences that have come to me, and for the way they have come. It's a great thing to have a sense of meaning in one's life, and that, in the tightest of nutshells, is what Christian Science has given me.

I was born in Auburn, Maine, on February 13, 1904, an only child. My parents were in very modest circumstances. My father worked chiefly as a printer, part-time farmer, and newspaperman. He was born in a little Maine village, the son of immigrant English parents. My mother was born and brought up on a Maine farm. I'm looking now at a faded, stained photograph of twenty-six tousled, unruly children whom she taught at the Fisher school in Webster before she was married. I have her bell, and pointer. My father's father was a weaver in the woolen mills, and my mother's father ran a farm and earned money by building brick chimneys. They were handsome chimneys, with tops a little like a Grecian urn, and you can sometimes see one still in the Maine countryside.

I get very sentimental about the way of life in which I was born and brought up. We lived very simply, on farm, in village, and in small city. There were many ties with the nineteenth century and ways of doing and looking at things that had prevailed in Maine since the early settlers.

My maternal grandparents came from pioneer stock. Their shed attic was crammed with handlooms, spinning wheels, cards, teazles, and many of the other tools of a handicraft age. These wooden, Yankee-craftsman gadgets had a clean smell, and I loved to play with them.

Electricity and running water came to our house only when I was in my teens. I helped my father and grandfather cut firewood and timber in the forests in the winter, and make hay— and many another crop—in the summer. I can milk a cow, plant a crop, stow a load of hay, harness a horse. Until I was five or six years old, I kept count of the number of automobiles I had ever seen. They could be numbered on my fingers. We did not get our own car, a used Model T Ford, until I was thirteen.

My parents and grandparents were wonderful people. With the perspective of time and distance I think so more than ever. We were always a very closely knit family circle, sharing joys and problems. During my early childhood, both my father and mother were employed on a newspaper. I was frequently left with my maternal grandparents. My grandfather read a great deal, but he liked to be read to, and so as soon as I could read fluently (I learned to read before I was four) he would get me to read to him, sitting in their farm kitchen. The big Glenwood range was very cozy, my indulgent and fiercely loyal grandmother would be making apple pies, molasses cookies, or cream-of-tartar biscuits, or churning her cream and patting into golden squares the butter she made and sold to city folks who knew a good thing. I enjoyed it all, and learned a good deal of homely wisdom and love.

During this early period, on Saturdays and in school-vacation time, my parents would take me with them when they went as news reporters to other small towns within a radius of thirty or forty miles of Lewiston, Maine, to cover local events and write up country correspondence. I was an eager observer on these trips. I enjoyed the times we went by train or by interurban trolley, but I liked it best when we had to go by horse and buggy down the leafy, winding gravel roads. I can feel under my toes the first macadam that came to the roads in our part of Maine.

In September, 1908, when I was four and a half, I started in the first grade of the country school, a half mile from our farm-house. It was the Durgin School at Peppermint Corner, Lisbon —a typical one-room schoolhouse with twenty-odd pupils of varying ages. The teachers, who sometimes boarded at our house, seemed to me (then and now) to be paragons of charm and learning. In 1912, I was promoted to the sixth grade in grammar school at Lisbon Village, a mile away. In late 1912 my father was hired to revive a moribund weekly newspaper in the town of Sanford, Maine. His employers were a group of younger professional men who supported Theodore Roosevelt and the Bull Moose cause.

Even before we left Lisbon for Sanford, I had my first taste of personal newspaper work. Sometimes, when my father was gathering village items to send to the nearby daily, he would assign me to the telephone. I was about eight at the time. I would stand on a chair or box in front of the wall telephone, and call the best news sources in the neighborhood—the country spinsters—to inquire what was going on. They would tell me whose daughters were home for the weekend, and whose cows had calved. My father would whack out the items on his ancient Underwood typewriter. I remember standing in back of the typewriter, resting my hand on the carriage, and letting it ride back and forth. My father, like myself, typed with two or three fingers by the hunt-and-peck system.

In Sanford, however, I plunged with the family into full-fledged professionalism. The *Sanford News* came out on Thursdays, and usually had eight pages. The old flat-bed press would print only two pages at a time. On Wednesdays my father would feed the press the inside four pages, and I would fold them. On Thursdays he would print the outside four pages, I would fold them around the others, and take an armful out on the street to sell. As the radical voice of Theodore Roosevelt's progressivism, we were not very popular around the mill gates. More than once I was chased away by the mill guards as I tried to sell the papers there. But this soon wore off, and the *News* became respectable.

It was in Sanford, in 1914, that the turning point came in our lives. Up to that time, happy as we generally seemed to a child, our lives were not in focus. We were badly beset by illhealth. My father was frustrated and unsuccessful. My mother had had a difficult time in bringing me into the world. I was so troubled by diseases in my infancy, and so dosed with strong medicines, that my baby teeth dropped out prematurely. My mother was very often bedridden, weak, and suffering.

We had always been a very religious household, attending and working in the Methodist church. My father's father was a lay preacher, and both my parents were always active in church affairs. I went to Sunday school from infancy. My father's diaries, written while he was courting my mother at the turn of the century, make a simple and appealing picture of the place of religion and health in their young lives. Sometimes they went to church three times on a Sunday. Before the days of radio, television or movies there wasn't much else for decent young folks to do on the Sabbath.

But, the diaries also record, they were frequently down with ill-health and the respected family physician didn't help them a great deal. Of course, it was out of the question for their religion to have anything to do with their health! They wouldn't have dreamed of mixing the two, except perhaps in the most extreme cases.

Thus it was that our lives moved along in a kind of overcast. Life had its joys and contentments. There were moments of resignation, and sometimes perhaps a touch of desperation. But there was little sparkle, little clarity, little direction in the things we did and felt.

Then came the moment of threatening tragedy. My mother was suddenly afflicted with growths in her throat, some kind of ulcerous condition. The kind family doctor and friend could do nothing for her. His diagnosis was that she could not live through the day unless the obstruction broke. At this time my mother remembered a copy of *Science and Health with Key to the Scriptures,* by Mary Baker Eddy, which had been left in our home two or three years before by a woman who had done housework for us. She had glanced at it, and Christian Science had made an impact on her thought, but she had not looked into it carefully. She also remembered a Christian Scientist in Sanford. This friend gave us the name of a Christian Science practitioner living some seventy-five miles away in Boston. Thereupon the Christian Scientist friend telephoned the practitioner and asked him to give my mother Christian Science treatment. Within a few hours the growths broke and ran harmlessly away, and my mother fell asleep, fully healed.

It was as if sunlight had burst into our lives for the first time. The swift, miraculous nature of the healing bespoke a truth new and powerful to us. My mother was radiant with joy. She began an intensive study of Christian Science, and so did my father and I. We entered and became active in the Christian Science church in Sanford. There was a little local turmoil, since one of my father's leading backers in the newspaper was the physician who had been unable to help my mother, but this wise man realized, I believe, that a power greater than his medical knowledge had been at work. We had the joy, the freedom of persons released from bondage.

From that day forward, my life experience—and that of my parents—was one of unfoldment. Within a year my mother had made such swift strides in the study of Christian Science that she was able to take what is called class instruction: a course of careful, organized study with an experienced teacher of Christian Science, so that she could engage in healing work professionally. For the rest of her human life, she was deeply and joyfully engaged in bringing this liberating, curative, regenerative truth to others. Her patients were numerous, and the marvelous, seemingly miraculous cures that came about, were the source of unending challenge and gratitude. Though my mother passed on a decade ago, after forty years of healing service, I frequently meet and am deeply touched by persons who express to me their gratitude to her for having helped them through trials and into the sunshine. Her own dedication and love were unbounded.

My father's life took on similar focus. His professional opportunities as a newspaperman expanded. In 1915 he became the publisher of a biweekly in Gardiner, Maine, and a little later returned to his earliest daily newspaper connection, the *Lewiston Sun* (and afterward the *Lewiston Journal*), of which papers he became agricultural editor. Thus he combined an interest in farming, which fascinated him so much, and his newspaper profession. He, too, was active in Christian Science work. He was a very cheerful, friendly man. People from all over our part of Maine still speak of his genial interest in their well-being. He passed on nearly a decade before my mother, his life filled with the joys of work, of friendship, and of spiritual commitment.

II. BURSTING OUT IN COLLEGE

With Christian Science the great clarifying force in our experiences, my own life began to develop with similar expansiveness. When the time came for me to go into senior high school, we moved to the nearby city of Auburn, where I entered a fine, academically solid, old high school. My teachers were thoroughly experienced and rigorous, especially in Latin, in French, and in English. Only the other day (in 1961) I had a reunion with my Latin and my English teachers, and their quality was as evident in their gracious retirement as it had been in the classroom.

I didn't do particularly well in high school studies until the last few months. Perhaps my grammar school training had not been good enough, perhaps I had not learned to study, perhaps

I had not come of intellectual age. Certain it is that my mother was striving continually to waken me through Christian Science to a better application of my capacities. One avenue of awakening was unused. A friend and classmate—a most talented and sparkling lad—suggested we collaborate in writing the senior class play. Nobody had ever done so before. And so we set secretly to work, spending long winter evenings in each other's homes pounding out a three-act social drama, *The Middle Path,* devoted to the bitter labor struggles which were coming to a head in 1920-21. Then, as now, I was a believer in moderation. We preached this sermon in our play.

The fact that we had written a play at all astonished our classmates and teachers. They delightedly approved it as the senior play. It was produced, with much comment in the local papers and notoriety for the authors. The experience gave me a sense of new possibilities, of new horizons, and I looked forward eagerly to college.

Meantime, summers and some weekends, I had worked on the local newspaper. In the wartime winter of 1918, only fourteen years old, I was sometimes sent out on actual reportorial assignments, though very modest ones. When my elders returned from the war, I was hustled back to the composing room, where I worked as a galley boy, carrying the short "takes" of type from the linotypes to the assembling stones, running proofs, inserting corrections, and otherwise doing handiwork from 6 P.M. to 3 A.M. through the Maine summer nights. At the end of every month, the year-round, I had a job collecting advertising bills for the newspaper, and would trudge all over Lewiston and Auburn, dunning those who would not pay by mail. When they would pay me, as they did surprisingly often, I would receipt the bill and thrust the money into my pockets. I'm glad it always came out even when I got back to the office. I was paid twenty-five cents an hour. It seemed like a lot.

In 1921, when I entered Bates College in Lewiston, I had to take four entrance examinations in order to qualify, so indifferent had been my high school work. Once in college, the spiritual and intellectual ferment that had been happily boiling up in me began to take hold. At the end of the first semester, to my total astonishment, I found myself with all A's and on the dean's honor list. I kept at this level throughout my college years, finding increasing zest and stimulus in the work. Let any parents, or any young person who hasn't found his studious wings in high school, recall that there are such things as slow starters. Let them strive to bring out the basic intelligence and diligence, which are man's birthright. Let them seek to reflect some measure of divine intelligence in human thinking, as my mother and I consciously strove to do for me. The young person is apt to move into a happy rebirth of interest and understanding.

In the spring of 1921, just before I entered college, Bates had sent abroad the first team of American college debaters ever to appear in the Oxford Union Society. There was a great furor locally, and some national attention. In the spring of 1922, the Oxford Union Society announced it would return the visit to Bates in September, 1922, just as the college was opening. While still a freshman, I tried out and was selected to take part in the debate. We prepared in late summer, before my sophomore year had begun.

Thus on a warm September evening I found myself speaking, first for our side, after the opening polished Oxonian oration by the Hon. Edward Marjoribanks, Eton and Christ Church, heir presumptive to the 3rd Baron Tweedmouth. I was a pretty callow Maine farmboy. I had been outside the state only once or twice in my life. But our debating preparation was careful, our professor was a very skillful coach, and somehow the lessons I had learned in Christian Science gave me a sense of reliance not on my own rather limited human capacities but on the reflection of true intelligence from God.

With this kind of mental preparation, I was not taken aback when Mr. Marjoribanks (subsequently an eminent barrister) heckled me in the midst of my opening remarks. Such interruptions were contrary to the rules of American debating, so the audience's sympathies were altogether with me, although my teachers and friends were breathless at what I would do under such shocks. Governor Percival P. Baxter of Maine was in the chair and he graciously silenced Mr. Marjoribanks. I went on with a little apology for the misunderstanding between us, and the audience breathed an audible sigh of relief. We won the verdict of the eminent judges.

This kind of seasoning, which was matched many times in my college debating experiences—in 1925 I led a Bates team that debated at seven British universities—gave me invaluable maturity for the professional duties I was soon to undertake. The preparation of debates was most useful for later newspaper work. The marshaling and organizing of fact and reasoning which constituted debate helped greatly in organizing news and analytical articles. The verbal side of debate, the quick thinking required, the encounters under competitive pressure, aided me for many of the crises in newspaper life and in the public-service tasks to which I was later called.

My college days were one constant experience of growth and development which I could not have conceived a few years before. All this time, living mostly at home, close to my spiritual-minded parents, attending Sunday school and discussing the elements of Christian Science, seeking divine guidance at every human step along the way, I felt only the natural unfoldment of opportunity. My happy experiences at college were un-planned fulfillment of God's unlimited goodness. Neither then nor now have I habitually tried to peer into the future, or tried to plan for bigger jobs. All of the opportunities that have come have been unexpected and uncampaigned for in any personal sense. I have always been perfectly happy in today's job, never asking and aspiring about tomorrow's. I never dreamed in my youth or early professional days of the chances to serve that would come. My goals were very much more modest.

Yet I have always been willing to undertake new tasks, always ready in the last analysis to say "Yes, I can." This has not been from reliance on personal abilities, but from a sense of divine support, divine power available to all men. Not, of course, that I ever felt God had selected me for any particular task, but that God had given me, like all men, the opportunity to reflect and manifest in as great degree as my own understanding permitted

His own qualities of intelligence, integrity, wisdom, and love.

A few months before I graduated from Bates, I was nominated by the college to be a candidate for a Rhodes scholarship. I appeared duly before the committee in Augusta, and was not selected. Some friends and well-wishers thought an injustice had been done. They charged collegiate politics, since the selection committee heavily represented another college. But not for one moment did my mother let me harbor any sense of resentment or disappointment. She reminded me that in God's plan, His responsive and obedient man would always be in what Christian Scientists call his "right place." I could only see the selection committee and the successful candidate as God's men, each seeking to do his duty honorably and lovingly. Nor did I accept the slightest sense of failure.

Then, in my final college days, came the debating tour to the British Isles. When we were in Edinburgh completing the tour, a cable came from Roland R. Harrison, executive editor of the *Monitor,* offering me a job as reporter. The cable came under rather unusual circumstances. We three debaters (there was no faculty member along) arrived in Edinburgh on a Saturday morning prepared to debate that evening in the Edinburgh University Union Society on the topic of cancellation of war debts. Our hosts, meeting us at the station, blandly informed us we would be debating on the question of prohibition, defending what was a palpably unpopular position in Britain.

We were not in the least prepared in the subject. The three of us conferred—all were very young—and as captain of the team I decided we should be agreeable guests and go ahead and debate the impromptu subject. This untroubled decision to go ahead, confident in our ability to do what was expected of us, is again part of the religious conviction which Christian Science has ingrained in my life. It is not a blind or shallow confidence. It turns totally to the one divine source of wisdom and understanding, and it seeks to implement prayer with hard work.

So the three of us shut ourselves in our hotel room, and for a long day made notes, organized arguments, and recalled all the facts we could about prohibition. On our way from Princess

Street to the university that evening—there was a formal dinner before the debate, and our leading opponent was not a student but a prominent young advocate (barrister) at the Scottish bar —we observed the rather squalid crowds pouring in and out of the public houses on an Edinburgh Saturday night. We made the most of the local arguments in our very informal appeals. Whether in response to our logic or out of perverse sympathy, the Edinburgh Union Society decided by a good majority that we had won the debate!

Then, upon returning to the hotel at midnight after such a strenuous test, all the debates over, my college days done, I received the cable from Boston offering me the job. Of course I accepted and a few days later reported for duty in the *Monitor* news room.

III. "A CHIEL'S AMANG YE TAKIN' NOTES"

I began my *Monitor* job with more than a little awe. Though I had worked for newspapers one way or another since I was eight, I had never worked in the big leagues—far from it. I had plugged away as a proofreader at the *Lewiston Sun* during the summer following my freshman year in college. Indeed it was as a potential proofreader that I had put in my first personnel application at the *Monitor*. In my sophomore-year's vacation, I had turned to the outdoors and worked as a counselor in a boys' camp in the White Mountains.

However, in my junior-year's vacation, I had unexpectedly been given the job of editor (that is, the entire editorial staff) of the *Hilltop,* a weekly magazine published at the then-widely known resort Poland Spring, Maine.

The emergence of this job was another example of totally unplanned opportunity. I don't know how it came about. The *Hilltop* was published under the editorial aegis of the *Lewiston Journal,* the rival of the *Sun,* for which I had worked. The resort magazine had for many years been edited each summer by a talented senior member of the *Journal* staff.

Suddenly to be called in and offered his job was quite breathtaking. The *Journal* editor who asked me to take the job was Arthur G. Staples, a brilliant essayist and political journalist. That I had met with his favorable attention from afar, was pleasant enough. I thought a bit and accepted the *Hilltop* job, again with a deep sense that what I needed to fulfill the job was mine as a part of the endowment of divine Mind.

The summer at Poland Spring was delightful, rich with growth. I also learned which fork to use, and how to order from an elaborate menu. As a professional employee, I did not eat in the back room with the help, but at the so-called "family table," in the sumptuous main dining room of the exclusive hotel. It was in the ripe and mellow Indian summer of the rocking-chair resort hotel, and the Poland Spring House certainly had rocking chairs! The menu was lavish and I could order what I chose without money and without price.

My charming tablemates were Frank Carlos Griffith, the life-long personal manager of Minnie Maddern Fiske, the great actress, and Mr. and Mrs. Carlos Penfield. He was first-violinist for the Boston Symphony and she a talented pianist. Mr. Griffith managed the library and museum the Poland Spring House maintained, and Mr. Penfield directed its admirable orchestra. For a young Maine farmboy to live, work, eat with such people, was an exciting cultural experience. I also earned good money. Though the hotel proprietors only paid me twenty-five dollars a week for my editorial labors, I was also correspondent for two daily newspapers apiece in Portland, Boston, New York, and Philadelphia. My earnings from them ran up to eighty dollars a week. Thus went the summer before my senior year at college.

The eight weeks at Poland Spring had definitely not made me into the kind of newsman the *Monitor* required. In the stern atmosphere of its news room, *city editor* Paul S. Deland set about that task. His sharp pencil and critical analysis were more challenging than the Oxford debaters or the Maine resort proprietors. You might assume, after what I have said about the confidence in man's capacities which Christian Science affirms, that the *Monitor* news-room atmosphere would be all bland assurance and perfection at the first try. Far from it! Many of us were Christian Scientists, of course, but we were all working under rigorous professional discipline. We had to prove our Christian Science, and we could only do it by good, hard work and the maintenance of challenging standards. Not all made the grade.

My sense of strangeness and rigor in the *Monitor* news room was soon mitigated in the most delightful possible way: by professional companionship. At the next desk was a bright-faced reporter who had a whole year's seniority. It was Roscoe Drummond, who became my closest professional friend. He was later the *Monitor's* executive editor, chief of its Washington Bureau, and still later, distinguished nationally syndicated columnist of the *New York Herald Tribune*. Roscoe put me at ease in the news room on my second day or so, and soon we were sitting up late talking over all kinds of professional problems.

Paul Deland, as I have written in *Commitment to Freedom: The Story of The Christian Science Monitor,* was an unrelenting critic. He taught me a great deal about the use of words, the choice of news materials, the questions to ask public officials.

Within a month of my arrival, I was sent up to the North Shore, where most of the Washington embassies maintained summer residences, to interview His Excellency the Baron Ago Von Maltzan, German ambassador. This gracious diplomat, knowing the *Monitor's* reputation and unaware that the voice requesting an interview over the telephone was a wet-behind-the-ears cub, kindly invited me up to lunch. My social experiences at Poland Spring came in handy as I approached the crested cutlery of the Weimar Republic.

Neither the ambassador nor his other guests showed their natural surprise at seeing so young a reporter, and he gave me a very useful interview. My most difficult moment came when, during lunch, he lifted his champagne glass and proposed a toast to Christian Science. The Church's postwar relief work had helped German children of his acquaintance. I was, of course, a teetotaler, but I knew I didn't have to drink the toast since it was to the cause I represented, however youthfully. I thanked him with fervor.

I write: "Of course, a teetotaler." This freedom from addiction, which my religious convictions have given me, has been one of the several freedoms for which I am most profoundly grateful. Alcoholism, at least in the past, has been the bane of the newspaper profession. Even now newspapermen are subjected to the temptation of an inordinate amount of freeloading. If only press-agents would realize that to make news material available in a straightforward manner, without impediment of refreshment, is far more appreciated by a newspaperman than a long-winded cocktail party. Indeed, it is usually the press-agent who has something to put over, rather than straight information, who baits the hook with liquor. My profession has required me to be present, for almost four decades, at a tremendous number of occasions when free liquor was served. I have sometimes wanted to calculate the cash value of the gift liquor I haven't consumed!

My professional friends soon learned that I don't drink, and my public friends are often most considerate in arranging substitutes. I have found a steadily increasing respect for nondrinkers. More and more of the people I meet, despite current fashions, are going "on-the-wagon." And the same applies to smoking. There is no reason whatever for the young person who is faced with the decision of whether to drink and smoke to feel embarrassed or "out of it" by abstaining. It is one way, and an excellent way, to affirm one's own individuality. That is something many modern young people like to do.

For the Christian Scientist, not to drink and smoke is a way to prove the individual's freedom from drugs, stimulants, or other bonds of materialism. It helps to prove individual freedom not to be addicted to anything. If I had to have a piece of mince pie every morning for breakfast, or a chocolate bar every afternoon, I would try to free myself from such addiction, too. It is the surrender of the individual's self-control which weakens and subjugates his precious sovereignty. Under God's sovereignty, he can be totally and gloriously free.

I have had countless happy experiences as a result of being free from addiction. Many a host, hostess, or companion has leaned over to me and whispered, "I admire your courage; I wish I didn't drink (or smoke)." Abstention, of course, was not exactly courage. It was simply freedom.

The most unexpected provision for abstention I ever had came in the Soviet Union, where I went in 1959 at the request of the United States Government. I was being given a formal lunch at a smart Moscow restaurant by the president of the all-Soviet Chamber of Commerce. I knew the Soviet official custom of abundant toasts in vodka and I was all ready to explain my teetotalism. It was not necessary. Somebody, I believe the American acting ambassador, had explained matters to our hosts. With great tact, they had provided copious draughts of fruit juice, and the toasts were drunk in this salubrious beverage.

Once a Protestant clergyman in Cambridge, Massachusetts, invited me to debate on the subject of alcohol with Bernard Devoto, who had just written *The Cocktail Hour*. I was eager for the debate, because as I confided to the clergyman, I intended to base my arguments on the virtues of absolute freedom for the individual from the slavery of any kind of addiction, and how to secure this precious liberty. Unhappily, Mr. Devoto was unwilling to debate.

Perhaps nobody has written more vitriolic attacks on prohibition and abstinence than the late Henry L. Mencken, and there aren't many people with whom I would disagree more on moral issues. But Mr. Mencken and I, while on newspaper trips, were on the best of terms. More than once he saw to it that I got my ginger ale or tomato juice, despite his panegyrics on beer. He had also written many ungracious and untrue things about Christian Science. I did not mawkishly ignore these elements in Mr. Mencken's character, but I always tried to see the true man of God's creation beneath his shell of cynicism and atheism. I admired his immense journalistic virtuosity and was vastly entertained by his presence. He seemed to like me, though he usually abominaetd and attacked religionists, and I felt it was because I tried to live rather than to proclaim my faith.

I believe with fierce conviction that self-righteousness is one of the cardinal sins. I hope these memoirs do not reek of it. My mother early dinned into me the eternal and practical truth caught in Paul's Epistle to the Galatians (6:3): "For if a man think himself to be something, when he is nothing, he deceiveth himself."

What Christian Science does for an individual's sense of self is one of its greatest boons. His concept of individuality and identity is affirmed by his awareness of being created spiritually in God's image and likeness. But this is not the same thing as ego. The one Ego, the I Am, is God. Man's being is created by God and reflects God. Man's selfhood is spiritual, eternal, perfect. It is expressed through individuality. Thus one can feel a tremendous, reassuring, confident sense of selfhood without in any way being selfish, self-centered, or—least of all—self-righteous. Identity becomes selfless when it is seen to be totally dependent on the ultimate selfhood of God.

Nevertheless, the Christian Scientist, in the tremendous happiness, confidence, and joy of his spiritual convictions, has to work and strive continually against smugness, self-satisfaction, and the pernicious, blinding delusion that he is not as other men. It is easy to inflate mere personal will into the delusion of a supposed divine leading. The struggle for humility and impersonality must be constant.

Personally I have found that the best way to seek escape from the vice of self-righteousness is to turn respectfully toward the other man, seeing and affirming his status as the child of God, loving and recognizing the dignity of his spiritual personality.

One needs also to keep a sense of balance and of old-fashioned common sense. Thus, for example, in considering the matter of abstention from drinking and smoking, one can remember that some who have not been liberated from these addictions may nevertheless have many totally fine qualities, such as generosity, magnanimity, unselfishness, love. Equally, some who eschew liquor and tobacco may have failed to be liberated from other vices, such as smugness, selfishness, lack of charity. Things have to be kept in perspective. These lessons came to me particularly as I was thrown increasingly into the company of worldly men and women, and learned to live with them and respect their good qualities, through which shone their eternal birthright.

IV. TO OXFORD AND GENEVA

My lessons as a *Monitor* reporter flowed rapidly through the summer and autumn of 1925. In the fall, because the "gentleman from the *Transcript*" had blackened the eye of the *Monitor*'s rather fragile State House reporter, I was sent up to Beacon Hill to hold the fort. It was a challenging assignment for a youth three or four months out of college, but I did not think of it in those terms. It was what they asked me to do: a natural opportunity to practice my profession.

In December, 1925, I reapplied for selection as a Rhodes scholar, with the hearty approval of the *Monitor* authorities, and this time I was chosen. The *Monitor* gave me a three-year leave of absence and in September I set forth for Geneva on my way to Oxford. It was clearly apparent why I had not been elected a Rhodes scholar in 1924. The thinking my mother and I had done—to avoid resentment, to realize that God would always direct my path and I would find myself in my right place—had borne fruit a year later. It is often the case in Christian Science work that a healing or unfoldment which is really a spiritual triumph does not become apparent until long afterward. Had I received a Rhodes scholarship in 1924, I would not have accomplished my basic training as a reporter before going to Oxford. I might not have been hired by the *Monitor* on leaving Oxford, in the summer of 1928. At any rate, I would have had to undergo the rigors and advantages of basic training three years later, with my Oxford ideas stiffened in me. Instead, when I went to Oxford I was already established and somewhat trained as a *Monitor* reporter at the time when my thinking was most responsive.

Moreover, the fact that I went to Europe as a *Monitor* reporter on leave of absence gave me perfectly invaluable advantages. It was the very heyday of the League of Nations—the year of the Locarno agreements and the admission of Germany to the community of nations. Hopes were high that peace had truly been made between the antagonists of the first World War and that the peace machinery might be made to work.

The atmosphere of Geneva, bright and sparkling astride its azure lake and under its mountains, was almost pentecostal. The leading statesmen of the world were there: the foreign ministers and ambassadors, the students of world affairs, and not least of all, to me, the great foreign correspondents. The historic day that Germany took her seat in the League and Austen Chamberlain, Aristide Briand, and Gustav Stresemann made their memorable speeches, I sat as a proud professional in the press gallery beside Frank L. Simonds. He was a famous war correspondent and foreign-affairs analyst, and a terse, effective stylist. For years I had read, studied, and emulated his approaches and style. He was most kind to the twenty-two-year-old cub reporter beside him, and we began a friendship which lasted until his passing in the 1930's.

It was an awfully heady atmosphere for a young fellow—professionally and in terms of idealistic hopes and dreams for an organized peace. The *Monitor* correspondent at Geneva was Hugh L. Spender. I was assigned to help him in any way he chose. Mr. Spender was a member of a most distinguished English journalistic family. His brother, J. Alfred Spender, had long been a pillar of liberal journalism. His nephew, Stephen, later a famous poet, was still a student when I met him at Oxford.

Hugh Spender did not know quite what to make of me at first but he soon found a young American cub useful on professional errands. I would pick up the texts of speeches and communiques, go to press conferences he couldn't attend, and help in getting copy to the cable office. Sometimes he dictated dispatches to me, for, as it was for some journalists of the old school, the typewriter was a mystery to him. Mr. and Mrs. Spender were most kind to me, partly because I was going up to Oriel College, his own Oxford college. They overlooked my naïveté. We grew well acquainted during the three years in which I returned to Geneva for the Assembly sessions in September.

Meantime I lived in a pension, practiced French, and got acquainted with students, professors, journalists, and foreign-office junior officials who swarmed over John Calvin's city. The Assembly sessions, including the speeches of the world leaders, were in the stark old Salle de la Reformation. As I walked to and from the sessions or the *Monitor* office I took the narrow cobbled streets of the clean old city, passing Calvin's cathedral, John Knox's house, and other storied memorials to men's struggles for the right to worship God as they chose. These reminders of Protestantism's vigorous history added to the depth of Geneva's tapestry. But there were also memories of Rousseau and Voltaire, and many an exile from despotism, while the street along the lake was Quai Woodrow Wilson—a recent poignant reminder. And from my pension window, up under the eaves, I could see across a little park the golden onion-domes of the Russian Orthodox church, which gave religious solace to many who had fled the Bolshevik revolution a few years before.

In the press gallery, in the delegations, among the observers, were many who had played prominent roles in the first World War, in the bittersweet years which had slid into the abyss of 1914, and indeed in the never-to-be-forgotten *fin-de-siecle* of the Victorian age. Thus I came into firsthand and sometimes emotional contact with lives that stretched far back beyond that great gulf of 1914-18 into a time forever gone. My youthful eagerness as a student of history to see and feel these embodiments of its continuity grew by feeding. Even today I feel particular pleasure in knowing that a friend of mine has clear memories of his grandfather, who had entertained the glorious Lafayette at dinner in Paris in 1826.

Three brothers at Geneva were on the Polish delegation. From them I learned something of the tangled loyalties of Central European politics. One had been an officer in the Imperial Russian armies, another wore the double eagles of Austria-Hungary's Hapsburgs, and a third bore an officer's uniform of the German empire. But each was above all a Pole. So, throughout the war, each did his best to impede the imperial forces he was supposed to serve. One was captured: the others made him very comfortable in captivity. Now, in 1926, they were proudly and fiercely serving the Poland that Jan Paderewski had helped re-create. It is sad that their kind of Poland has again been submerged, but it will not be forever.

I also met Olga Masaryk-Revilliod, the daughter of Thomas Masaryk, the father of Czechoslovakia, her brother Jan, later a martyr to Communist pressures, and Edouard Benes, who carried his nation bravely through the 1920's and '30's until Hitler's legions moved after Munich. Mme. Masaryk-Revilliod is an active Christian Scientist. The church in Geneva was itself a vital, cosmopolitan place. Its base of membership began with the Genevese, a fine, sturdy people, proud of their Protestant heritage, definitely akin to the New England congregationalism from which Mary Baker Eddy came.

But the Christian Scientists in Geneva also included very interesting people from all over the world. The Marquess of Lothian, who, as secretary to Prime Minister David Lloyd-George, had had much to do with drafting the League of Nations covenant, was frequently in Geneva and at church. A regular member was Col. H. H. Wade, the League's chief interpreter. He had the task of turning the French speeches into English and he handled M. Briand's organ-toned oratory with circumspection. Often, during the Wednesday-evening testimony meetings at church, Colonel Wade would rise and convert into either English or French some particularly helpful testimony of healing.

To see and participate in the work of Christian Science in Geneva alongside the glamorous trappings of diplomacy, the worldly glitter of the great hotels, and with the thrilling waves of hope for world peace, intensified my awareness of the transcendent mission, individual and universal, of spiritual revelation. I felt Christian Science was playing its part in the unfolding pageant of men and nations. I was grateful to be in this movement, assured of my birthright as God's man, respectful toward the fine idealists—Christian Scientists and others—among whom I found myself. I could see that my religion was not only the wonderful healing truth that had saved my mother in our little Maine town in 1914, thus opening our lives to rich personal fulfillments, but also a universal principle available everywhere and applicable to collective as well as to personal problems.

Not all of these experiences in Geneva took place in that exciting September, 1926, but in the succeeding Septembers, when I returned, and in the years from June, 1930, to September, 1932, when I was in charge of the *Monitor* Bureau there. In early October, 1926, I had to leave Geneva for Oxford, going by way of Basel and Strassburg. I took my first airplane flight from Strassburg to Paris, sitting on a pile of mail sacks in a creaking old French biplane. It seemed like a good idea—I had long wanted to fly. And thence to Oxford.

How I wish space allowed an adequate account of my three years at Oxford. They were pleasant and beneficial beyond words. Among the best things they did for me was to make me a better American, to give me perspective, balance, and appreciation for the values of my native country.

In later years there have been unprincipled attacks on Rhodes scholarships in extreme quarters, describing them as some kind of conspiracy to bring the United States into a British orbit. Whatever may have been in Cecil Rhodes' thought—and many things were, at various times—neither I nor any Rhodes scholar of whom I ever heard was required to assume any sort of obligation except to engage in honorable postgraduate study. There was no conspiracy, no commitment. Some of us became Anglophile, some Anglophobe, and some completely objective. We were all entirely free to grow and develop mentally as we were able.

Some of my closest friends were Americans, from parts of the country I had never seen or known. They helped develop a sense of kinship in diversity.

But a broader sense of kinship in diversity came from friendship with students of many other lands. And the Oxford methods of making a student learn to study and grow for himself, its picturesque traditions, its total embodiment of the continuity of history, its very beauty and charm, all left their inevitable impression. I did not, however, adopt an Oxford accent.

I "read"—specialized—in modern history. My tutor, G. N. (later Sir George) Clark, had been editor of the *English Historical Review*. He learned that I was on leave of absence from the *Monitor,* for which he and my other teachers had a healthy respect, and I believe he was genuinely interested in helping me become a better journalist. Writing weekly essays (the Oxford method of tutelage) on historical subjects, and then receiving the acute criticism of G. N. Clark was an excellent experience for a reporter who hoped to become a foreign correspondent. I was still very green, professionally and personally. The analytical techniques, the critical judgment of Oxford modern historians, were of top value. And the cultural, social, personal side of Oxford life, matched by about six months' "vacation" on the Continent each year, seasoned my personal inexperience. One has those six months of vacation to settle down to solid, quiet study. The term-time at Oxford is too lively for that kind of work.

Again through my Oxford years, development as a Christian Scientist was of utmost importance. There is a modest Christian Science church in the town and its membership is a cross-section of earnest folk—trades people, professionals, housewives, farmers—and persons connected in some way with the university. There were undergraduates, some American but many more British.

I attended church regularly, Sundays and Wednesday nights, and thus met and came to know and respect local people with whom few overseas students would have had personal contact. One gracious lady opened her home to Christian Scientist undergraduates, and there I enjoyed the company of both girls and lads who had a common dedication and life purpose. One of them is now one of Queen Elizabeth II's most distinguished ambassadors; another has been a successful world-trading businessman; another heads a fine college in the Western United States; still another is an editor, and another is one of Britain's two or three most eminent drama critics. With them one formed lifelong bonds of shared experience.

On the Continent, apart from my annual Geneva interlude, I coordinated my travels with my historical studies. For five periods I went to university towns—Göttingen and Heidelberg in Germany, and Aix-en-Provence in France—to concentrate in libraries on the history of these two great Continental powers and to savor and appreciate more of their ways of living and thinking. In Göttingen in 1928-29 I had vivid and horrifying warning of the torrents of hate and resentment controlling the emotions of many Germans, victims of inflation, against the would-be democratic institutions of the Weimar Republic, and against the Jews.

To see and feel these destructive passions in otherwise fine, loving, culturally rich people helped me to understand the phenomenon of Nazi Germany in the 1930's, and especially the bemused support of that regime by some German Christian Scientists. These things often dawn on one as a result of small episodes, little flashes of insight. One such came in Göttingen, where I lived in the home of a retired German admiral who was somewhat reduced in circumstances due to inflation. He and his wife were charming, gracious people, and I grew very fond and grateful toward them.

At Geneva I had observed and interviewed German cabinet members and Reichstag deputies. Some of them seemed to me to be dedicated, intelligent leaders. I mentioned the Reichstag to the admiral, and his usually kind and generous lips drew back into a hateful grimace: "The Reichstag—that *schweinekoben!*" —pigsty—he snarled. So, for the first time, five years ahead, I saw the face of Nazi Germany. I saw it again as a correspondent in Berlin in the grim winter of 1932, and in Geneva and Lausanne later that summer, when Nazi stooges came to attack and ruin the fine journalists who had for years represented the upstanding newspapers of a Germany in which for a century liberalism had been fighting a losing battle with militarism and hate.

From the perspective of Europe, the strong and the weak points of an America in the grip of the delusive 1920's were quite clear. I was an emotionally and politically loyal American, defending the cultural and national attributes of my native land in many midnight arguments with fellow students. Sometimes I would dig out of my trunk the few articles of American campus clothing which I had kept—a cap, a gaudy striped sweater, a sports shirt—and delight as well as appall my cronies in the staid Oriel quadrangles. Or I would join them at American movies or musical shows, lustily praising (in the manner of Oxford's often absurd dialectic) the exaggerated mores Hollywood had contrived. In stiff debate at the Oxford Union Society, I supported the Monroe Doctrine, though it was in the last phase of a rather bad period of dollar diplomacy, against the impassioned attacks of a man who was later a revolutionary leader in Latin America.

In the summers of 1927 and 1928 my mother and father, respectively, came to spend some time with me. With what joy I opened the delights of Oxford, of Britain, and of Western Europe to these dear folk who had never before strayed far from New England. We had long, natural, and wonderful talks about the spiritual significance of all that was happening to us. Their pleasure in my progress was always balanced by a deep impersonal sense of God as the giver of all good. What had come, they saw quite clearly, was not the result of any personal qualities of my own, but the realization and emergence of attributes and opportunities which are divine blessings available in countless different individual ways to all men.

If they had any sense of pride in their only son it was utterly and beautifully transcended into gratitude. They had an intensely vivid awareness of the dangers of personal pride, of satisfaction, of arrogance, spiritual, cultural, or otherwise. Many times during their visits to me they took me down from the high horse of ego, to which my heady experiences tended to boost me. With patience, humility, and love they would bring me back to earth—and yet, not to earth really, for the ego of vanity and pride is profoundly earthy, but to the heavenly directed consciousness of God's infinite goodness and availability to the humble, honest, impersonal, rightly motivated seeker.

Two sentences in *Science and Health with Key to the Scriptures* were often in my thoughts at this time. My mother had reminded me of them long before. They are: "Love inspires, illumines, designates, and leads the way. Right motives give pinions to thought, and strength and freedom to speech and action" (454:18).

On one dark morning in 1923 my mother had given me the illumination of these sentences when I began a long journey alone, and they had helped protect and save me when the lighting system of our car suddenly broke down at a hazardous spot. And in debating, college work, etc., I had found it essential always to re-examine and clarify my motivation. Then I felt the assurance of soaring thought and strong, free speech and action. To this day, seeking to protect mentally the safety of a journey by aircraft, I remind myself of the importance of right motivation for the journey, and feel the pinions of divine support which spring therefrom.

In June, 1929, I took my final examinations, passed, and was back in the *Monitor* news room in Boston. It was a period of rapid evolution on the staff, and there were not too many qualified staff members. The legal battle over the control of the paper, ending in 1922, had required large-scale restaffing. Many of those hired in and after 1922 had not worked out, so by 1929 great opportunities were available to those who had really made good, both at home and abroad.

The London Naval Disarmament Conference had been convened for January, 1930. It was felt that the *Monitor's* London Bureau was not altogether equipped to handle the coverage, and so I was assigned for a few weeks of training in Washington and thence to London with the American delegation. Here was an assignment far beyond my twenty-five-year-old expectations, and in all conscience, far beyond any talents I had proved.

I was to take full charge of the conference coverage. Having spent six weeks working in the London Bureau, during an Oxford vacation, I was on warm personal terms with its members. They accepted my invasion of their territory with good grace. In Washington, preparing for London, I was given the best possible contacts with American correspondents who were also handling the assignment. I had met a few of them in Geneva.

Again lifelong friendships grew up with such rare people as Raymond Clapper, then of the United Press, Charles G. Ross of the *St. Louis Post-Dispatch,* Jay Hayden of the *Detroit News,* William T. Stone of the Foreign Policy Association, Arthur S. Henning of the *Chicago Tribune,* Frederick William Wile of CBS, and many another. These well-informed, shrewd, seasoned veterans of Washington reportage, were extraordinarily kind and helpful to me. I reciprocated with my junior-level contacts with members of Geneva delegations.

But again it was only a turning to God and receptivity to the strengths, attributes, judgment, alertness, which are man's heritage as image and likeness of divine wisdom, that made it possible for me to carry out an almost absurd assignment. Again I did not feel self-conscious, or either exalted or overwhelmed by the job and its fulfillment. Again I felt natural, zestful, but above all, impersonal. Nor was I a special instrument of divine power— far from it.

All around me were able journalists doing fine professional jobs, journalists whom I greatly admired, who were not Christian Scientists, or even religious. They were consciously applying their best human qualities, and unconsciously they too were exhibiting and living the attributes of God's man. One difference between us was that my early study of Christian Science led me to turn prayerfully to God at all times, to realize man's ever-available potential of service and accomplishment.

I was also able to turn to God for physical healing, as well as for professional and moral inspiration. Unfailingly, from the dawn of Christian Science in my boyhood consciousness, I have been wonderfully protected and healed in physical adversity. I have met with many physical problems, and any that could have kept me from my work have swiftly been healed. One physical problem of maladjustment has not been met: I have worn glasses since I was a youth, to correct physically a condition of nearsightedness. I should have been able to realize and demonstrate my full, unimpaired physical vision long since. I firmly believe that I shall be able to do so some day. I offer no excuses. Meantime, neither my eyes nor my thought ever accepts any sense of strain or weariness, and I accomplish much more than my share of intensive reading. Otherwise, I have been grateful for unremitting physical well-being, with occasional challenges quickly met and resolved.

Among the many physical healings I have enjoyed was one which gave me a sharp awareness of the powerlessness of drugs to touch the individual. In 1947, Secretary of War Patterson invited me to go to Japan as guest of General MacArthur to observe the Allied occupation. I knew that numerous medical inoculations might be required. Like all Christian Scientists I am willing to observe the law and submit to inoculation whenever the established authorities have decided inoculation is required. But, like other Christian Scientists, I seek exemption from compulsory medication on grounds of religious conviction whenever my exemption is recognized not to harm the supposed protection of others. I turn to God for my own protection, feeling that His power, as manifested particularly by Christ Jesus, is the supreme preventive or curative healing for mankind's ills.

So I asked Secretary Patterson for exemption from the many shots then required for a trip to the Far East. I was told that the surgeon-general of the army had issued the exemptions, though I had nothing in writing. When our flight arrived at Fairfield-Suisun Air Base ready to take off for the Orient, the technical sergeant responsible for clearing our medical certificates naturally paid no heed to my claims of verbal exemption nor the assurances of the Major shepherding our party. Either I took the shots then and there, or I didn't board that aircraft!

I reasoned that it was my professional duty to the *Monitor* to go on the inspection tour, that I had made every available effort to obtain conscientious exemption from medication, and that the drugs which might be shot into me could have no effect upon me, since they were powerless to touch the individual, save as he might give them apparent power in his belief. So I told the sergeant to go right ahead, and he jabbed, or scraped, me three times on each arm with presumably potent injections and I walked aboard the plane for the twenty-hour grind to Hawaii, followed by equally long flights to Kwajalein and Guam.

I had not the slightest perceptible reaction to any of the six injections. When, nowadays, under special circumstances, small-pox shots are required of me and exemption is impossible, the medics enter "reaction: immune" on my yellow card. This, of course, is not unusual medical experience, but I believe that total immunity from six various shots is.

I am aware that doctors themselves in their study of psycho-somatic medicine have documented many cases where power-ful drugs have been followed by opposite reactions when patients were told they were receiving an opposite drug. I know, too, that placebos—drugless treatments such as pills of sugar and water—have long been known to produce in patients exactly the reaction physicians tell their patients to expect. What such experiments do to the faith of people in drugs, I cannot say, but for myself I have seen abundant proof of the mental causation of physical sensation. Sometimes, of course, a Christian Scientist comes under the pressures of the world's belief in an epidemic or a drug power and has to check himself sharply to "come out and be separate" from contagious human thinking.

V. MOVING TO THE NATIONAL SCENE

Returning from London to Boston in May, 1930, I had the joyous experience of getting married. My bride, Thelma Whit-man Hart, came from North Truro, on Cape Cod. Her own path to Christian Science had been self-discovered. As a young girl she had grown totally dissatisfied with religion as she knew it, and began a systematic investigation of the principal churches. In her humble, eager search she came to Christian Science and recognized it at once as the answer to her longings. I had known her in 1925-26, when I first came to Boston. We became engaged in November, 1929, just before I went to London.

It would take another volume to describe the great spiritual riches of striving to demonstrate Christian Science as a family. Whatever I write from this point on reflects the joint efforts of my wife and myself to understand and implement our place in God's scheme of things. The complete happiness of a marriage in which both partners are following the same spiritual path is beyond praise. Our eldest daughter, Carolyn, was born in Geneva in 1931, and a second daughter, Elizabeth, in Waban, Massachusetts, in 1942. Carolyn is married and we have three grandchildren. One's gratitude in watching children and grandchildren strive to learn and understand the same truths about God and man is one of life's deepest joyous experiences.

A few weeks after our marriage we were sent back to Geneva, where I succeeded Hugh Spender, who had passed on, as *Monitor* correspondent. The climate was swiftly changing there. The general disarmament conference opened in 1931, and not long thereafter the Manchurian and Shanghai incidents marked the outbreak of violent aggression, which was to lead ultimately to World War II. The hopes and visions of 1926 were tarnished by power rivalry. Looming on the horizon was Adolf Hitler. Soviet delegates appeared, led by Maxim Litvinov, and began what has become a habit: the presentation of total disarmament proposals which simply would not work and are advanced for their propaganda values.

Meantime, world economic problems were growing apace. I went to Basel to cover the Bank of International Settlements, and to the Reparations conferences in Lausanne. I covered the gallant efforts of Henry L. Stimson, American secretary of state, in the dark spring of 1932, as he went from Rome to Berlin to Paris to London in a desperate effort to halt the slide into monetary collapse.

In August, 1932, I was transferred to Washington as chief of the *Monitor*'s News Bureau. Here was a more challenging job than ever. It was the paper's principal news office. There had been difficulties over its management. The atmosphere was disturbed. But, as often before, I was led by my study of Christian Science to expect nothing but good, and to deny and reject any assumptions of trouble. The members of the bureau, far more experienced in Washington affairs than myself, helped me with fullest loyalty and friendship.

In October I was flung into the throes of the presidential campaign and traveled with Herbert Hoover as he made his last intensive transcontinental trip to avoid defeat. I heard the crowds jeer and boo in many cities where unemployment was high, and witnessed faithful loyalty in Republican territories. On Sunday morning before the election, on the empty station platform at Omaha, Lewis Strauss, later chairman of the Atomic Energy Commission but then an aide to Mr. Hoover, came sprinting along looking for a Bible. He was on the point of sending a Western Union boy to the nearest hotel to get a Gideon Bible, assuming that nobody on the train traveled with a copy, when I spoke up and offered the President my own Bible. I read it, together with *Science and Health*, every day. Mr. (now Admiral) Strauss took the good book gratefully and gave it back after the President had finished.

The morning after the election, so dismal for Mr. Hoover, I went up to his house on the Leland Stanford University campus to see him. The election results had been a blow. Never would I have thought that the man with whom I talked on that day, whose career had gone back to the early years of the century, would still be serving his country and the world almost thirty years later.

I wish there were space to do justice to my seven years in Washington. From March 4, 1933, onward, they were the years of the New Deal. It was an exciting, precedent-shattering time. For a newspaperman the years were filled with professional challenge. One had to write about the New Deal and its glamorous leader, President Roosevelt, with accuracy and perception. One had to avoid being carried away by that skillful charmer at biweekly press conferences and yet not lapse into negativism on the opposite side. The writing one had to do was apt to be criticized by conservatives as too sympathetic with the Roosevelt Administration, and by liberals as hopelessly reactionary. I am prepared to leave the verdict to the historians, but I believe their conclusions today will be far kinder to the *Monitor*'s Washington file in the years from 1933 to 1940 than were many impassioned readers at the time.

In 1933 I was sent back to Europe to cover the London Economic Conference, and in each succeeding year across the United States to cover domestic politics. Thus I got much better acquainted with my own country, its regional leaders, and my newspaper colleagues from Coast to Coast. In 1935, I was assigned by the *Monitor* to be guest of the Philippine Government on the inauguration of its commonwealth, and my wife came along at our own expense. We visited Japan, China, and the Philippines just a few years before full-scale war broke out in the Pacific. It was a world soon to be profoundly changed.

On our trip, as in every detail of our lives, the effort to understand and demonstrate spiritual truth was dominant. Our dearest friends on the trip were those much-beloved Kansans, Mr. and Mrs. William Allen White. They were not Christian Scientists, but they appreciated what it had done and was doing for us. At one sweet, never-to-be-forgotten moment, gracious Sallie White drew us aside on the ship's deck and said, "My dears, Will and I want you to know that you are living the way we think young people ought to live. Keep it up. You will be very happy." Their own idyllic marriage had many of the elements of ours: they did not drink or smoke, they turned to God prayerfully, they shared their lives lovingly. And they gave us, as they had given so many others, a world of inspiration.

On the trip to the Philippines, some fifty members of Congress were the chief guests. Naturally we came to know them intimately on the long voyages across the Pacific. Among them was one well-known senator (who shall not be identified), who carried with him a number of copies of *Science and Health*. He was not a Christian Scientist, and his life had had many jarring elements in it. But whenever anybody felt ill, or got into trouble, he would call upon them with a *Science and Health* and tell them to read it: it would do them good. When a high

Philippine official—who also shall be nameless—affected illness because he feared an assassination attempt, the worthy senator pressed upon him his last copy of Mrs. Eddy's book. I never knew whether it really brought about a mental cure of a mental complaint, but the official soon emerged from his "sickbed."

The 1930's were full of other rich personal and professional experiences. Men and women who were soon to carry heavy responsibilities in World War II were close personal friends. Presidential campaigns added their spice and conflict. I covered Governor Alf M. Landon's campaign closely in 1936, and came to respect an ill-prepared candidate who had a lot to learn, knew it. The fact of our dedication to Christian Science seemed to arouse interest and create a bond with public men and women who were themselves not Christian Scientists, but wanted desperately to believe truths of spiritual importance.

Rarely indeed have my wife or I discussed our religion with these many friends in public life. But almost invariably the contact between these public officials and ourselves was deepened and enriched by their indirect reaching out for spiritual values. We hoped that our lives spoke for themselves, so that our way of life might be convincing without being doctrinal. More than once the hand reached out for a cup of cold water, and we tried to have it ready.

Thus on one grim night, a brilliant journalistic colleague—his name known to all—cried out in his drunken delirium for help to prevent suicide. I spent the night with him and in the morning he came to himself. Another time, another colleague came to the office with a dreadful hangover, of which he was properly ashamed. With trembling fingers he tried to extract a cigarette. I told him we didn't smoke in the *Monitor* office. He straightened up, didn't smoke again, went on the wagon and saved his career.

Always there were opportunities, seen or unseen, to show people that the life of a Christian Scientist can lead to spiritual fulfillment, professional balance, and the zest and happiness which are normal to God's man. You never have to preach. Into the *Monitor* office in the National Press Building drifted a constant stream of colleagues, seeking not only information; we were glad to share with them, and they shared with us. We were not regarded as religious stuffed-shirts. Casually, indirectly, personal problems would be mentioned. Our job would be to help without appearing to do so. Very often the lives of colleagues or public men had been touched at some time in the past by Christian Science: a dedicated mother or aunt, a spell in the Sunday school, a healing not understood but remembered. Again the task was to try to exemplify, not exhort.

In 1937, as a kind of status symbol on the Washington newspaper scene, I was elected to the Gridiron Club. Only fifty Washington correspondents are members, and its dinners are memorable. The night I appeared as a dragon, in a skit written in collaboration with the presently dignified head of the Dow-Jones Corporation, which produces the *Wall Street Journal,* was the end of my histrionic career.

In the mid-Thirties I was asked to contribute a weekly letter of private guidance to a well-known news-weekly. I was also asked to do a weekly interpretive broadcast over the Columbia Broadcasting System, and I have been broadcasting a bit in my spare time ever since. It has been a fine opportunity to reach a different and numerically extensive audience.

In December, 1939, the *Monitor* decided to bring me back to Boston as general news editor, and my Washington days were ended. Of course, I have been in and out of Washington every few weeks since, but my basic responsibilities have been in Boston. A year later, I became the chief editorial executive of the paper, responsible to the Christian Science board of directors for its news and editorial operations, and to the board of trustees of the Christian Science Publishing Society for the business conduct of the editorial department.

From 1940 to 1945 my work was concentrated on the wartime service of the *Monitor.* Correspondents had to be extricated from areas that fell into enemy hands and dispersed in the vital news zones of the world. Younger men, and some women, were going into military service, and many older staff members were borrowed for important governmental tasks.

Those of us who stayed in the home office had our hands full. There were constant urgent needs to know the protective power of God's love and care in a world at war. The paper's mission to help lead the nations back to peace was impelling.

The light which Christian Science throws upon the false dream of mortal existence, as compared with the order and harmony of spiritual being, was doubly beneficial in wartime. In 1940 and early 1941 the paper had to explain why it felt a buildup of American armed forces was necessary in the face of Nazi and possibly Soviet aggression, in aid to the embattled Allies. The difference between a nonresistant pacifism and a thoroughly aroused support of the human footsteps needed to protect free society had to be made clear to readers. It was quite possible, and necessary, to affirm the unreality of war as the truth about God's man and yet to go forward, vigorously supporting and participating in the war effort. The *Monitor's* wartime record was useful, indeed distinguished.

In late 1945 a new phase in my experience began: the emergence into public affairs. Maurice J. Tobin, then governor of Massachusetts and later secretary of labor, asked me to be a member of a committee (eventually its chairman) to try and persuade the United Nations to make its home in Boston. Governor Tobin, President Karl T. Compton of the Massachusetts Institute of Technology, myself, and others, went to London to present our case to the organizing sessions of the U.N. assembly. The effort went on, covering both sides of the Atlantic, for about a year. When the Rockefeller beneficence finally persuaded the U.N. founding fathers to settle in New York, there were Bostonians who breathed sighs of relief. On the whole, the sighs have grown more heartfelt ever since. It is interesting to speculate on whether the U.N.'s development would have been any different had it not been ensconced in a turgid, electrically stimulating metropolis like New York, but in a more livable community like Boston—or Geneva.

One experience in public activity led to another. Throughout the mid-Forties I had been progressing through the offices of the American Society of Newspaper Editors, and became its president in 1948, three years after I had received the title of editor at the *Monitor*. President Truman appointed me one of several newspapermen to serve on the American delegation to the Conference on Freedom of Information, held in Geneva in 1948. A year later, I was a member of the American delegation to the United Nations, charged with the task of helping draft a treaty on freedom of information.

The cause was good and American editors had supported it for years. Indeed they had demanded that such a treaty be negotiated. Before long it appeared, as the treaty took shape, that the views of many other governments were deeply against freedom of information. The Communist states in particular made the issue a device for propaganda attacks against the United States and the free press in an effort to mask their own suppression of press freedom.

In Geneva in 1948 and New York in 1949, my colleagues and I tried hard to make the best of a bad business. We strove particularly to obtain guarantees against censorship, suppression of sources of news, free movement of foreign correspondents, and the untrammeled transmission of news across frontiers. We failed. The United Nations is still, nearly fifteen years later, pursuing the cause of freedom of information, but often with plans and devices which would perpetrate new barriers.

My months as an amateur diplomat were strenuous. Continually I had to realize my right to capacities and qualities which I had never before exercised. My connection with the *Monitor*, and with Christian Science, was well known to my colleagues and opponents. It was a big help. I remember once, when an Arab delegate had made a bitter attack on the American press, that he turned graciously to me and observed, "What I have said does not apply to the American delegate and the newspaper he represents. He is a rose in a garden of thorns!"

I was most grateful to be exposed to the rigors of international negotiation. It helped me to understand what the statesmen and diplomats have to face continually. The Soviet member of my committee at the U.N., for instance, was Semyon Tsarapkin, who later became the chief Soviet delegate at the negotiations on nuclear testing. I was glad to have some personal insight into his character and techniques.

My service was in the good old days of U. S.-Latin-American relations, so I shall not soon forget the South-American delegate who came up to me at the first session of our U.N. committee and said: "My instructions are to vote the way you do. But for goodness' sake get your hand up quickly." I did. And high, too.

Another form of public service and communication increased in the Forties and has not been easy to keep within due limits: that is the giving of public speeches and lectures. The demand, indeed the need, for oral communication is very great. I have acceded to it perhaps more than I should. The lecture which drew most attention, and is still extensively circulating in printed form eleven years after it was first written and delivered, was "The Authentic Revolution," presented as the Frank Ellsworth Spaulding Lecture at Yale University in 1950.

In this paper I developed the thesis that free society, stretching back to the emergence of monotheism and the law in Judaeo-Christian experience, is the true revolution and that all forms of totalitarianism, from the pharaohs to nazism and communism, are reactions.

A series of lectures I gave at Leland Stanford University in 1953, like most of my other work of this sort, was turned into a *Monitor* series, then into a book, *New Frontiers for Freedom,* six years before the phrase "new frontiers" was used as a political slogan. The book has been translated into some fifteen European and Asian languages. Thus the spoken word, turned into the written word, has provided a major opportunity for the ideas which it is the *Monitor*'s role to spread.

Various other public-service tasks followed steadily throughout the 1950's. I was one of the initial members and sometime chairman of the United States Advisory Committee on Information. This five-member group, set up by Act of Congress, had the thankless task of advising the State Department and later the United States Information Agency on the difficult, urgent operations of the nation's global-information program.

President Eisenhower drafted me for several other tasks, culminating in membership on his Commission on National Goals, which produced a survey and recommendations he left with the nation as his presidency ended. All these and many others were challenging, gratifying tasks. They could be accomplished —with some exceptions—in my spare time. As an editor I had to keep in touch with Washington affairs anyway, and service on official boards gave me a useful behind-the-scenes look at men and operations. But when both President Truman and President Eisenhower, through their secretaries of state, urged me to accept certain full-time appointive offices, I felt no hesitation in declining, on the plea of more urgent responsibilities.

These, of course, were my *Monitor* duties. I believed at all times that no influence could be more helpful to the affairs and service of our nation, or the cause of freedom and understanding in the world, than the practice of daily journalism in *Christian Science Monitor* terms. I could do far more for the good of all in my *Monitor* job than in all the governmental jobs I was offered. This was particularly true because of the *Monitor's* transcendent mission as a part of the Christian Science movement.

Humankind's thinking must be regenerated. The true path to peace lies through spiritual awakening. Christian Science is enlisted in this task, and every Christian Scientist has his part to play in this mighty army. The battle for peace takes place initially and basically in the individual's own consciousness. The *Monitor's* role is to inform and to awaken those who must move toward this awareness. Its service is not alone to Christian Scientists, but to awakening thought everywhere. There can be no greater individual fulfillment than to serve in such a cause.

There were, however, other public-service tasks which I could perform without subtracting heavily from my *Monitor* work. One such was the presidency of the Chamber of Commerce of the United States. In the pattern of total unexpectedness which has run through my life, I found myself called to the telephone in 1954 and asked if I would serve out the unexpired term of a New England director of the national Chamber. After considerable thought, in which important pros and cons had to be weighed, it was decided that I should accept the appointment. It would bring me into intimate and extensive contact with many American business leaders. I was already well acquainted in the field of newspaper leadership and among the colleges and universities; my diplomatic and governmental phases had shown me national and international policy in operation. But my contacts with business and financial leadership had been minimal.

It was a most invigorating and informative experience to serve with such men, and after five years I expected my terms in office would run out and I would retire from the Chamber scene. My surprise was never greater than when the nominating committee asked me to be president. Once more it was necessary to weigh still more urgent pros and cons. Only after very prayerful thought was it decided that the service I might perform in helping articulate the role of private enterprise in a world where it is under the most severe attack, would justify the acceptance of the office. It required, on the average, perhaps as much as twenty per cent of my professional time for some nine months.

My appreciation of the importance of free competitive enterprise, a form of economic life which helps sustain other freedoms, grew as I saw American business, its problems and shortcomings, its strengths and weaknesses, at close range. I sought to remain blind to no problems, no unfinished business, no conflicts of interest, no mesmeric waves of self-righteousness. I tried time and again, however, to put the facts of free enterprise in positive terms. This was one way to counterbalance the waves of statism which were—and are—sweeping the world.

These partial distractions from my basic *Monitor* duties came to an end. They were all opportunities, and some of them continue in proper proportion. But whatever I can do as a Christian Scientist and as a journalist finds itself concentrated in the vehicle of the *Christian Science Monitor*.

Contacts and opportunities in the world of affairs, normal parts of my editorial duties, continue. Nothing I do on the boards where I serve, in the public contacts which must be maintained, in the speeches or broadcasts or telecasts I am called upon to make, would be the same if I were not a Christian Scientist.

I hope I have made it clear that reliance on God's power and awareness of spiritual reality are the complete and dominant influences in my life as a Christian Scientist. Naturally I do not buttonhole people in clubs and board rooms and preach religion to them. My language, in the dialogue all of us have with the world, is the world's language. But the best—the only real—language I can utter is the language of a way of life. What I may be in human experience is the result of the influences I have tried to describe frankly in these pages. It is not easy for me to do so. Somebody else, no doubt, should be saying these things if they are to be said at all.

I hope and believe there is some utility in such declarations of faith. "This I Believe" was the title of a fine radio series, published in later books, in which many Americans were invited to expose their inner convictions. I was profoundly appreciative when Edgar Comee, without any consultation with me at all, wrote in the "Newspaper Editor" series of the *New York Herald Tribune*: "Mr. Canham is the creature, exponent, reflection and partial embodiment of an institution, in this case the Christian Science Church."

I hope I may be more worthy of such a characterization. But I know that nothing that I ever had the opportunity to do, no task that I was privileged to undertake and fulfill, ever came to me except as a part of God's divine plan for every man.

Christian Scientists in these days are not particularly large numerically, but they are a mighty army nonetheless. Their capacity to help their fellow men and human society depends above all on their fidelity to the Truth, which they have learned, and they must seek each day to understand and live more faithfully.

The Christian Scientist, like everyone else in this troubled time, bears the heaviest responsibilities men have experienced in the history of the race. If the night is dark, what of the dawn?

The engines of material power have become incalculably destructive. Yet it is no longer possible for any rational person to rely upon matter for the salvation of mankind. This era was foreseen by Mrs. Eddy when she wrote (*Science and Health with Key to the Scriptures,* 97:11): "The more destructive matter becomes, the more its nothingness will appear, until matter reaches its mortal zenith in illusion and forever disappears."

How earnestly enlisted, how committed, must the individual feel whose life is dedicated to the task of spiritual awakening —not to survival but to salvation! Such is the role of the Christian Scientist in today's world.

Bibliography

(1) WORKS BY MARY BAKER EDDY

The following writings by Mrs. Eddy are quoted in the text. All of them are published by the Trustees under the Will of Mary Baker Eddy in Boston, Massachusetts. The abbreviations in parenthesis are those used in the text to identify these books.

Manual of The Mother Church (Man.)
Message for 1900 (Mess. for 1900)
Miscellaneous Writings (Mis.)
No and Yes (No.)
Retrospection and Introspection (Ret.)
Science and Health with Key to the Scriptures (S&H)
The First Church of Christ Scientist and Miscellany (My.)
Unity of Good (Un.)

(2) WORKS BY OTHER AUTHORS

Adler, Mortimer J., Interview in *U.S. News and World Report*, February 22, 1960.

Adolph, Paul Ernest, "God in Medical Practice" in *The Evidence of God in an Expanding Universe*. New York: G. P. Putnam's Sons, 1958.

Barth, Karl, *The Word of God and the Word of Man*. New York: Harper and Brothers. 1957.

Beasley, Norman, *The Cross and the Crown: The History of Christian Science*. New York: Duell, Sloan and Pearce, 1952. *The Continuing Spirit: The Story of Christian Science Since 1910*. New York: Duell, Sloan and Pearce, 1956.

Chute, Marchette, *The Search for God.* New York: E. P. Dutton Company, Inc., 1941.

Conant, James B., *Science and Common Sense.* Connecticut: Yale University Press, 1951.

Davenport, Russell W., *The Dignity of Man.* New York: Harper and Brothers, 1955.

Decline of Materialism Seminar. Rye, New York: Wainwright House, 1957.

Dresser, Horatio W. (ed.), *The Quimby Manuscripts.* New York: Thomas Y. Crowell Company, 1921.

du Nouy, Lecomte, *Human Destiny.* New York: Longman's Green and Company, Inc., 1947.

Eiseley, Loren, *The Immense Journey.* New York: The Modern Library, Random House, 1957.

Epps, Bryan Crandall, *Religious Healing in the United States. 1940-1960: History and Theology of Selected Trends* (unpublished Ph.D. thesis, Boston University, 1961).

Fitch, Robert E., "The Obsolescence of Ethics" in *Christianity and Crisis,* November 16, 1959.

Frankl, Viktor E., *From Death Camp to Existentialism.* Boston: Beacon Press, 1959.

Leishman, Thomas L., *Why I Am A Christian Scientist.* New York: Thomas Nelson and Sons, 1958.

Messer, Mary Burt, *The Science of Society.* New York: Philosophical Library, Inc., 1959.

Moehlman, Conrad Henry, *Ordeal by Concordance.* New York: Longman's Green and Company, Inc., 1955.

Moffatt, James A., *The Bible: A New Translation.* New York: Harper and Brothers, 1934.

Neil, William, *The Rediscovery of the Bible.* New York: Harper and Brothers, 1954.

Orcutt, William Dana, *Mary Baker Eddy and Her Books*. Boston: The Christian Science Publishing Society, 1950.

Peel, Robert, *Christian Science: Its Encounter with American Culture*. New York: Holt, Rinehart, and Winston, 1958.

Powell, Lyman P., *Mary Baker Eddy: A Life Size Portrait*. New York: The Macmillan Company, 1930.

Ramsay, E. Mary, *Christian Science and Its Discoverer*. Boston: The Christian Science Publishing Society, 1935.

Reiff, Philip, "The American Transference: From Calvin to Freud" in *Atlantic Monthly*, July 1961.

Schneer, Cecil J.. *The Search for Order*. New York: Harper and Brothers, 1960.

Shapley, Harlow, *Of Stars and Men*. Boston: Beacon Press. 1958.

Smith, Clifford P., *Historical Sketches*. Boston: The Christian Science Publishing Society, 1941.

Snow, C. P., *The Two Cultures and the Scientific Revolution*. New York: Cambridge University Press, 1959.

Steiger, Henry W., *Christian Science and Philosophy*. New York: Philosophical Library, 1948.

Tillich, Paul, "The Lost Dimension in Religion" in *The Saturday Evening Post*, June 14, 1958.

Index

canham

201 — Slow starters — "basic intelligence and diligence
man's birthright."

208 — Exp with H.L. Mencken

207 — Abstention
209 — Identity — free smugness — human will instead
of divine will
210 — wisdom of not being chosen
Rhodes Scholar in 1924 — closen 1925

219
220 — Healings — eye-glass situation

224 — Inspiring marriage — mr.+mrs. William Allen White
231 — chamber of Commerce Exp.   mr.+mrs Canham